Christianity In Conflict A
Catholic View Of Protestantism

John A. Hardon

CHRISTIANITY IN CONFLICT

A Catholic View of Protestantism

by John A. Hardon, S.J.

The publication in 1956 of *The Protestant Churches of America* established John A Hardon as an acute and perceptive Catholic scholar of Protestantism. In this entirely new, sequel work, Father Hardon has produced a superbly readable appraisal of contemporary Protestant thought and practice. The book is, in his own words, "neither a polemic defense of Catholicism, nor a personal witness to the faith, but the more modest work of seeing the Protestant religion through Cathol'

Outspoken and frank, but balan charitable throughout, *Christianity in Conflict* evaluates from the Catholic standpoint current Protestant positions on the Christian ministry on marriage and divorce, on church and state relations on religious education and the ecumenical movement. There are, as well stimulating chapters on Protestant doctrinal variations social ideas and practices. With rare exception, only Protestant sources were used in writing the present work; it is moreover the fruit of several years of study and reflection, and is based on much experience with Protestant churchmen and educators.

As Father Hardon notes in his Introduction, a number of books by Protestant authors have been published in recent years giving an appraisal of Roman Catholicism, but there have been few, if any, works written by Catholic authors giving an appraisal of Protestantism. *Christianity in Conflict* corrects this deficiency brilliantly and effectively.

CHRISTIANITY IN CONFLICT

Christianity
in Conflict

A Catholic View of Protestantism

by John A. Hardon, S.J.
PROFESSOR OF DOGMATIC THEOLOGY
WEST BADEN COLLEGE
WEST BADEN SPRINGS, INDIANA

The Newman Press • Westminster, Maryland

1959

Imprimi Potest·   William J. Schmidt, S.J.
                    Provincial of the Chicago Province

                    March 27, 1959

Nihil Obstat.   Edward A. Cerny, S S., D D.
                    Censor Librorum

Imprimatur   Francis P. Keough, D D.
                    Archbishop of Baltimore

                    November 23, 1959

The *Nihil Obstat* and *Imprimatur* are official declarations that a book or pamphlet is free of doctrinal and moral error. No implication is contained therein that those who have granted the *Nihil Obstat* and *Imprimatur* agree with the opinions expressed

ACKNOWLEDGMENTS

THE most substantial contribution to this volume was made by the many Protestants, especially in professional circles, who have personally and in correspondence shared their religious convictions with the author. While remaining anonymous, they deserve special gratitude for their assistance along with the assurance that any critical judgments in the following pages have not the shadow of personal imputation behind them.

The writer is indebted to about thirty copyright holders for permission to quote from the books and periodicals published by their respective firms. Complete titles and authors are given in the Notes.

To Brother Luis Tomas, S.J., are due my sincere thanks for his meticulous care in typing and arranging the manuscript, from hand-written copy to the finished stage. His generous cooperation was invaluable.

CONTENTS

CONTENTS

CONTENTS

INTRODUCTION

CATHOLIC evaluations of Protestant faith and practice have a long and respectable history that goes back to the time of the Reformation. One of the earliest was John Eck's disputations *Against Luther and Others,* which the writer has before him in a heavy wood-bound edition of 1535. One of the best known is Edmund Campion's vigorous *Ten Reasons,* that passed through forty editions in the original Latin and is still read as the testimony of a martyr whose only crime was devotion to the Holy See.

The present volume is neither a polemic defense of Catholicism nor a personal witness to the faith, but the more modest work of seeing the Protestant religion through Catholic eyes and giving the impressions accordingly.

Many factors contributed to the writing of this book. There were frequent suggestions to publish a sequel to *The Protestant Churches of America,* whose kindly reception prompted the need for a Catholic analysis to supplement the earlier volume. More urgent considerations are the duty to live in peace and harmony with those whom we recognize as fellow-Christians, but whose principles may be alien to the Catholic mind. If the basis of personal tolerance is mutual understanding, increased knowledge of the other side will help remove obstacles that can be removed, even when the differences remain. Today more than ever, Protestants and Catholics should cooperate to stem the tide of agnostic secularism, which threatens our Christian heritage and has already infected American literature and higher education. Intelligent cooperation presupposes more than passing acquaintance for both sides with their basic agreement and differences. Protestants are given a full diet of studies in Catholicism, some highly imaginative like Blanshard's trilogy, and others more objective like the *Primer on Roman Catholicism for Protestants* published for the Young Men's Christian Association. But Catholics are less fortunate and the present volume is intended to supply the deficiency.

Another and pressing motive for evaluating the Protestant way of life is the extraordinary interest in Christian unity which the ecumenical movement has crystallized and which the twenty-first general council of the Catholic Church has envisioned as one of its principal aims. The very desire for unity assumes there are fundamental divergencies between Catholic and Protestant faith and polity; and no greater disservice can be done than to gloss over differences while stressing only the common beliefs. Protestants are different, and they know it, more often, in fact, than many Catholics know how different they are from Protestants. In reply to Pope John's convocation of the general council, the World Council of Churches emphasized that "progress towards unity is made when churches meet together on the basis of their deepest convictions." These convictions must first be understood and their variance appraised before anything approaching the true ecumenism of the Gospel can begin or be assured the grace of God without which human efforts are vain.

A final reason for looking into the subject is the frank desire that Catholics have to communicate their religious faith. To elevate this desire to something more than a vague apostolic urge, it should be supported with motivation and based on sufficient evidence. The Vatican Council solemnly defined that the great benefits which the Church confers on her members, her potential for exalted sanctity, her unity and unshaken stability are signs of divine approval which may lead persons outside into the Mystical Body of Christ. Catholics will better appreciate these benefits and be ready to share them with others if they see what Protestants lack and how willing they can be to regain what others had lost for them.

With rare exception, only Protestant sources were used in making the present study. Denominational books were consulted along with writings of the more important figures in contemporary religious thought. But more valuable than printed material was the friendship which the author has had over a period of years with Protestant churchmen and educators, whose integrity and dedication to ideals he has learned to respect. In fact, this volume would not have been written except for the knowledge that religious differences can be discussed with unemotional objectivity, provided the norms of charity are faithfully observed. The writer has honestly tried to be fair, especially keeping in mind the distinction between Protestantism as a religious system and Protestants as devoted believers. The latter may be quite un-Protestant in their outlook on life if they have lived among Catholics with any sympathy; but the former is opposed to Catholicism on principle, and its very existence is a "protest against the errors of Rome."

Our concern in the following pages is mainly with the system, and with personalities only as they shed light on what needs explanation, if for no other reason than because millions of Christians are seeking to find "the whole Christ" in His Mystical Body and millions of others are waiting to show them.

CHRISTIANITY IN CONFLICT

I

THE BIBLE

ACCORDING TO its own apologists, Protestantism was born in a rediscovery of the Bible and nourished almost exclusively on its devoted study. The Reformation gave a great impetus to the vernacular translation of the Scriptures, and the newly invented printing press made the Bible more widely read and diffused than any book had ever been before. Commentaries multiplied, and the Reformed preaching concentrated on the exposition of the Scriptures. Lutheran and Calvinist churches exerted themselves to see that their people understood the Bible. Later the Puritans in England and America, and the kindred movements in Germany and Holland, found their inspiration in the reading and study of "the inspired Word of God."

In our own times, the growth of numerous Bible societies shows the enduring vitality of the Protestant belief in the plain text of the Bible as the greatest single agency of propagating the Gospel. Protestant missionaries entering a new field consider one of their primary tasks to have the Bible translated into the language of the people among whom they work. In the field of publication, the majority of books deals with biblical subjects, and in Protestant church-schools the main text is a copy of the Scriptures. Ostensibly, therefore, Luther's exhortation, "Let us not lose the Bible," still remains active among his followers.

Contents of the Protestant Bible

The difference between the Catholic and Protestant concept of the Bible is manifold and begins with the contents, which the Reformers determined should be otherwise than the Church had believed since apostolic times. As currently received, the Protestant Bible has seven books less in the Old Testament by excluding Tobias, Ecclesiasticus, Judith, the Book of Wisdom, Baruch and the two Books of Maccabees. Behind this mutilation stands a whole system of theology that epitomizes the spirit of Protestantism even to the present time.

At the dawn of the Reformation, Luther and Calvin were faced with a difficult problem. By substituting the Bible for the Church as the ultimate ground of the faith, they put a heavy strain on the Scriptures. There was one way they might have logically tried to carry out their plan. They might have refused entirely to discuss the question of inspiration or canonical authority, and simply accepted the Bible from the Church as a primitive document sanctioned by time and prestige and having the sure claim to authority possessed by any Christian writing that was more than fourteen centuries old. After taking the Scriptures on these terms, they might have built on them a new religious structure to replace the Catholic Church they had left. But this would have seemed like compromise. With the Reformers it was an essential postulate that mere tradition, however old, or Church authority counts for nothing. Consequently, as the basis of their theological system, they set the principle that the Holy Spirit, speaking in the heart of every godly man, identifies the books which He inspired.

As the pioneer in this iconoclasm, Luther was more crude than some of his successors. Shortly after his defec-

[4]

tion, when faced with texts from the Old Testament which contradicted his teaching, he boldly answered that the questions were from books which he denied were canonical. When told that the Church had always considered them inspired, he retorted that "the Church cannot give more authority or validity to a book than it has already."[1] Later on, when he published a German translation of the New Testament and relegated to an appendix the Epistles of Sts. James and Jude, the Epistle to the Hebrews and the Apocalypse, it was on the score that they were not apostolic. He defined an apostle as one who "preaches the suffering, resurrection and works of Christ, and thereon lays the foundation of his faith." Accordingly, "whatever does not teach Christ is not apostolic, even though Peter or Paul should teach it; on the other hand, what preaches Christ is apostolic even though Judas, Annas, Pilate and Herod produced it."[2] Since four books of the Catholic New Testament did not preach Christ to Luther's satisfaction, they were put outside the biblical canon. Fortunately for the spiritual welfare of his followers, this treatment was too drastic, and Protestant Bibles now include without qualification the writings he had disclaimed as unapostolic.

More clear-sighted than Luther, John Calvin reduced to a simple rule the method for determining whether a book belongs to the Scriptures or not. Conscious of the centuries-old tradition against the new Bible, he admitted "there has generally prevailed a most pernicious error, that the Scriptures have only so much weight as the authority of the Church confers on them, as though the eternal and inviolable truth of God depended on the arbitrary will of men." With great contempt of the Holy Spirit, Catholics inquire "who can assure us that God is the author of the Scriptures? Who can persuade us that this book should be read with reverence, and another removed from the sacred number, unless all these things were regulated by the decisions of the Church?" The answer is almost too simple, says Calvin. "It is just as if someone inquired, how should we learn to distinguish light from darkness, white from black, sweet from bitter. For the Scripture manifests the evidence of its truth as clearly as black and white objects show their color, or sweet and bitter things their taste." The operative agent in this manifestation is the Spirit of God. "For, as God is an adequate witness of Himself in His own word, so also the word would never gain credit in the hearts of men, till it be confirmed by the internal testimony of the Spirit. Consequently, the same Spirit who spoke by the mouth of the prophets must penetrate into our hearts, to convince us that they faithfully delivered the oracles which were divinely entrusted to them."[3]

Thus Calvin raised a pure hypothesis to the level of an objective fact and changed one element in the recognition of Scripture into the whole process. Theoretically God might have chosen to inspire each man individually on the canonicity of a book in the Bible. But then He should have dispensed with the communal structure of Christianity and given some indication that every Christian personally and not just ecclesiastical authority was infallible in matters of faith and morals. Moreover, what Calvin and the Reformers never so much as hinted was the historical record of a plethora of gospels, histories, acts, and epistles, all allegedly inspired, that arose in competition to the authentic writings of the New Testament. With every new heresy arose another gospel. The *Gospel of the Egyptians* was created by the Gnostics who rejected matrimony, the Ebionites wrote the *Gospel of the Twelve Apostles* as an attack on the birth and genealogy of the Savior, the *Gospel of St. Peter* was a

Docetist fabrication which made Pilate a hero and questioned the reality of Christ's bodily death and resurrection. We have record of twenty-five gospels, exclusive of other apocrypha, on which the Church had to pass critical judgment and out of which she admitted only four to the biblical canon. Hence the axiom of St. Augustine that, "I would not believe in the Gospels unless moved by the authority of the Catholic Church."[4]

No doubt the internal guidance of the Spirit helps a man believe in the Church's right to decide on the writings of inspiration, but the guidance does not supplant the authority. In fact those who ignored that authority in the early centuries were branded heretics, and against their penchant to create their own "Scriptures" the first lists of inspired books were assembled by the popes, with high probability in the second century and certainly by the year 400. It mattered nothing to the Reformers that the canon issued under Pope Damasus in 382, Siricius in 397 and Innocent I in 405 was identical with the Catholic Bible which they were excising. For, "being illuminated by the Spirit, we now believe the divine original of the Scripture, not from our own judgment or that of others. It is such a persuasion as requires no reasons, such a sentiment as cannot be produced except by a revelation from heaven."[5] And who would argue with a divine communication?

To give substance to his rejection of seven books in the Old Testament, Luther appealed to St. Jerome who questioned their canonicity as a private opinion in which he submitted to the authority of the Church. Jerome's doubt came from the fact that the Palestinian Rabbis in the time of Christ rejected all writings not composed in Palestine and originally in Hebrew or whose author was not gifted with prophetic charism. The books in question did not meet these specifications inspired by the Jewish nationalism that Christ Himself had reprobated. For a thousand years, Jerome's opinion remained a historical relic, contradicted by the stream of patristic tradition and a series of papal declarations, until popularized by Martin Luther to serve his own polemic ends. In 1534 he completed his translation of the Bible from Greek and Hebrew into German, but, instead of keeping what he called the Greek Apocrypha in their regular place, he put them after the Old Testament with the bare remark that, "Although these books are not considered Holy Scripture, they are still useful and worth reading."

Luther's example was immediately followed by Myles Coverdale, in the first printed English Bible, which appeared the next year, 1535. His "striking innovation," as a Protestant writer calls it, "in gathering the Apocrypha out of the Old Testament and putting them by themselves" was soon taken up not only by Coverdale but from him by all the Protestant English Bibles that followed. The Geneva Bible produced by the Puritans in 1560, the Bishop's Bible in 1568 and the King James version in 1611, all segregated the "Apocrypha" from the Old Testament but still continued to print them. By the end of the sixteenth century, however, the Puritans rebelled against even this concession to Romanism, and as early as 1599 copies of the Geneva Bible began to omit the sheets containing the seven rejected books. Within a generation, the King James Bible did the same, so that now it is difficult to find the "Apocrypha" in any English version of the Protestant Scriptures.

Yet in recent years a heartening reaction has taken place, not indeed to restore the biblical canon which Luther had mutilated, but to publish his deletions under Protestant auspices and write commentaries on what has been "almost forgotten by the Christian public." For the first time in centuries, scholars of the Reformed persuasion are saying that "no one can have the complete Bible as a source book for the cultural study of art, literature, and religion, without the Apocrypha (decanonized by Luther), and as an aid to understanding the New Testament the Apocrypha are indispensable."[6]

Biblical Inspiration

There was no doubt in the minds of the Reformers that the Bible is divinely inspired. "You are so to deal with the Scriptures," Luther told his disciples, "as to bear in mind that God Himself is saying this." Many Protestants in America still believe the same. Seminarians are taught "there is no real difference, but only a difference of expression, between the two terms, 'Holy Scripture says,' and 'God says.' Holy Scripture and the word of God are interchangeable terms."[7] Billy Graham has been preaching this message to thousands in America and elsewhere as the only hope "in this hour of confusion and crisis." Sixteen hundred years were needed to complete the writing of the Bible. "It is the work of more than thirty authors, each of whom acted as a scribe of God. These men acted as channels for God's dictation; they wrote as He directed them; and under His divine inspiration they were able to see the great and enduring truths, and to record them that other men might see and know them too."[8] Perhaps the largest factor in the phenomenal response to Graham's evangelism is the solid scriptural basis of his sermons with their constant appeal to the infallible word of the Bible.

It would be comforting to say this concept predominates among Protestant churchmen. More typical is Reinhold Niebuhr's estimate of Billy Graham, whose "uncritical biblicism" he considers a hazard to the acceptance of the Gospel and a kind of faith that must be "irrelevant to any mature person" who understands the true dimensions of life. The late Albert Knudson, dean of Boston University's school of divinity, fairly represents the majority attitude. He frankly admitted that the old Reformation idea of Bible authoritarianism is dead. "During the past century and a half, it has crumbled under the impact of biblical and philosophical criticism. And as it was gradually discarded, a new kind of authority took its place; an authority that was no longer regarded as external and coercive but as inner and spiritual. It was implicit in the individualism and subjectivity of such early Protestant doctrines as the right of private judgment, the witness of the Spirit, justification by faith, and in the Methodist emphasis on religious experience. But it was not until the time of Kant and Schleiermacher that it received what might be called official philosophical and theological ratification. Since then it has become increasingly clear to thoughtful people that religious faith does not need either an infallible Book or an infallible Church to establish its validity. It validates itself."⁹

This self-validation of faith is a euphemism for denying the supernatural order. It asserts the power of the human mind to pass judgment on revelation at the bar of reason and personal experience. Both factors are essential. The appeal to reason applies the principles of Kantianism to the Christian religion. By the use of its a priori judgments, the human mind can determine the truth or error of what God has allegedly revealed. The appeal to experience invokes the sentimentalism, or feeling theology, of Schleiermacher, for whom the validity of doctrine depends on the emotional satisfaction it gives, or fails to give, to the one who believes. In either case, the evidence for truth is purely subjective.

But Protestantism in some quarters has gone still further. Not satisfied with demanding that revelation be judged by human standards, it reduces the word of God to purely natural intellection. Biblical Protestants and Christians in general believe the Scriptures are not a product of mere human genius; that in writing them the hagiographers were supernaturally influenced to write only what God intended so that He became the author of the sacred books produced. Liberalism rejects this bibliolatry that would enslave us to a deposit of faith once given to the ancients and now closed except for interpretation. " 'Word of God' is an ambiguous term. It is often used in the sense of the written word of the Bible." Actually, "the 'Word of God' is every reality through which the ultimate power breaks into our personal reality, (since) revelation is revelation to me in my concrete situation, in my historical reality. If I am asked to make a leap from my situation into a situation of past history in order to receive revelation, what I receive is no longer revelation *for me*, but a report about revelations received by others, for instance, in A.D. 30–33, by people in Palestine."[10] In this concept of the Bible, Reformation theology goes the full circle of subjectivism. Following the principle that no authority has divine sanction to determine the canon of sacred Scripture, the same freedom by which I decide (on my own) what books are inspired, allows me to say that none is inspired, or that everything religious in my life is a revelation of God.

Private Interpretation

Protestant historians until modern times used to say there were two fundamental principles of the Reformation, an objective and subjective one. The former was the unique authority of Scripture, independent of tradition; the latter justification by faith alone without good works. While still considered important, these principles are now subordinated to a deeper issue from which they were both derived. Underlying them was the Protestant belief in the inspiration of the individual and the corresponding right of private judgment in matters of faith. Consequently, the real point of difference between Protestants and Catholics was not the canon or authority of Scripture, but who has the right of interpretation. Catholics believed the infallible Church, Protestants said the inspired or enlightened individual.

The dichotomy has not substantially changed. Against the Church's claim that only she has the right to explain the inspired text, contemporary Protestants hold the opposite. They may not agree on the conditions required for valid interpretation, but on one point they all concur—it is not an ecclesiastical body and least of all the Catholic Church.

Though widely different and apparently contradictory, two streams of thought came out of the original Lutheran concept of private interpretation. Divine grace through Jesus Christ speaks directly to the heart of the believer. Consistent with this principle, Luther threw out the so-called Apocryphal books, declared that in many places the Scriptures had erred and even conceded that another New Testament might be written to improve on the first one. His fundamentalist followers blandly teach that "Christians are individually taught by the Spirit of God, so that they are slaves to no one as they study the Scriptures. Each individual believer is able by the grace of God to read the Scriptures for himself, receiving the benefit of divine illumination."[11] Extreme forms of this illuminism are found among the minor sects of Pentecostals, the Holiness movement and, on a more respected plane, among the Quakers. A variant form of Bible individualism dispenses not only with special guidance of the Holy Spirit but with any kind of scientific inquiry into the proper meaning of the text. Since "the entire Christian doctrine is revealed and set forth in Scripture passages so clear that the learned and unlearned alike can understand them, they do not stand in need of 'exegesis' for explanation. If Scripture did not have this quality, it would not be for all Christians 'a lamp unto their feet and a light unto their path,' nor would all Christians be able to establish the truth of their faith by Scripture and in the light of Scripture to mark and avoid false teachers."[12] As an expression of biblical Protestantism, this statement could scarcely be improved. Sectarians who wished to hold on to some form of dogma could not follow Luther to the conclusion of his premises; that way lay chaos and the end of organized Christianity. Neither would they accept the Catholic magisterium. They took the middle course of setting up the Bible as the only and ultimate norm of Christian belief. Thus authority was met with authority, a book against an institution or, as the fundamentalists prefer, the word of God instead of the word of man.

However, the more common idea of private interpretation took Luther at his word. It seemed a trifle to insist on a special illumination for interpreting the Scripture. Enough to know that every one has a spark of the divine within him to sift the wheat from the chaff in the Bible and derive what he can from the wisdom of the ancients. His tools in the process are historical and literary criticism. With these he recovers the true Jesus of history. Following the lead of men like Harnack, for whom the Gospels are "not altogether useless as sources of history," and Bultmann, who marveled, "what a primitive mythology, that a divine being should become incarnate," liberal Protestants still use the vocabu-

[13]

lary of dogmatic Christians, but they no longer believe in the concepts. No major denomination has escaped the solvent of rationalism, not excluding traditionally conservative bodies. Lutheran churchmen tell the people "with new light and more adequate interpretation of the biblical writings, changes in doctrine are not only anticipated but necessary," and although highly recommended as the literature of a nation, "the Episcopal Church does not ask you to make a formal statement of belief in the Bible." You may, therefore, be a professed Christian and believe in the Scriptures, but you are not obliged to accept them as divinely inspired and still less hope to find there any security of doctrine.

Conflict with Catholic Principles

Since Reformation times, the Bible has been a favorite target for Protestant criticism of the Catholic Church. The original complaint was that Rome kept the people in ignorance of the sacred text, in order better to exploit their submission to her authority. Her priests, according to Luther, had conspired "to lead us away from Scripture and make themselves masters over us, that we should believe their dream sermons." While the accusation is still made by some evangelists, the issue, at least in America, now turns on a different plane.

Catholic apologists for years had answered the charge about Rome's hiding the Bible by showing that, except for the Church's exercise of authority in the first centuries, not even the Protestants would have a New Testament. A few critics, mostly in the South, persist in challenging the Church's right to say that she determined the biblical canon. "The books of the canon are their own apologists," according to one Baptist divine. "For the Bishop of Rome to lay claim to the New Testament Scriptures is absurd. All the churches and all the Christian people, everywhere and in all ages, have accepted and loved these books as the word of God."[13] However, such innocence of religious history is comparatively rare. Normally, Protestant writers explain that about the middle of the second century a brilliant, but unorthodox, leader by the name of Marcion, published his own list of the Scriptures which he considered inspired along Gnostic lines. Violently anti-Semitic, he said that only the letters of St. Paul and an expurgated edition of Luke and Acts were canonical. "It was" therefore, "to counteract the influence of Marcion that the Church began in the middle of the second century A.D. to make lists of books that were to be considered authoritative for the life and faith of the Church." Most non-Catholic scholars would subscribe to this explanation.

The same disposition to respect the so-called Apocrypha of the Old Testament, rejected by Luther, has been gaining ground. No doubt the blurring of a real distinction between divine and literary inspiration has something to do with the tendency to accept Tobias, Wisdom and Maccabees as "highly inspirational." Yet, there are notable exceptions. "Why does the Catholic Church hold on to these uninspired writings," ask the fundamentalists. "Because their fictitious teachings endorse the doctrines of the Church, such as prayers for the dead, almsdeeds delivering from death and sin, and salvation by works." Then follows a series of texts from the objectionable books with appropriate comments: If charitable offering could purge our sins, we would have no need for the blood of Christ. Sins are not pardoned by prayer. If that were true we would have no need of Jesus.

All heathen people pray, but sins are not pardoned by prayer alone. Money flows into the Church's coffers for Masses for departed souls "beyond the imagination."

Equally divergent are the current estimates of that stronghold of Reformation theology, the absolute sufficiency of the Bible. As a general rule, conservative and evangelical churches like the Southern Baptists and Synodical Lutherans will have nothing to do with tradition. The Scriptures are the only norm of faith and channel of salvation. More liberal groups are never so hide-bound. In fact, when their freethinking shades into mysticism, as with the Quakers, or lapses into naturalism, as among Unitarians, even the Scriptures are not essential. Not infrequently, this ambivalence is found in a single denomination. Thus in their Articles of Religion, the Episcopalians still protest that "Holy Scripture containeth all things necessary for salvation, so that whatever is not read therein, nor may be proved thereby, is not to be required of any man, that it should be believed as an article of Faith, or be thought requisite or necessary for salvation."[14] But too much has happened among Anglicans since that piece of Lutheranism was put into their creed. While still giving it token adherence (in a fine-print appendix to the *Book of Common Prayer*), the church's "official" stand has become more lenient. Now "it is in accord with the ethos (of evangelical Catholicism) that Anglicanism has asserted that there is an essential place for tradition in the Christian religion. Those who believe that Christianity is indeed the true religion, based on the mighty acts of God, cannot doubt that the guidance of the Holy Spirit has been with the Church in its development, as in the growth of the primitive preaching into the Apostles' and Nicene Creeds and Christian dogma."[15] Such realism among church leaders suggests a definite break with the past.

[16]

One form of opposition, however, remains the same. When the Reformers castigated Rome for keeping the bread of Scriptures from the starving people of God, they added a censure of the Church's claim that only she may explain the Bible and communicate its interpretation to the faithful. Luther called this "a mark of the Anti-Christ," Zwingli said it was "a reproach cast upon God," and even the mild Wesley spoke against the Papal bigotry. Those who inherit their spirit continue in the same tradition, instinctively sensing that any compromise on this point would strike at the roots of Protestantism. Their criticism sometimes descends to personal invective. After modestly conceding that "the authoritative theological doctrine of the Scriptures is not always unambiguous in the Protestant reading," a Presbyterian adds that "those things can only be absolutely and finally ascertained by Roman Catholic methods of reading them in where they are not, and if one prefers those things to the living Word, he can dispense with the Bible altogether." And worse still, "the entertaining but saddening caricature of scholarly argument by which Roman Biblical interpreters regularly proceed from a show of historical method to predetermined orthodox conclusions can be readily recognized by those who have seen the degradation of scholarship to propaganda in Nazism and Bolshevism. No totalitarianism, even the most humanitarian, can tolerate the free search for historical truth." This contribution from a respectable school of divinity (Chicago University) becomes less surprising when seen as only the gesture of a more radical animus against anything Catholic. A more revealing observation tells the reader that "Romanist doctrine releases the faithful from the obligation to tell the truth to 'heretics' when the interests of the Church are at stake,"[16] with the expressed implication that only on Protestant territory can religious faith and uninhibited human inquiry flourish. While fairly common, this attitude is by no means universal. Professional scholars often rise above denominational bias to recognize the Church's contribution to the Scriptures. Cooperative ventures, like the American Schools of Oriental Research, bring Catholics and Protestants together for scientific work in the Holy Land, with consequent breakdown of prejudice against Roman hostility to an objective study of the Bible. Catholic archaeologists are sometimes given the highest praise, as the French Dominican, Père Vincent, whom Albright describes as *facile princeps* and "the tutor of all" in the field of Palestinology. And currently, "no institution has exerted itself more nobly in the acquisition and study of the Dead Sea manuscripts than the *École Biblique*," which is under Catholic auspices.

Equally encouraging is the change of attitude in historical circles to consideration of the Church as the guardian of Holy Scripture, and even, in a carefully defined sense, its creator. The studies of Lightfoot and Harnack must be held responsible for the concessive statement, "that the Church is responsible for the canon of Holy Scripture is certainly true." Further concessions that Catholic Christianity has always exercised "a wise vigilance over the purity of the biblical text" are the fruit of more than a half century of research in Christian origins, which show how absolutely the Scriptures depend on the Church's guidance and care.

However the most promising feature of Protestant studies of the Bible is the light they shed on the essential unity of the Church as founded by Christ. It seems almost like a reversal of history to say, as Cullmann does, that the Petrine text in St. Matthew is genuine. "Jesus promises Peter that he will build upon him the earthly people of God; he promises that in this people Peter will have the leadership, both in missionary work and in organization. What is said of Peter as the Rock refers only to him, the historical apostle; he represents once for all the earthly foundation, the beginning who supports the whole structure of the *ekklesia* that is to be built in the future." Cullmann's restraining distinction that Christ's immediate thought probably deals only with the time of Peter should not obscure what many writers are coming to see, that "as regards the current problem of 'Catholics and Protestants,' if we study the New Testament from the viewpoint of its authors, every page tells us that our separation is a scandal."[17] While this judgment was born in Europe and has more followers there, its growing acceptance in America is a welcome balance to the more familiar prejudice against the Catholic Church.

I I

CHRISTIAN MINISTRY

"ONE OF THE weaknesses of Protestantism today is that so few Protestants know what they believe and why." If this self-criticism from a leading theologian is valid for any aspect of religious faith and worship, it is eminently true of the Christian ministry, whose complications and varieties are confessedly baffling even to scholars, let alone to the rank and file members of the denominations. The complexity exists not only between different churches, mutually excluding each other's ministry, but within the same religious body are positions held by one party which another faction, in equally good standing, repudiates.

Still there are common factors in this medley and a certain constancy of practice which sharply distinguish the Catholic from the Protestant clergy. On them will depend whatever success the current ecumenical movement may achieve, as through them a Catholic can learn how deeply the Reformation severed its followers from Roman unity, and how any hope of reunion is possible only when the problems of a divergent ministry have been solved.

Reformation Origins

The Protestant concept of the ministry cannot be understood without an examination of its origins in the Lutheran denial that the Catholic priesthood was instituted by Christ as a distinct sacrament, empowering those who receive it to offer Mass and forgive sins in the name of God. "If there were no higher consecration than what the pope or bishop can give, there would never be a priest," according to Luther, who proclaimed the spiritual priesthood of all Christians in virtue of their faith in Christ.

Yet, Luther was shrewd enough to see the necessity for some kind of ministry. His purely invisible Church with a universal priesthood was only a convenience to explain the rejection of Rome. His aversion to authority was limited to the Pope and the hierarchy. Within a few months of his break with the Church, he saw the need for instituting a public ministry of his own and, although often uncertain about its nature, he never once doubted how important it was to the cause of the Reformation. Armed with a number of texts from St. Paul, he fought against the old idea of two classes in the Church, clergy and laity, but at the same time promoted his own division of the spiritual priesthood of the many and the public ministry of the few. The instruments of grace, he held, have the same power and effect, whether administered by common Christians or by ministers in their public office. In a famous passage which summarizes the Protestant idea of the clergy, he said, "we firmly maintain there is no other word of God than the one all Christians are told to preach; there is no other baptism than the one all Christians may confer; there is no other remembrance of the Lord's Supper than the one any Christian may celebrate; also there is no other sacrifice than the body of every Christian."[1] Accordingly, every believer has the power to preach, teach and administer the sacraments, and any limitation of this faculty is contrary to the plain words of Scripture.

Nevertheless, though all Christians have the power, not

all should exercise it whenever they please. There must be order and discipline in the church, as much as in other societies. "Though all of us are priests, we should not on that account all preach, or teach or govern. But from the whole congregation some must be selected and chosen to whom this office is to be committed; and whoever holds this office is now, because of it, not a priest (like all the rest), but a servant, or minister, of all the others. For this office is no more than a public service, which is delegated to one by the whole congregation, though all of them are priests together."[2] Thus the title of "minister" in the Protestant churches has more than a symbolic meaning; it designates the clergy as delegates of the congregation and nothing more. Any assumption of power or authority beyond this range is, by Reformation standards, a deviation from evangelical theology.

John Calvin and the reformed school likewise rejected the idea of a sacrificing priesthood, specially ordained by bishops with apostolic succession to administer the sacraments and offer the Sacrifice of the Mass. "The priesthood of the Catholics," wrote Calvin, "is a damnable sacrilege, and it is impudent to call it a sacrament."[3] With minor changes, all the confessions of faith in the Calvinist tradition said the same thing. On the continent, the Gallican, Belgian, Heidelberg and Helvitic creeds plainly called the Roman Mass superstition and Roman priests usurpers of a right that belonged to Christ alone. In France and the Low countries, this preaching led to a wholesale destruction of Catholic churches and shrines and a persecution of priests and people, which gave the Church a series of martyrs to the Eucharist. In England, the Westminster Confession of Faith (professed by all Presbyterians) called "the popish sacrifice of the Mass, most abominably injurious to Christ's one only sacrifice," and consistently professed only a spiritual sort of ministry for "offering of praise and thanksgiving to God," with no consecration of the Body and Blood of Christ.

Although Luther and Calvin were agreed in denying an ordained priesthood with unique powers to offer Mass and forgive sins, they differed widely in their explanation of the public ministry which they both allowed. Luther thought the ministry was divine only in the general sense that trustees of a church are appointed to carry out the "divine ordinances" of teaching, baptizing, and giving the Lord's Supper. Calvin made the ministry part of his scheme of predestination. "It is by vocation," he said, "that ministers are destined for preaching the Gospel and administration of the sacraments." This divergence has been the seedbed of bitter controversy between the two sides and still divides Protestant theologians who favor one or the other interpretation. The Lutheran concept nurtured a crop of "free churches" of the Baptist and Congregational type that wanted no compromise on the priesthood of the laity, and to this day jealously guards the autonomy of each congregation to elect and depose its ministers who are absolutely responsible to the community which put them into office. Calvin's notion of a divinely elected clergy, to be merely recognized and approved by the people, has found its way into Lutheran communions and is generally accepted, though modified, by religious bodies that are still concerned about doctrinal and ritual conformity. They feel that unless the laity consider their pastors "chosen of God" and respect them accordingly, the urge to independence will dissolve the churches' ecclesiastical structure and leave them (as it has) a collection of fellowship societies.

The Established Church in England resisted the Protestant dilution of the ministry until the middle of the sixteenth century. But in 1552 a new Ordinal was issued by Archbishop Cranmer, following a Lutheran pattern, from which every mention of a priesthood offering sacrifice was carefully removed. Under pretext of returning to the primitive form, Cranmer and his associates radically changed the liturgical rite of ordination in line with the continental Reformers. For, as Cranmer taught, "there is no more promise of God, that grace is given in the committing of the ecclesiastical office than it is in the committing of the civil office." Both are equally human creations, except that one deals with spiritual and the other with temporal affairs of state. A hundred years later (1662), the old Ordinal was revised to include once more the words of ordination "for the office of work of a priest." But it was too late. In the course of a century the Anglican hierarchy had died out through using a mutilated form and the majority of the English clergy and bishops came to believe in a ministry which excluded the powers of Eucharistic consecration. To remove the last vestige of doubt, the 28th of the Thirty-Nine Articles, promulgated by Elizabeth in 1563, declared that "transubstantiation cannot be proved by Holy Writ: but is repugnant to the plain words of Scripture." The result in England as on the continent was a functionary clergy divested of sacred powers and exercising only what "every godly Christian" had the faculty to do without ordination.

Comparable to the Reformation changes in the concept of the ministry were the alterations introduced in ecclesiastical authority. Luther was satisfied to leave local conditions to determine whether a monarchical bishop should be recognized. Thus in Prussia bishops were continued without discussion, and similarly in Hesse and elsewhere. But in Brandenburg a system of consistories and superintendents was, after a few years, preferred, until this type of church government prevailed in many places and was later imported to America. When bishops were accepted, it was assumed that the nature of the office was "reformed," as in Pomerania, where the people decided that "Bishops should continue and remain; not anointing-bishops, nor ordaining-bishops, but such as preach and teach and expound the pure word of God and preside over the Church."[4] Luther was even prepared to put up with a secular prince as *Nothbischoff* where no ecclesiastic was available. Lutheran churches in Europe still have bishops, but not in the States. Church conventions, which elect presidents and other officials, are the main instruments in the American churches.

But the Lutherans were inconsistent. Though logically they should have disclaimed ecclesiastical authority on the principle of private inspiration, they allowed an episcopate or, as in America, a convention to be elected and vested with the trappings of juridical power. Again, the free-churches were more faithful to the Reformation. They would have no judges over them, and proceeded to organize a chain of congregational bodies which, at least in the States, are becoming the normal type of Protestant church government. The freedom of the congregation in this polity is inviolable, "because the congregation is better able to consult the mind of Christ than is any outside group. No minister beloved by his people can be removed by external pressure." By the same token, no minister remains in office unless he caters to the congregation.

By a strange anomaly, which their own theologians find it hard to explain, the Anglican Church has a full-blown episcopate which claims direct succession from the Apostles and, when meeting in solemn conclave, has authority (more or less) to bind the consciences of the faithful. Several factors contributed to England's attaching a historical episcopate to the main trunk of Protestantism. One reason was the national character of the English Church, whose bishops became ecclesiastical arms of the civil authority and instruments of the king and parliament to exercise their political will. Also, the insular character of the country isolated her people from the reformed spirit of independence on the continent, which atomized so many of the churches and either destroyed the episcopate altogether or reduced it to a symbolic nonentity. When the American Church became free of the parent body after the Revolutionary War, the tradition was already crystallized. But authentic Protestants eye the Anglican structure with misgiving; to them it looks like a compromise with the evangelical ideal that no human agency, papal or episcopal, should mediate between God and the Christian soul.

Although the Methodist Church was born in England, its ecclesiastical beginnings were in America. When the Bishop of London refused to ordain ministers for Methodist societies in the colonies, John Wesley on his own authority first ordained three laymen and then consecrated one of them, Thomas Coke, to the episcopacy. "I can scarcely believe it," wrote his brother Charles, "that in his eighty-second year my brother, my old, intimate friend and companion, should have assumed the episcopal character, ordained elders, consecrated a bishop, and sent him to ordain our elder preachers in America."[5] Some have defended Wesley against the charge of unauthorized assumption of episcopal powers on the score that he called Coke only a superintendent; but all the evidence is against him. Long before consecrating Coke, he had ordained twenty-seven men for the work of preaching and administering the Lord's Supper in the American mission. But this alone would not guarantee succession after his death. "Here, in England," he wrote, "there are bishops. In America there are none." So he imposed hands on Coke and declared he was making him a superintendent. Coke understood himself to be a bishop. Within a year he exercised what he believed were episcopal powers by imposing hands on a man named Asbury. In two years, the latter realistically changed the title "superintendent" to "bishop" for himself, Coke and Wesley, with the approval of the General Methodist Conference (American) in 1787. If anyone should have known Wesley's intentions, it was his brother Charles who summed up his views in a bitter quatrain:

> How easy now are Bishops made
>   At man or woman's whim!
> Wesley his hands on Coke hath laid,
>   But who laid hands on him?

When pressed on the point, Wesley defended himself in a formal manifesto, declaring that, "I, John Wesley, think myself to be providentially called, at this time, to set apart persons for the work of the ministry in America."[6] Even today, the official *Discipline* defines a "bishop (as) a general superintendent of The Methodist Church," thus retaining Wesley's ambiguous term to describe what he actually intended, namely, the episcopal dignity.

Presbyterianism as a form of church government has a long and controverted ancestry, going back to the conciliarist theories of the fifteenth century which made a council of bishops superior to the pope. Condemned by the Church in the middle ages, the concept was revived by Calvin and John Knox, who needed some kind of organization into which their ideas could be set. Presbyterian polity is essentially a reaction against two extremes, the control of church discipline by one person, whether pontiff or bishop, and the practical elimination of control by making each congregation its own authority. Instead of either, a group of churches bands together to dictate policy and direct the parishes which belong to the presbytery. In the early days, there was no fixed number of local groups required for a *presbyterium*, and even now the membership follows geographical, or language and racial lines. Below it is the session or parish, and nominally above is the synod, but for all practical purposes the presbytery governs the modern followers of John Calvin

The word *presbyterium* occurs in St. Paul, who exhorts Timothy not to "neglect the grace that is in thee, granted to thee by reason of prophecy with the laying on of hands of the presbyterate,"[7] which Calvin explained to suit his theology as a college of presbyters. At this point he introduced a revolutionary idea into church government. After studying the Catholic system he disliked it. "All the right of the people to choose has been entirely taken away," he complained. He would restore the laity to what he considered their original privilege of voting power in the choice of ministers and, by extension, of active voice in church discipline. His contribution to Protestant ecclesiology was therefore monumental. He spelled out in precise and legal terms the principles inherent in the Reformation, by which the new *ecclesia Christi* was to be governed not only by the clergy but equally by all the people.

Verbally, presbyterianism seems to have derived from presbyter, which in New Testament language means an ordained minister of the altar. But the name and meaning are really based on a new form of authority, residing in a presbytery, whose membership in Calvinist theory is composed of ordained ministers and so-called ruling elders, representing the congregations. The church that Calvin invented, therefore, was more radically different than many historians believe. He conceived its structure as both laic and clerical, with enough stress on the first element to create a type of religious society that now permeates all existing Protestant churches. Writers dispute on the amount of credit that Calvin should be given for setting the pattern of modern Presbyterianism; but they agree that his insight saved all churches in the reformed tradition from clerical control and domination. More than Luther, Zwingli or Cranmer, he "emancipated the layman and restored his honorable position in the Church of Christ." It was no coincidence that practically alone of all the original Reformers, he never took sacred orders or exercised the function of the priesthood.

Inherited Problems

The changes in the ministry effected by the Reformation were the most decisive factor in alienating Protestant Christianity from its Catholic ancestry. Differences in doctrine and ethical values were disruptive in any case, but the breach would have been less radical and even possibly healed if the principles of Reformed theology had not become fixed in a clerical system that was tailored to fit the new heresy. After four hundred years of experimentation, the inherent defects of the system are recognized by those who are part of it, who begin vaguely to see the damage sustained when the priesthood was discarded as blasphemy.

Except among Anglicans, the general conviction is still that sacraments and worship are subordinate to subjective faith, and that "a man's relations with God are not to be hindered by ritual display." But a reaction has long been setting in. Clergymen who cannot be suspected of Roman leanings believe that "We need a revival of worship at the heart of our Protestant churchmanship." They admit it will be hard to escape the shell of tradition. Their inheritance gives them a distrust of the altar and its liturgy. They are more familiar with the pulpit and its sermon, which makes it difficult to put the sacrament and the word together. Their training gives them an erroneous concept of the Catholic liturgy. "The Reformation brought us out of the Roman Church, where worship was regarded as an end in itself. To the devotees of the far-flung Roman Church, worship is a contribution to God, pleasing to him apart from any effect it may have upon the worshiper." Yet, though critical, they are also envious. "Even in so potent a conception as the Roman Mass a human means is used in communicating the divine. While we dismiss for very good reason all the superstition clustering about the Mass, in repudiating the defect we are likely to throw out the accompanying reality. I believe that modern psychology is going to teach anew the values and demand a fresh interpretation and more rational cultivation of the forms and ceremonies of liturgy and ritual which are part of our (Catholic) inheritance."[8] The plea in many quarters is for "great music, noble liturgy and worthy symbolism," in a word, for the art of worship by which the faithful become aware of the presence and reality of God, and comport themselves accordingly. Why be surprised, they ask, if the world passes us by? "It knows that too often in Protestantism, Sunday-morning church is a this-world function, with pious gossip and a decorous sort of human friendliness, with a not-too-strenuous intellectual fillip thrown in. We try to make our services attractive to the secular tastes, to the non-religious attitudes in man's nature. We have naturalized and domesticated our very offices of devotion. We call men to be list-

[31]

eners of contemporary event rather than participants in eternal purpose. Instead of bringing men face to face with God in awe and reverence, we introduce an affable and comfortable season of spiritual entertainment."[9]

These sentiments are not the opinion of a single man. All the major denominations, including the most unlikely, in the past three decades have promoted a liturgical revival that has no counterpart in American Protestant history. Churches without a previous set hymnal and ritual prayers have acquired them; others have recast their "orders of worship" to make for more communal participation; church buildings and furnishings are being designed according to liturgical lines; denominational catalogues advertize a complete line of ritual miscellanea—the Evangelical and Reformed offers "altars" and "church candles," the Lutheran "an attractive variety of vestments and paraments," the strongly Calvinist Southern Baptist several hundred choices of "octavo anthems" and a variety of sacred pictures for use in the churches. Books on symbolism are sold by evangelical supply houses, to provide "practical help in choosing chancel equipment with understanding and taste," and answering such questions as "How should candles in the chancel be lighted? What colors should be used at the various seasons?" These do not include the well-known Episcopalian propensities to follow Catholic liturgical customs, including a recent modification of the Eucharistic fast that is almost verbatim with the decree of Pope Pius XII.

Sacramental confession is another aspect of the ministry which reflective Protestants are missing. The Methodist Bishop, Francis McConnell, advised his co-religionists to look into the practice of confessional absolution as a logical response to human demands. He felt that Protestants underestimate the value of Catholic confession when they equate it with moral counseling where delinquents are helped with psychological insight and understanding. The real value lies much deeper. "The penitent believes that the priest is speaking as the actual agent of God and that when the priest pronounces forgiveness and prescribes the method of penance the case is closed. There is no need of the penitent's thinking of reopening the case. The priest considers himself as the spokeman of God, who is the source of all authority. The relief to the penitent comes from the official assurance that God has forgiven his fault." No such assurance can be given the Protestant, "confessing in his prayers to God or even to a discerning counselor." He is "never sure that the case is closed. The Protestant conscience, assuming it to be sensitive at all, is prone to review its own decision sometimes to the point of becoming morbid."[10] It can never receive what the churches are unable to give, the sense of perfect security which comes from a ministry that professes to speak in the name of God.

The Lutheran principle of a universal priesthood has produced a lay-controlled church polity that Catholics can only imagine. As far back as 1800, Bishop John Carroll of Baltimore wrote against the Protestant-inspired state laws which favored the trustee system for local churches. If ever the principles of trusteeship prevailed, "the unity and catholicity of our Church would be at an end. It would be formed into distinct and independent societies, nearly in the same manner as the congregational Presbyterians of our neighboring New England States."[11] Catholic parishes withstood the legal pressures and came through unscathed; but Protestant churches without exception became responsible to lay vestries, elders or trustees, whose authority is now part of the ecclesiastical structure. For ten years, the Episcopalians in Brooklyn have been plagued with rival claimants to the pastorate of Holy Trinity Church, both parties supported by conflicting vestry interests. In 1955, when several Wisconsin ministers were convicted on "heresy" charges, the trial ended in a stalemate because the lay congregations denied any judicial authority in the Lutheran Synod. One of Norman Vincent Peale's earliest impressions as a clergyman's son was "the pressure that 'leading members' of a congregation could exert on the minister and his family." The resulting suspicion of lay interference was to stay with him for the rest of his life.

Yet Protestants commonly accept this "mutual ministry of believers" without complaint. They are even proud that their clergyman "can never claim the distinct spiritual status and the peculiar prerogatives of a priest in the Orthodox or Roman Catholic senses," that "on all fundamental matters he is only another 'believer,' of the same rank as the 'ministers' in the pews." If he assumes a unique religious position, either his conduct is ignored or, if he persists, he is accused of leaving evangelical grounds, as "a new presbyter but old priest writ large," and out of harmony with the spirit of Protestantism.

A Catholic may ask whether the clergy and laity are really distinct under these conditions. The ministry seems to be purely functional, or less, a kind of appendage to lay ecclesiasticism. In most Protestant churches this is actually the case. Without sacerdotal powers, the clergy never rise above the lay state. Objectively and intrinsically, a minister is only a delegate of the congregation, commissioned for services that anyone else can perform. No matter how elaborate the ordination ceremony (usually very simple), he remains before and after the same. No divine power has been given him to consecrate the Eucharist or absolve from sins, no faculty to bless and sanctify as found in the Catholic priesthood. Ordination, like marriage, is not sacramental; it confers no grace in virtue of the imposition of hands and no rights from God, but only a delegation from men.

While these are the principles demanded by Protestant theology, they are not always consistently followed and at times prove highly embarrassing. For years the Lutherans have been struggling with a dilemma raised by their own speculators. The evangelical party grants that the ministry is divinely ordained, but only in the sense that everything wise and useful comes to us from God. Against this position is the "strongly Romanist doctrine" which claims that ministers receive spiritual power at ordination, transmitted immediately from the Apostles through their successors to the present day. Most of the schisms in American Lutheranism are traceable to conflict over these opposite interpretations.

Presbyterians face the same problem. Their difficulty is resolving the status of elders in church polity. Are they laymen or clergy? Since the time of Calvin and Knox, their main concern was "the spiritual well-being of the people." Attention was in practice concentrated on external breaches of the moral law, sabbath-breaking, sexual offenses, domestic and local quarrels, charges of frivolity and extravagance in dress. With the passage of time, the emphasis shifted from cure to prevention, leaving to civil authorities the preservation of public order and decency. Yet even now they are described as "representatives of the people, chosen by them for the purpose of exercising government and discipline, in conjunction with pastors or ministers."[12] The description is ambiguous. It leaves untouched the prickly question of whether elders belong to the clergy or laity. If to the latter, why ordain them; if to the former, why give them ecclesiastical authority? Presbyterians in the States partly avoid the impasse by "installing" elders instead of ordaining them, or making them "commissioned workers" of the congregation. Even so, "there is confusion as to what happens on any such occasions, and we have the problem of the meaning of grace, and a real difference regarding objectivity and subjectivity as in the doctrine of the sacraments." Whether elders should be ordained by the minister or presbytery, and whether with or without laying on of hands; whether an elder may officiate in a church court, are all "questions which have been discussed with passion in different parts of the Reformed and Presbyterian world, and different opinions and practices are to be found side by side even in the same Church."[13] An example of one policy was the religious service performed during the Suez crisis by John Foster Dulles, ordained Presbyterian elder, and attended by the President of the United States. At the other extreme are elders who never officiate at church ceremonies and may not even be consulted by the local ministry.

The most critical effect of this ambivalence involves the Protestant Episcopal Church which still professes to believe in a historical episcopacy. The climax was reached in 1958, when the Lambeth Conference of the Anglican hierarchy and the General Convention of American Episcopalians approved intercommunion with the Church of South India. Anglicans throughout the world were deeply affected by the move which compromised their doctrine on the ministry beyond everything in the history of the church.

The Church of South India, numbering about a million members, is a curious amalgam of Anglicans, Congregationalists, Methodists and Presbyterians, who formed a new denomination in 1947. As an ecclesiastical experiment the C.S.I. has been called the boldest venture in the ecumenical movement. Never before had episcopal and non-episcopal bodies joined together on such a large scale, and ever since the Anglican churches in various countries have toyed with the idea of giving the C.S.I. full recognition as an affiliate member of the communion. Catholic-minded Episcopalians resisted the invitation and protested in a spate of books, pamphlets and articles that acceptance of the Church of South India's ministry would destroy the Episcopalian Church as a doctrinal institution. Their objections were unassailable. Canon du Bois, head of the resistance movement in the States, identified the Church of South India as a group which does not require assent to any of the Christian creeds from its members, which intends to remain permanently in communion with the most liberal elements in the Free Churches, and, above all, "which has presbyters and not priests, and nowhere defines the eucharistic doctrine it holds or the purpose for which the eucharist is celebrated."[14] In England more than a thousand members of the clergy formed the Annunciation Group as a united front to stop the intended recognition. But protests were futile, except to make the final approval more diplomatically worded. Following the lead of the Bishops at Lambeth, the American Episcopalians in solemn conclave accepted the orders of the South Indian clergy, allowed celebration of Eucharistic liturgy and reception of Communion between the two churches and without qualification subscribed to the creedal vagaries of the Church' of South India. Under fire from High Churchmen and Anglo-Catholics they inserted a proviso which does not mitigate the gravity of these concessions. The clergy are acceptable if they have been episcopally ordained; but the Church of South India considers priests on a par with presbyters. At the time of merger in 1947, free-lancing parsons of the Congregational sect were allowed to continue in the ministry along with the Anglican

[37]

clergy. For thirty years, until 1977, new candidates for the ministry must be ordained by bishops, but after that date another ruling will be made to decide about mitigating episcopal ordination. In other words, the keystone of Anglican theology, the historic episcopate, is an open question for the Indian hybrid. Yet now the Anglicans remove the keystone by accepting the Indian theory and, by implication, deny the doctrinal basis of Christianity. In the Church of South India, the Trinity, the Incarnation and Redemption, sacramental grace and the Real corporeal Presence are permissible opinions, but not required dogmas. To hesitate about episcopal ordination while making these huge concessions is straining the proverbial gnat with a vengeance.

What effect has the South India question had on the Episcopalian Church? For a while it looked as though the Anglicans in England would split wide open and another Oxford movement was in the offing. There was even talk of forming a Continuing Church of England in opposition to the Establishment which the Annunciation Group accused of defection. But when the ax fell and the Anglican hierarchy approved the South Indian heresy, only a handful had the courage to face the consequences. The rest either lapsed into silence or turned about-face to defend what they had shortly before condemned. About thirty of the English clergy have so far come into the Catholic Church, in many cases at great social and material sacrifice to themselves and their families. In the United States, the American Church Union, dedicated to "maintain and defend the Catholic heritage of Anglicanism" made desperate attempts up to the last minute to forestall intercommunion. They protested against the projected "false unity, basely purchased by the betrayal of vital trusts and precariously sustained by the combination of indifference to the things of God." Except for the courtesy of being aired in the religious press, the complaints were simply ignored. If American Episcopalians are generally less disturbed by this action of their leaders, the reason can only be that the Protestant hold on dogmatic principles is less firm in the States than in England or in Europe as a whole. Yet both in Europe and America, the Anglican Church must now be identified with the principles of the Reformation and its ministry denied any semblance of sacred orders. When individual clerics have themselves validly ordained by (or through) bishops of the Oriental and Old Catholic Churches, this gesture itself confesses a doubt that perhaps, after all, Pope Leo XIII was right when he declared that "Ordinations carried out according to the Anglican rite have been and are absolutely null and utterly void."[15] The present approval of the Church of South India confirms this judgment to a striking degree. Is it conceivable that ordination would be valid, in a Catholic sense, in a religious body which formally recognizes a church whose own clergy do not have to be ordained by a bishop, or believe in the Real Presence, and may even question the Incarnation, without which a Christian priesthood does not begin to exist?

More than a century ago, Newman was led to embrace Catholicism at seeing how the English Church of his day acted in a similar situation. An act of Parliament in 1841 authorized ministers of any Protestant sect to become subjects of Anglican bishops, without examining their doctrinal orthodoxy. He observed that at the very time when the Bishops "were directing censure at me for avowing an approach to the Catholic Church not closer than I believed the Anglican formularies would allow, they were on the other hand fraternizing with Protestant bodies and allowing them to put themselves under an Anglican bishop, without any renunciation of their errors." This, he said, was the last blow "which finally shattered my faith in the Anglican Church."[16] The South India crisis may evoke like sentiments in modern Episcopalians.

III

MISSIONARY ENTERPRISE

FROM A CATHOLIC viewpoint, the most serious aspect of modern Protestantism is the missionary outreach that leaves the home front to bring the "blessings of the Reformation" into foreign lands. Twenty years ago the Cardinal Prefect of the Propagation of the Faith urged priests and the laity to labor for the conversion of sectarians in their own countries "to check," as he said, "the grave obstacles which Protestant missionaries sent from Europe and America place in the way of the Church's evangelization." It was this problem which inspired Pope John XXIII to call a special meeting of the Latin American hierarchy within a few weeks of his elevation to the papacy.

For American Catholics the major issue is the impact which Protestants from the States are making on Latin America. On their own testimony, the Protestant Reformation of the sixteenth century did not fail in Spain; it was retarded, only to emerge triumphant years later in Spanish America. Never before, throughout the four hundred fifty years of its presence in history, has Protestantism reached such heights of apostolic fervor and ecumenical strength as of today in Hispanic America. From the days of the Reformers in Europe and the Pilgrim Fathers in New England down to the present, history does not register such a phenomenon as the emergence of a Protestant community in twenty countries that have been regarded as traditionally Roman Catholic.[1]

These observations are not idle rhetoric, as anyone familiar with the situation can testify. They are at least a challenge for Catholics to better understand the efforts which a declining Protestantism at home is making to reclaim its evangelical strength overseas.

Historical Background

Religious historians are a little surprised that for two hundred years after the Reformation, except for a few isolated voices, the Protestant churches showed no concern over the condition of the heathen world. Several reasons may be given for this apathy. Their time and attention were occupied with urgent matters at home. They had to entrench themselves in their own countries, England, Germany and Scandinavia, where the reform movement was threatened with submersion by the political power and a resurgent Catholic vitality. Theological differences had to be composed into working agreement; creeds had to be written; new church organizations devised and set up; the Scriptures had to be translated and circulated. In due time the early religious fervor of Reformation days cooled down to a life of religious formalism, worldliness and skepticism. But most significantly, Protestant nations like Denmark, Britain and Holland, had not yet begun to expand as great colonial and commercial powers, which might offer soil and scope for missionary work.

Sporadic experiments in foreign evangelization date back to the mid seventeenth century, when John Eliot (1604–1690) labored for forty years among the Indians of Massachusetts, translating the Scriptures and gathering his converts into Christian settlements to better wean them from pagan customs. His zeal was quickened by the firm belief that the Red Indians were the Ten Lost Tribes of Israel. Eliot's Catechism (1653) is said to have been the first book ever printed in the Indian tongue. His complete Indian Bible appeared in 1663—a triumph of scholarship in the face of almost insurmountable difficulties.

But the first real beginnings of the modern missionary movement among Protestant Churches date from 1792, when a small group of English Baptists organized a mission society and sent William Carey to India, where he labored with his companions for forty years. Most of their time and energy were devoted to translation work, publication of literature, preaching and the founding of a seminary and college at Serampore, which still survives. Within thirty years of Carey's landing in India, most of the influential foreign mission societies in the Protestant world had been founded.

By the end of the nineteenth century, these societies had grown and diversified to a point where the whole work of Protestant evangelism was threatened unless some kind of unity were achieved. In 1910, therefore, missionaries from all the major countries met at Edinburgh and agreed to form what eventually became the International Missionary Council. Organized at London in 1921, it divided its work with a co-ordinate office in New York from 1924 and has since provided for an agency in the Far East. It is now the chief organ of liaison for the Protestant missions and a major factor in the whole ecumenical movement.

The Council derives from its thirty constitutive bodies the mandate to promote consultation, investigation, publication and co-operation in "the work of presenting the Gospel to non-Christian peoples." Variety of belief is recognized as a fact, but subordinated in practice to "fellowship in the total task of the missions." An official statement covers three principal areas of policy:

The International Missionary Council is the chosen instrument of the churches for world-wide missionary cooperation. It is a Council of councils. Its constituent national and regional cooperative organizations are all bound together by their common missionary purpose. Five world conferences have been landmarks in the history of the modern missionary movement. Jerusalem, 1928; Madras, 1938, Whitby, Canada, 1947; Willingen, Germany, 1952; Ghana, 1958.

The International Missionary Council is a consultative and advisory body. It furnishes information to its constituent members and assists them to initiate strategic cooperative projects in areas of need. It studies policy and strategy for the world expansion of Christianity. It seeks to function as an agency through which all the forces of world-wide missions can think and act together.

The sole purpose of the International Missionary Council is to further the effective proclamation to all men of the Gospel of Jesus Christ as Lord and Saviour.[2]

Current estimates place sixty per cent of all Protestant missionary activity under the auspices of the International Council, which at its 1958 convention in Ghana voted to integrate with the World Council of Churches. At the same meeting a four million dollar theological education fund was made available to members of the I.M.C. "to render a new and more far-reaching service to the training of the ministry and the Christian world mission." Typical of the American support of the Council, half of this sum is the gift of John D. Rockefeller, Jr. The other half came from nine major U.S. boards of missions. As a result of this heavy financial backing from the United States, delegates to the Ghana conference publicly stated that "Americans are resented because they provide the dollars" which practically keep the International Missionary Conference in existence. There is no doubt that Americans in the I.M.C. fairly control its policy as illustrated in the latest move to unite with the World Council of Churches. All the proponents of the merger were Americans, including such eminent liberals as Drs. MacKay and Van Dusen, while a substantial block in the I.M.C. is still conservative and properly suspicious of the slippery theology in the Council of Churches.

Although in literature on the subject the International Missionary Council may appear to hold a monoply on Protestant evangelism, it is actually in competition, by a ratio of 3 to 2, with other societies who prefer to sacrifice material advantage in favor of a more evangelical and frankly biblical form of apostolate. "Faith Missions" they are called by others than themselves, because of their continued insistence on faith in God to provide the necessary means. More accurately their express function is to preach the word of God and not primarily, as with less dogmatic groups, to promote the temporal welfare of their clients. The best known of these groups, the International Foreign Mission Association, affiliates more than thirty lesser bodies with a personnel of some 5,000 members. It is sharply critical of the International Missionary Council.

In the face of the disposition today in some missionary circles to disparage and discard evangelism in favor of a more popular program of social studies, higher education, and other things, we boldly assert that the substitution of any other policy or program of work has signally failed in achieving anything like equal returns for the energy and money expended.

Critics have claimed that the evangelistic policy of Faith Missions does not make for the effecting of a strong and enduring structure for the future, as does work along educational and community service lines. On this point we must emphatically differ with our critics. We are strongly convinced that the truest criterion of a missionary's success, judged by the test of time, is the degree in which his efforts are the means of producing truly regenerated men and women who, united together in indigenous churches, will propagate their faith, win others to Christ, and exert a vital and ever-increasing spiritual and moral influence in the community and the nation. We fully recognize the social, industrial, political, and all other implications of the Gospel. And as for the term, "applied Christianity," so much upon the lips of champions of social service, we are of the opinion that any Christianity which does not find practical expression in daily life is not the real article but only a spurious imitation.[3]

Catholics who wish to evaluate Protestant missions should be fully aware of this basic divergence of attitude and know which method, the social or evangelistic, or their combination, is operative in a specific locality.

Growth and Variety

Due in large measure to the generous support from America, Protestant missions throughout the world have grown in number and influence to a degree unparalleled since the Reformation. In estimating the size of these missions, however, a number of careful distinctions should be made. Otherwise the real picture becomes distorted or even falsified.

First we note the difference between indigenous Protestant population in a given territory and what are reported as recent converts. The former may go back several generations and are safely authentic, the latter are often too recent and fluctuating to give anything but a vague approximation. Thus in 1930, before the recent crusade to "convert" Latin America got under way, the Protestant figure for Brazil was reportedly 1.3 per cent of the total population. In 1950 it rose to 3.3—which fails to distinguish between old time conservative bodies like the Igreja Evangelica

Luterana and evanescent American imports like the Assemblies of God. A reported growth of 460,000 in five years for the Assemblies (one of forty sects in Brazil), or one fourth of all the Protestants in Latin America, is certainly an exaggeration that can be dismissed.

More pertinent is the disproportion between what are ambiguously called "Christian communities" and actual communicant members. According to the latest *World Christian Handbook* the Adventists have 110,000 persons attached to the Philippine "community," but only 51,000 communicants; in Southern Rhodesia, the Methodist Church claims 42,000 adherents but only 15,000 members. Consistently the two figures vary, to such extremes as 100,000 in the Mennonite "community" of India, with only 13,000 recognized members. One calculator known to the writer estimated the number of Protestants in Guatemala by the size of a parade commemorating the Presbyterian Diamond Jubilee!

Still, no matter how severely qualified, Protestant missionary zeal has been phenomenally successful, to the point where it seriously hinders the apostolate of the Catholic Church.

For sheer numerical increase, Latin America offers the most sobering example. Unsupported figures now range as high as ten million Protestant "adherents" below the Rio Grande. More objective estimates reduce the number to about five million. This represents a growth of more than one hundred per cent in less than ten years. On the eve of World War II there were half a million sectarians in Hispanic America, or less than one-sixth the present calculation. Heaviest concentration is in Brazil, with close to two million, and Mexico with 900,000. Asia reports fifteen, Africa thirteen, and Australia eleven million adherents respectively. Preferred churches in Latin America are fundamentalist bodies like the Baptists, and fringe sects from the United States, especially the Pentecostals and Seventh-Day Adventists.

Some idea of the motley variety of churches on the missions may be gained from the situation in India. By actual count, 159 juridically distinct and autonomous Protestant bodies are currently active in the country. They fall into six classes or types: national organizations like the one million member Church of South India; national societies with no denominational affiliation and negligible membership; Australian and British groups, of which the largest is the Church Missionary Society of England; a handful of church-affiliates from the continent; and about forty denominations from the United States and Canada, among which the American Baptists (700,000) claim the largest membership. It may be surprising to know that many Protestant converts on the missions do not belong to any denomination, like the Methodist or Lutheran. They are simply joined to whatever society gave them baptism and instruction in the Bible. Better than a book on the subject, this peculiarity shows the shapeless character of Protestant faith and worship; you become a Christian without belonging to any church, except the nebulous society of those who accepted Jesus Christ as their Savior.

Methods and Techniques

The method of evangelism is determined by two factors in particular: whether the mission agency stresses the social aspect of Christianity or direct and personal indoctrination. In practice, of course, the two functions will be closely related; but as one or the other predominates it affects the orientation of missionary effort down to the smallest details.

Easily the best example of an organization mainly concerned with the social Gospel is the Young Men's Christian Association. What may be less familiar is a century-old tradition of promoting the Protestant missionary apostolate throughout the world. The Y.M.C.A. has fully established national alliances in forty-five countries, including India, Iceland and Japan, besides local foundations in twenty-seven other territories like Madagascar and Thailand. Its program is to advance the kingdom of Christ under Protestant auspices, as appears from the whole structure and history of the Association. For twenty years (1926–1947) the international president of the Y.M.C.A. was John R. Mott, one of the pioneers in the Protestant ecumenical movement and vice-president of the World Council of Churches until his death in 1955. His administrative genius and dozen volumes on the Christian apostolate under such titles as *Cooperation and the World Mission* and *The Larger Evangelism* played a major role in setting the tone of Protestant missionary work among the member churches of the World Council.

As far back as the last century, delegates to successive world conferences have been told to "look on the Young Men's Christian Association as an important and practical auxiliary to the Foreign Missions' effort." Over the years, this policy has not changed except to be intensified. Leaders in the Protestant mission field had long sensed the injury done to their cause by the sectarian divisions in their ranks. Something had to be done to neutralize the bad effect and the Y.M.C.A. furnished the answer.

In 1888, when the offer was first made to Association representatives at Stockholm, they were told how "when the devotees of other religions are asked to embrace the religion of Jesus it does appear to them a stumbling block of no small moment to find that the followers of Jesus, instead of presenting a united front and walking side by side with each other in loving harmony, are often so rent asunder by ecclesiastical strife that all traces of Christian unity disappear." No section of the pagan world is more aware of this sectarianism and therefore prejudiced against Protestant missionaries than educated and intelligent young men, the future leaders of their people. Consequently, "if, side by side with the missionary efforts of the Churches on the foreign field, there were placed an effective Young Men's Christian Association holding forth its all-embracing arms to everyone who loves the name of Jesus and cooperating in loving harmony with every earnest effort of every faithful section of the Christian Church, much of the evil resulting from sectarian division would be dissipated, and the essential unity of the followers of Jesus placed upon a platform that all might see. This is a kind of testimony no argument can refute, and the relation of the Young Men's Christian Association to Foreign Missions would be felt to be no uninfluential one, if in all our Foreign Missions' centres it thus let its light shine."[4] In the years since this proposal was made and adopted, the Y.M.C.A. has done yeoman service in every major country of the world.

Competent observers rank the Association among the leading instruments of Protestant evangelism; some would have it as the most influential. Certainly its concentration in urban areas and access to American revenue, both secular and sectarian, make it a heavy competitor with Catholicism in the Christian apostolate.

On a broader scale the building and maintenance of welfare institutions are the main vehicle for the Protestant message in the Foreign Missions. When the question arose whether they are merely instrumental or positively integral to the Christian Gospel, the answer was unequivocal. "Christian institutions," the World Council of Churches was told, "are the exhibitions in collective and social life of the new power in Jesus Christ and therefore part and parcel of the declaration of the Gospel." The impressive network of Christian hospitals, dispensaries and other organizations of service, which stretches from one end of a mission country to the other, has grown out of the impulse to express the power of the Gospel, however dimly conceived, in the presence of immediate need.

Hence the problem is only one of balance and proportion, and perhaps of deciding how far a hospital, for instance, should go in proselytizing among its patients. Some institutions, notably those connected with the ecumenical movement, consider the proclamation of the Gospel beyond the scope of their immediate purpose. But this is rare and frequently criticized, within and outside the Council of Churches, as a "half-hearted" attempt to prepare for Christ without openly declaring His message.

An Asiatic conference on *Hospital Evangelism* showed that a great deal of proclamation of the Gospel takes place in medical institutions.[5] Some hospitals in the Far East were criticized for being used as means of indoctrination. To which a large medical college replied that "We rarely find a non-Christian patient who does not ask for Christian services." And again, "We decided it was not right to have prayers in the wards with non-Christian patients. So we stopped. After twenty-four hours we had to resume as the protest from the patients was so strong." The current model for combining Protestant evangelism with high-minded social welfare is Albert Schweitzer, whose volumes in liberal theology pale in comparison with his care of the sick in French Equatorial Africa.

As a promotional medium, educational institutions are the most permanently effective. They will differ according to the needs and, incidentally, according to the weight of proselytism that a local situation will bear. In Latin America schools enjoy the highest priority for long-range Protestant evangelism. The current figure is more than 900 institutions, from elementary grade to university, with an enrollment approaching 100,000 students. Their impact has been immense.

Early in 1957, the National Council of Churches invited the American ambassador from Bolivia to address its Committee on Cooperation in Latin America. Victor Andrade, the ambassador, used the occasion to give a personal testimony to the influence that a Protestant high school—Instituto Americano, of La Paz—had exerted on his life. During the plastic years of his adolescence, he said, "we learned there the great teachings which are not written in books. We learned there the spiritual values of evangelical love which translated itself into the good life as to morals and into the democratic style of government as to politics. And now in retrospect I realize that these values are nothing but the Protestant style of life."[6] Not only the ambassador, but most of the government officials in 1957, including the Bolivian president, were reportedly graduates of that Methodist institution. Here, according to a commentator, is perhaps one clue to the secret of Protestantism's success. When the president of Bolivia and his cabinet were ready for high school, the only good one available in La Paz was the Instituto Americano.

A Catholic is naturally interested in the dogmatic side

of the Protestant apostolate. What sort of doctrine do the missionaries preach? How liberal or conservative? Do they tailor Christianity to meet the existing needs? No general answer is possible because the method varies so much among different churches and even in the same mission working the same locality.

At one extreme are fundamentalist bodies whose ideas of God and the supernatural life are closely akin to the Catholic. The Gospel Mission of South America, active in Chile and Ecuador, requires of all its members (including office workers and staff) unquestioned faith in the divine inspiration of the Bible, the Trinity, the fall of man, his need of regeneration, salvation through Christ, the divinity and bodily resurrection of Christ, heaven for the saved and eternal punishment for the lost, and, typically, Christ's premillenial return before the last day.

More common are the huge sending societies sponsored by the International Missionary Council, whose individual members or even constituent churches may be quite orthodox, but which tolerate almost any quantity (or absence) of Christian belief.

As reported by a Protestant missionary resident in China before the Communist invasion, the General Conference of the Methodist Church authorized a new translation into Chinese of the church's *Discipline and Ritual,* to conform to the latest American edition. Needless to say, the English version had not touched the Apostles' Creed, which is part of the historic basis of Methodism. But the Chinese committee had no scruples. It reduced the twelve articles of the Creed to eight, by removing the whole section on the life of Christ, from "conceived of the Holy Ghost, born of the Virgin Mary" to the Ascension and the Second Coming "to judge the living and the dead"—also the "Communion of

Saints and the Resurrection of the Body." There were also notable additions, in the form of explanatory clauses.

More instructive, however, than this manhandling of the Creed by educated Christians was how little attention the pastors and missionaries paid to the changes, after they appeared in print and were circulated among the people.

In Hispanic America, Catholics see themselves "face to face with Anglo-American Protestantism which means to repeat with its neighbors to the South what its ancestors did in Europe in the sixteenth century. We face a true invasion, systematic and perfectly synchronized and perfectly planned."[7] In 1936 one out of fourteen Protestant missionaries in the world came to Latin America, in 1952 the ratio was one out of four. In Argentina, to give only one sample, the number of sects had increased from 20 to 147 in less than twenty years. Missionary imports, mostly from the United States, are now in the neighborhood of 6,000 every year. Small wonder, then, how promising the harvest looks to those who are promoting and financing the movement. "In few parts of the world is there more continuous and more fruitful day-to-day evangelism than in Latin America. Visitors are impressed by the immense vigor of the work and the determination to grasp to the full the almost fantastic opportunity which confronts the Church."[8] This in turn has stimulated a missionary zeal in North American Protestantism that has no parallel in modern history. It is the Reformation come to life again.

A number of factors explain the shift of emphasis. They were thoroughly discussed at the Madras missionary convention in 1938, where the basic strategy of the new approach was formulated. Delegates at Madras correctly sensed the rise of a spirit of nationalism in Asia and Africa that would certainly inhibit the preaching of Christianity as a foreign commodity. Since then China fell into the hands of the Communists, and India had placed restrictions on visas to prospective missionaries. Spanish America offered a likely substitute for the oriental apostolate. Actually, Latin America was more than a substitute; it was a deliberate choice. A singular unity of language and culture, material conveniences and protection from the politically interested States made the diversion from the Orient highly prudential. Only one difficulty arose, which for years had checked the Protestant advance—Latin America is already Catholic and possesses what the sectarians claim to propagate, except for allegiance to Rome.

To get around this difficulty psychologically, various expedients have been used. The least intelligent solved the problem by ignoring it. Catholics are victims of mass delusion from which the Protestants must come to rescue them. A typical piece of vocation literature, entitled *Symbol or Saviour?*, pictures the huge Cross that towers above the Chilean Andes. It also helps to explain why American missionaries are sometimes "persecuted" by the reluctant people. "Everywhere one sees the cross," says the brochure, "and everywhere, too, one sees tragic evidence of the total ineffectiveness of that mute symbol to stay the power of sin, to alleviate life's burdens, to cheer in the hour of grief, to give hope in the time of despair. Worn paths lead to crosses near the roadside where flickering candles burn unsteadily, left by those seeking peace who do not know it is the *Living Saviour* and not the symbol that can grant soul's ease. And because they do not know it is Christ, and not the cross that saves from sin, they make endless pilgrimages to image and shrine. None but the *Living Christ* can answer the needs of these souls. They do not know. They must be told." Hence the need of men and women "who know that God has called them to carry the Message of Life in Christ to these people."⁹ Unless they are enlightened, the invitation concludes, thousands will remain in superstition, mistaking idol for reality and never hearing the secret of salvation.

More frequently the argument for sending missionaries is not professedly religious at all. Great poverty, undeveloped natural resources, sickness and a scaling death rate, widespread illiteracy and the need for social reform are sample motivations to inspire many Protestants, often at great sacrifice, to enter South America. When doctrinal differences are considered unimportant, this attitude has a degree of logic on its side but not enough to say that "today the Protestant faith down South is a sociological rather than a theological presence." The presence is sociological only for those who take their religion so lightly that cardinal mysteries of Christianity are ignored without concern.

American apologists are offended when the inroads of Protestantism in Hispanic America are called a foreign invasion. They object that the records point to an invasion from within rather than from without, on the premise that the spearhead of the movement is really native. At least in Brazil, Chile, Cuba, Argentina, Mexico and Guatemala the growth should be called indigenous and a product of the soil. The "invasion" occurred two generations ago; it was the sowing of the seed. It was Paul crossing the Hellespont into Macedonia and the West. "At present the problem for our Roman Catholic brethren would be rather to stop the tropical growth of the Evangelical forest." Nowadays there are numberless Protestants in Hispanic America who speak of their religion as "the religion of our fathers and of our grandfathers." It may be. Perhaps the financial support of Protestant enterprises in countries like Mexico can now be shared by the native population. Also it may be conceded that the invasion began two generations ago, around the turn of the century. But until the late thirties it was more a reconnaissance and testing of the ground than a full scale operation. Since then it has been carried on with the combined strength of American evangelism.

The essential feature of this movement is its invasive character. No one from the pope down denies that "the grave and ever growing problems of the Church in Latin America are not yet solved, especially the one which with anguish and alarm is justly called the most serious and dangerous, the shortage of priests."[10] When people are spiritually uneducated, they tend to superstition and become lax in the practice of their religion. The Church is moving mountains to correct these evils and remedy the situation. But where do Protestants get the right to exploit the weakness to their own advantage, by attributing what is bad in Latin Americanism to the Catholic faith? With eighteen hundred million non-Christians in the world who need the teaching of Christ, how explain the concentration of Protestant forces in a continent that has been traditionally, albeit weakly, Christian and Catholic for centuries?

A revealing page can be read on the subject from the address which Archbishop Michael of the Greek Orthodox Diocese of the two Americas gave at the Evanston Assembly of the World Council of Churches. He spoke to a plenary session of the Council on *The Tensions of the World and Our Unity in Christ*. His message, in brief, was a solemn protest against proselytism of one Christian denomination among the communicants of another, particularly of the projected Protestant evangelism among the Greeks and Russians behind the Iron Curtain, once those countries are opened to missionary enterprise. He said this was "most disquieting, and saddens us profoundly, because we believe that this interest is derived from selfish motives entirely incompatible with the spirit of love and of mutual understanding that should characterize not only every Christian but everyone who has a Common Father, our God in heaven." Instead of planning grandiose schemes for conquest among fellow-Christians, "the first responsibility we have toward these brothers of ours is prayer on their behalf, regular and systematic prayer." And instead of competing with one another, Christian Churches should meet together, through accredited representatives, "for the friendly discussion of such matters as keep us apart."[11] More prayer and examination of doctrinal differences are needed among the members of the World Council.

Change the Archbishop's complaint from a future possibility to present fact and we have a fair statement of the Catholic case against Protestant activity in Latin America. It is competition whose principles are alien to Christian charity.

I V

MARRIAGE, DIVORCE AND CELIBACY

OF ALL the areas of difference between Protestants and Catholics, none is more serious or affects American society more deeply than the institution of marriage. Sectarian literature on the subject emphasizes the tension with disarming bluntness: "Protestants cannot agree with Roman Catholics concerning marriage, divorce, the family, and birth control."[1] What makes the disparity critical is the effect of an alien theology on the modern mind, by creating attitudes, setting up standards and even codifying laws which contradict the principles of the Catholic Church. Unlike other phases of Christian doctrine, marital differences touch the lives of thousands of Catholics who enter marriage with persons whose religious ideals are derived from Protestant ancestry.

Sacrament Denied

When the Reformers broke with the Church, they followed the logic of this breach by removing from the category of sacred objects as much of the sacramental system as pleased their fancy. Five of the seven sacraments were dropped, simply and without scruple, though not without elaborate apology that filled volumes of controversy in the sixteenth century. Among the eliminations was marriage. "The last of their [Romanist] sacraments," wrote Calvin, "is matrimony, which all confess to have been instituted by God, but which no one, till the time of Gregory, ever discovered to have been enjoined as a sacrament. And what man, in his sober senses, would ever have taken it into his head?"[2] Calvin's diatribe was refuted many times over by his Catholic contemporaries, notably Bellarmine, who quoted a dozen authorities before Gregory I testifying to the sacramental character of marriage. Thus St. Augustine, who lived two hundred years before Gregory, reduced marital union among pagans to a purely natural contract, "whereas among the people of God it belongs to the sanctity of a sacrament."[3] Again, "in the City of the Lord, that is, in the Church, we recognize not only a bond of matrimony but also a sacrament."[4] Bellarmine's observation on Calvin was to call his statements "malicious lies" and "evidence of gross ignorance."

Calvin's modern disciples repeat the same arguments with minor variations. Protestants are told that in the early days only baptism and the Lord's Supper were regarded as sacraments. Ignoring the whole sweep of patristic evidence, supported by Christian archaeology (as in the catacombs), otherwise serious writers accuse St. Thomas, or Peter Lombard, or St. Bernard, of inventing the seven sacraments "since it had already been decided that there were seven deadly sins." So, as many sacred rites were developed, each to meet and complement a corresponding vice. Then the facile conclusion that "a sacrament was therefore of no great antiquity when in the sixteenth century the Protestant Reformers liberated marriage from this ecclesiastical entanglement"—which imitates the earlier bias without the pretense of plausible reasons.[5]

But if marriage is not a sacrament, is it purely secular? Most of the Reformers seemed to think so. Calvin compared the "sacredness" of marriage to "agriculture, architecture, shoemaking and many other things," which are also legitimate ordinances of God and yet certainly not sacraments. However, this concept has been greatly softened with the passage of time, until now the liturgy and writers generally prefer to stress the holiness of the marriage vows. In the *Book of Common Prayer*, matrimony is "an honourable estate, instituted of God"; the Congregationalist *Book of Worship* says that God "so consecrated the state of matrimony that in it is represented the spiritual marriage and unity betwixt Christ and his Church"; according to the *Lutheran Agenda*, "holy matrimony was instituted by God for the welfare and happiness of mankind and blessed by our Lord Jesus Christ." Ministers are told to treat marriage "as almost a sacrament," in protest against the pagan standards that have crept into Christian families and even the Christian pulpit.

Yet the original deposit remains. No matter how embellished with religious terms, the universal Protestant attitude regards marriage as noble indeed and even holy, but not sacramental. Only two sacraments, baptism and the Lord's Supper, are recognized even nominally. The other five, along with matrimony, "are not to be counted for Sacraments of the Gospel, being such as have grown partly of the corrupt following of the Apostles, and partly are states of life allowed in the Scriptures." In any case, they are not sacraments because "they have not any visible sign or ceremony ordained of God."[6] The solitary exception among certain Episcopalians only proves the rule, since High Church people of the Anglo-Catholic variety are anomalies to their own communicants by professing "Catholic" ideals within the structure of a Protestant denomination.

From the Catholic viewpoint the consequences are enormous. The Church teaches as a matter of faith that matrimony is one of the seven sacraments of the New Law, instituted by Christ to confer the grace it signifies. If Protestants do not believe this, they lose or deprive themselves in a variety of ways of what faith and experience teach is indispensable for a lifetime fidelity to marital obligations, namely, the grace of God. Certainly if two baptized Protestants enter valid marriage, they receive the sacrament of matrimony with a corresponding title to the sacramental graces. But even here a series of postulates must first be verified. The partners to the contract have to be validly baptized, since without baptism there could be no question of receiving another sacrament. Yet on principle the denominations do not consider baptism necessary for salvation and, therefore, do not require the first sacrament as a condition for valid matrimony. Moreover, though juridically the Church regards Protestant baptism as valid until the contrary has been proved, in practice she hesitates enough to rebaptize most Protestant converts who enter the Catholic fold. More serious still, though all the conditions required for a sacrament are present, sacramental graces will not be received unless a person is in the state of grace. Hence the Church's solicitude about Catholics making their peace with God by a good confession before entering marriage. A careful examination of the marriage rite of all the major Protestant bodies showed not a trace of awareness about the need for purity of conscience and the friendship of God to profit supernaturally from the marriage contract. In fact, any hint in that direction would contradict a principle of sectarian theology, that, in Luther's words, Christian marriage has no more claim on the divine favor than miscegenation among the pagans.

The issue remains no less serious even where a Protestant marriage was contracted sacramentally and fruitfully, and all the graces intended by God were received to bring the natural love of the spouses to perfection, to strengthen their indissoluble unity and sanctify them and their children. But in order to profit from these graces, there must be generous cooperation, which by the laws of psychology presupposes their existence is admitted. Why cooperate with something I do not believe has been given to me? Also grace once received may later be lost through indifference or neglect. And, in any case, what effort will a person make to preserve and fortify what his religious background has taught him to ignore and even deny?

Theology aside, Protestants labor under a grave handicap. Common experience teaches that nothing more surely gives courage and stamina to husband and wife than the calm assurance that in spite of whatever trials they suffer, power will not be wanting to see them through every crisis. Spokesmen for the National Council of Churches properly urge married people to recognize that "a resolute will to succeed no matter what comes, a refusal to give in to difficulties, a realization that even problems which cannot be solved can be outgrown, a determination to give their best in a relationship vital to the happiness of others and, above all, a reliance upon God's help are of great importance to strong home ties."[7] But where obtain this resolution and strength of will, and the guarantee that God's help is at hand and more than sufficient to weather any storm? Even on purely natural grounds, Catholic belief in the sacrament of matrimony begets confidence in divine assistance of which Protestants have no experience.

Under Civil Authority

Among the revolutionary changes created by the Reformation, none was more drastic than the secularization of marriage. What the Christian conscience had always considered a sacred institution which Christ committed to the Church, the Reformers proclaimed free from ecclesiastical authority and dependent on the political power of the State.

Calvin had no doubt why the Church usurped this authority over marriage. Once the Papists established that matrimony was a sacrament, "they assumed to themselves the cognizance of matrimonial causes, for matrimony was a spiritual thing and not to be meddled with before lay judges."[8] Luther concurred in the same judgment. Since marriage was "a physic against sin and unchastity," it belonged wholly to the natural order. No doubt, lawful wedlock was "the chief in the world after religion," but it had no immediate connection with religion, and meant no more to a Christian than any other amenity. It was a civil contract and nothing else. There were certain revelations of the purpose of the Creator in regard to it, as there were in regard to just dealing in the market place, but in both cases justice should be administered only by the prince and his officers. The Church was not appointed to judge and rule in such matters. Luther carried these notions into his own ecclesiastical system. "I advise," he said, "that ministers interfere not in matrimonial questions. First because we have enough to do in our own office; secondly because these affairs concern not the Church, but are temporal things, pertaining to temporal rulers. Therefore we must leave them to the lawyers and magistrates. Ministers should only advise and counsel consciences, out of God's word, when the need arises."[9] Historians of political theory see in this conception the birth of the modern State which, at least in the western world, had not received such rights over the family since the fall of the Roman Empire.

Protestantism not only inherited this legacy but, as in

America, wove it into the fabric of civil society and made it almost a part of the juridical status of marriage in modern times. However the process was a slow one. The change effected by the ideas of Luther and Calvin did not reach fruition until much later. In Germany, after a time, the liberal teachings of Luther were generally ignored, and until the seventeenth century the ecclesiastical (Anglican) courts still continued to try matrimonial cases in the spirit of the Roman canon law. Under Cromwell, however, the Civil Marriage Act was passed in 1653 to become the basis for matrimonial laws in the English-speaking world, and to a large extent also of Western Europe. Substantially the Act placed all jurisdiction over marriage in civil tribunals and a civil ceremony was required in all cases of valid marriage, although the wording of the ceremony remained religious in character. By providing for the authority, registration, publication and every aspect of marriage in the nation, this Act was declared to be "good and effective in law; and no other marriage whatsoever within the Commonwealth, after September, 1653, should be held or accepted as marriage according to the laws of England." Subsequent amendments to permit the use of "accustomed religious rites" in the ceremony in case the parties so preferred, did not alter the essential fact that "this law placed matrimonial jurisdiction in the hands of civil, instead of spiritual, tribunals and asserted unequivocally the secular nature of marriage."[10] Its philosophy became part of the legal structure of the English colonies and eventually the guiding principle of American legislation.

As a Protestant heritage, therefore, every phase of marriage falls, in American theory, under the competence of the State. Students of juridical history declare without hesitation that "marriage is recognized by American law as a civil contract for which the approval, assistance or blessing of the Church is legally unnecessary."[11] And consequently, "a minister, in undertaking to perform a marriage ceremony, does not act strictly as such, but rather as a minister of the law or quasi-officer deriving this authority from the statute."[12]

Consistent with these principles, Protestant churchmen accept the *status quo* in the United States, where the civil law and not the churches has final jurisdiction over the marital contract and its implementation. Occasionally they encourage people to marry in church at a religious function, and argue that "a marriage solemnized by a minister is more likely to last than one with a civil ceremony." But they practically erase even this mild recommendation by officially providing in their liturgy for a ritual of "Consecration of a Civil Marriage," in which the married pair (who have come to the entrance of the chancel) are told by the minister that, "Whereas you have been duly united in wedlock by an official of the civil State, and have presented yourselves here to have your marriage consecrated by the Church of Jesus Christ, it behooveth you to hear what the Word of God teacheth concerning marriage."[13] Then the vows are renewed in the past tense, "Hast thou taken. . . . I have," to remove the least suspicion that the church considers her ceremony anything more than a religious ornament to an already existing bond.

The baneful results of this transfer of authority from Church to State are manifold. Legal recognition of divorce with remarriage will be treated under a separate heading. But other aspects of civil intrusion may be quite as harmful. About half the States require no waiting period before a marriage license may be secured, and practically no State requires any waiting after the license is issued. Resulting "novelty marriages," "thrill marriages," "runaway marriages" contribute to the growing tide of family instability. Such marriages are not intended to last and generally do not. "Our lax marriage laws," according to one observer, "which do not provide for adequate waiting periods between issuance of a license and marriage ceremony, which have inadequate curbs on juvenile and adolescent marriages and which require no preparation for marriage, are largely responsible for the swelling ranks of divorce."[14] Yet the removal of such curbs becomes inevitable once religious sanctions and motivation are removed.

At times the civil law directly interferes with a natural right, as in the case of miscegenation. Thus marriages between a white person and a Negro or Oriental are generally held by statute to be invalid. According to Missouri law, "All marriages between . . white persons and Negroes, or white persons and Mongolians . . . are prohibited and declared absolutely void."[15] In context the prohibition reduces interracial marriages to the level of unnatural incest, by equating them with the mating of parents and children, or brothers and sisters. Here a salutary comparison might be made with the practical solution of the race problem in countries like Mexico and Brazil, where a Catholic mentality forestalled legal discrimination against "alien" races. In America the existing statutes on miscegenation simply reflect the bias of certain communities that create their own marriage laws without reference to Christian principles.

More grave than anything else, however, is the attitude which may now be considered inbred in the non-Catholic American mind, that getting married is a private affair which the State has surrounded with certain formalities, and that marriage itself has no more bearing on religious issues than any other institution operating under the civil law. Denominational leaders are painfully conscious of the situation and try to strengthen the people in their marital obligations by appealing to spiritual motives. "Today," they confess, "there is a special need for a clear statement of the Christian conception of marriage." And "one of the most important tasks of the church today is to keep these ideals from reverting to their primitive and unspiritual levels."[16] Yet, for all their evident high purpose, these appeals to *The Christian Ideal for Marriage*, to *Building the Christian Family* and to making *Home and Church Work Together* seem like pathetic after-thoughts to any one familiar with the secular concept of marriage introduced by the Reformation.

Divorce and Remarriage

As early as 1520, or three years after breaking with Rome, Luther refused to assert the indissolubility of the marriage bond. Very soon the complaint raised against him became fully justified, that, in his own words, "he arbitrarily trifles with the dissolution and confirmation of matrimony."[17] Though he regarded divorce as injurious to Christian polity and the State, he found that adultery is an immediate ground for divorce, with liberty to remarry. After reinterpreting the biblical doctrine and ignoring the voice of tradition since apostolic times, he proposed wilful desertion as a second ground for divorce. He did this in order to come to the aid of those "unfortunates" who had been forced to adopt celibacy. Other grounds which he recognized were persistent irascibility and pronounced uncompatibility of temper. If either party cannot restrain himself, he says, "let him (or her) woo another in the name of God."[18] Finally, he extended the so-called Pauline privilege to Christian couples and to cases where one party urges the other to "unchristian conduct," to "theft, adultery or any unrighteousness towards God," always with the option of remarriage.

The bridge between Luther's libertarian teaching on the marriage bond and the modern divorce crisis in Europe and America is the position he was forced to take with regard to the civil authority. Although Luther had consorted with the civil powers from the beginning of his Roman defection, his later philosophy on subordination of Church to State did not grow out of any tyranny from partisans like Frederick of Saxony or the Landgrave Philip of Hesse. If anything, Luther dominated the civil magistrates; he was not their puppet creation. But as the Reformation spread and the doctrinaire liberties which Luther unleashed began to assert themselves, he realized the need for some staying force to control the aberrations that his own theology had encouraged and to give some kind of unity to the new Christianity that had come on the European scene. Splinter sects of the Anabaptist type were symptomatic of the inherent tendency of the early Reformation to break into fragments, and only the restraining hand of the civil power, invoked by Luther and his disciples, succeeded in quashing the incipient fragmentation. In the same way, the dictum, *cujus regio ejus religio*, coined by the Reformers, consolidated the Protestant churches by the easy method of imposing a common profession of faith on all subjects in anti-Roman territories.

Given Luther's thesis that "marriage is a purely civil affair, subject only to civil authority like clothing, food, and lodging," it was only a matter of time before theory was reduced to practice. Once the State took over, marriage not only lost caste as a Christian sacrament, but all the grounds for divorce that Luther permitted on religious principle became solidified first as mere concessions and then as established custom recognized by the civil law.

The granting of divorce with the right to remarry was practiced in America since colonial times. However divorces were rare in the early days, largely due to the more rigid English tradition which differed from continental Protestantism on this point. With American independence, a radical change took place. Authentic records show that ten thousand divorces were granted in 1867, for a population of thirty-seven million, with a ratio of one divorce to eighteen marriages Current figures show a yearly average of 400 thousand divorces in the States, or one to approximately four marriages, to give the highest divorce rate of any nation in the world.

While notoriously differing in minor details, American divorce laws follow the pattern set by the Reformation on the legal grounds for dissolving marriage. Adultery is the universal solvent, with cruelty (physical or mental), desertion and neglect to provide, recognized by most of the States.

All the Protestant churches in America, without exception, accept the dissolubility of marriage as part of their theological system. Some manuals of doctrine, like the *Methodist Discipline*, put the matter obliquely by forbidding a minister to solemnize the marriage of a divorced person whose wife or husband is still living and then qualifying that "this rule does not apply to the innocent person in case of adultery or other vicious conditions which through mental or physical peril invalidated the marriage vow." Subsequent marriage of the innocent person also gives his guilty partner the right to remarry.[19] But most churches are unambiguous. Thus, according to the *Presbyterian Constitu-*

tion, "Remarriage after a divorce granted on grounds explicitly stated in Scripture or implicit in the gospel of Christ may be sanctioned in keeping with his redemptive gospel."[20] The explicit grounds are said to be adultery and desertion, the implicit are all others, as neglect of support or emotional incompatibility.

In defending the scriptural warrant for divorce with remarriage, the older school still uses Luther's exegesis to make Christ's words "except for adultery" refer not to legitimate grounds for separation but to a sanction for second marriage during the lifetime of the first (adulterous) spouse. Also following Luther's explanation of the Pauline privilege, the term "unbeliever" is stretched to cover every contingency, not excluding mental cruelty or the loss of romantic affection.

However, the more common approach admits that Christ's condemnation of divorce is a "hard saying," and then qualifies its application. "It is impossible," the argument runs, "without incurring great evils, to follow the saying literally in a world where there are criminals and predatory nations." In the same way, "Jesus' condemnation of divorce defines the norm for Christians, but there may be cases in which divorce should be permitted them in order to avoid greater evil. This is the basis of the Protestant view that, while divorce is a tragic thing, it is advisable under certain conditions when two persons have definitely failed in their marriage." Consequently marital indissolubility should be ranked with forgiveness of one's enemies as something idyllic. It must not be considered a moral law binding on all Christians, and much less become the basis of civil legislation. In fact "any attempt by the state to enforce any part of the Christian ethical ideal destroys the religious character of that ideal." An act of obedience motivated by fear of the law degrades an action from the religious to a purely social sphere, unworthy of dedicated children of God.[21]

Inevitably this approval of a practice reprobated by Christ exerts a variety of moral pressures on Catholics in a country like the United States. Divorce laws are not of their making. In the Irish Free State, for example, where Catholic principles guided the national legislature, the Constitution provides that "no law should be enacted for the grant of a dissolution of marriage, (and) no person whose marriage has been dissolved under the civil law of any other State but is a subsisting valid marriage shall be capable of contracting a valid marriage during the lifetime of the other party to the marriage so dissolved."[22] In America, legal recognition to the contrary exposes Catholics to severe temptations to "try again" in spite of the Church's prohibition. Add to this the practice of Christians in good standing in their churches, including ministers and bishops, along with the media for creating a general atmosphere of tolerance in the highest ecclesiastical circles. The effect on Catholic consciences can best be seen from the number of those who finally barter their religious heritage in favor of the easier, yet ostensibly Christian, practice of their non-Catholic neighbors. With almost half a million divorces annually, twice that many people every year become marital "free lancers," legally permitted to marry yet in most cases forbidden to Catholics because of a previous valid marriage. Not to compromise under these circumstances requires courage and moral convictions that not everybody has.

An equally grave problem faces Catholics who contemplate or actually enter marriage with Protestants after receiving the necessary dispensation from the Church. The issue involves more than appears on the surface. Since the

Protestant party has been taught that marriage can be dissolved, his Catholic partner is exposed to the danger of being stranded by the divorce courts, with no prospect of remarrying except at the price of estrangement from the Church. Everything in the Protestant's background and current practice conspires to weaken the marriage bond. "Too often," ministers are told, "the church has been used to frustrate and suppress spiritual growth through insisting that mismated couples remain married even after it is recognized that they will not be able to reach a union emotionally through affection for each other."[23] They should be advised, according to this Methodist counsellor, to give up the notion that divorce is wrong from a religious standpoint.

One aspect of the problem not only affects the harmony that should prevail in Christian marriage but touches on the validity of the marital contract between Catholics and Protestants. As expressed by canon law, indissolubility is among the essential properties of marriage. Consequently, if a person, in contracting marriage, excluded it by a positive act of the will, he contracts invalidly.[24] This does not mean that mere ignorance or erroneous belief would invalidate the contract. Thus in the famous Gould case, the Protestant wife was known before and after marriage to regard it as subject to termination by divorce. Yet the Roman Rota decided against nullity on the grounds that "such an erroneous opinion and intention invalidate the marriage only when it has been made a condition *sine qua non*." A positive act of the will to that effect, even by only one of the parties, not to be married unless the union be dissoluble, would suffice, provided the will act were clearly proved. In the case of Anna Gould, the intention was not proved to be sufficiently explicit, and her Catholic partner was not permitted to remarry.[25] In other cases, however, declarations of nullity have been granted by the Holy See, as in the decision where it was "fully proved by witness testifying to statements made by the man, both before and soon after the marriage, to the effect that he would not marry and did not marry otherwise than in contemplation of possible divorce."[26] It would be disastrous to cast suspicion on the average non-Catholic marriage in the light of these norms. The preponderance of Roman decisions favors a valid contract for want of sufficient evidence to the contrary. Nevertheless, the prevalent notion on marital dissolubility is one of the guiding principles in trying nullity cases before Catholic matrimonial courts.

Celibacy and Evangelical Chastity

The Protestant theory of marriage cannot be properly understood without considering the attitude towards abstention from marriage, or virginity, which the Reformation introduced into modern theology. Underlying this attitude is a whole system of ideas that runs counter to Catholic principles on the nature of man, original sin, the power of divine grace and the will of God as manifested in the precepts or evangelical counsels. Its beginning must be traced directly to the writings of Martin Luther whose great contribution to Christianity, according to one admirer, was to have liberated matrimony from over a thousand years of Roman tyranny.[27]

More restrained observers, however, believe it was fatal to Luther's teaching on marriage that it grew out of his twofold struggle against the state of virginity and against the Church's authority.

The sexual overtone of his doctrine derives from the antagonism to virginity that scandalized even his contemporaries. More recently, Sigrid Undset said, "I had read what Luther wrote about virginity, and it made me very anti-Lutheran," leading to her conversion. Luther's hostility to the sacerdotal and monastic states drove him to calumniate celibacy beyond all reason. In order to assail the Catholic position more effectively, he assumed, as the basis of his own doctrine, that the sexual instinct operates as an irresistible law of nature and tolerates no restriction in the form of vows. In his invectives against the vow of chastity, human dignity and decency are set aside to a point that modern editions of his works frequently omit the more offensive passages. He simply ignores the means of grace offered by the Church for controlling the sexual passions and leading a life of perfection. Nature, in his opinion, forces practically all men to embrace the married state. It is a "miracle" if anyone manages to live continently. Then, contrary to what the Church ever held, he declared the sexual instinct sinful in itself and refused to consider the involuntary sex movements not sinful, and much less as virtuous if resisted for the love of God or in obedience to a previous vow.

Coupled with this preoccupation with the libidinal drive, Luther's attitude towards Rome cut him off from the sacramental system and ascetical practices which centuries of tradition had proved sufficient to conquer the bodily instincts. As a result, the historic confessions of faith which stabilized Protestant theology commonly repudiated celibacy and inveighed against the evangelical counsels. Romanists, says the Confession of Augsburg, "would persuade men that these invented religious orders are a state of Christian perfection," and the fourteenth of the Anglican Thirty-Nine Articles still reads, "Voluntary works besides, over and above, God's commandments, which they (Catholics) call works of supererogation, cannot be taught without arrogance and impiety."

While less crude in our day, the original prejudice has not changed. But now the stress is on the blessing of marriage which Rome allegedly denied the people by her exaltation of celibacy. "Under the Papacy, marriage was regarded as an estate of lesser value, while celibacy, or the unmarried state, was praised as a specially sacred calling, meriting divine grace. For this reason the work of Christian fathers and mothers was greatly despised, while that of monks and nuns was highly exalted as meritorious to salvation. Priests were compelled to abstain from marriage, and the blessing of Christian homes. The Reformation changed all this by restoring the pure doctrines of the Gospel to the Christian people."[28] St. Paul's commendation of virginity is dismissed as a piece of masculine ignorance. Since "he had very little idea of the Christian family as an equal partnership of the sexes," the apostle "seems to have thought celibacy the preferable state, with marriage as a sort of prophylaxis against incontinence."[29]

Occasionally bias stimulates the imagination to conjure up reasons why the Church introduced the law of celibacy in the first place. A major consideration, we are told, was to keep the priesthood from ever becoming a hereditary caste. In the same spirit, with a trace of malice, Protestant readers are informed that religious chastity "also includes sexual continence outside of marriage, but that, though often ignored in practice, is an undebatable general requirement in all systems of morality."[30] More often, when celibacy figures in denominational literature, the treatment is soberly objective and serves to emphasize the fundamental difference in doctrinal principle which the acceptance or rejection of a life of virginity implies.

Superficially, it might seem that rejecting celibacy is only an inherited relic from the sixteenth century, when many priests and religious disgraced their profession by not living up to its high demands. Luther himself was a prime example, along with Cranmer, Bucer, Zwingli and Knox, all of whom had broken their monastic or sacerdotal vows. Actually the Protestant position on celibacy cuts across the whole field of dogma to illustrate how radically the Reformers had changed the teachings of Christian tradition.

The Catholic Church had always taught that, in spite of the fall of our first parents and inherited original sin, man's nature was not absolutely vitiated. We are indeed deprived of many gifts previously enjoyed by Adam and Eve, but still we are not utterly depraved. Due to concupiscence, the intellect has been darkened and the will notably weakened in their struggle against the lower instincts. With St. Paul, we are inclined to do the things we would not and leave undone the things we should. But we do not say that "reason can only blaspheme and dishonor everything God has said or done," nor that "man's will has no power to work the righteousness of God" because freedom is a pure fiction since the fall of Adam.[31] Consistently, therefore, on a theory of total depravity, not only the counsels, like virginity, but even the precepts of the Decalog are impossible of fulfillment. The irritant as regards celibacy is the implied Catholic teaching that celibacy can be kept, that with divine grace the will can so far rise above passion as to observe the commandments of God and even generously offer the sacrifice of perpetual chastity.

Tied in with the depravity theory is the more familiar denial that good works are needed for salvation. Having denied that man has enough will to keep the divine mandates, good works are not only unnecessary but impossible Merit is a misnomer and, quite logically, "it is more impor-

[77]

tant to guard against good works than against sin."[32] For sin cannot be avoided, whereas good works are a blasphemous claim that we and not God alone perform anything virtuous. If good works in general are not possible or meritorious before God, *a fortiori* not the pretended evangelical counsels which contradict the plain teaching of Christ who said, "When you have done all that was commanded you, say, we are unprofitable servants."

On principle, Protestants recognize no difference between precepts and counsels, even as they deny any distinction between mortal and venial sin. They conceive the divine will as uniform in all directions because the human will is equally impotent, whether to avoid evil or do good, to obey the commandments or follow the counsels. What place could perfection or celibacy have in a system whose author believed that "Judas' will was the work of God" and whose theorists even now believe that "the fulfillment of God's will is an accomplishment beyond our capacity. It is not we who do the will of God. To Him belongs the plan and execution, and its time of fulfillment."[33]

Yet we know that Protestant anti-asceticism was born of more than pure theory. Its rise and continued existence are less the fruit of dogmatic ideas than the rationalization of certain courses of action, notably severance from the Church's authority and discipline. From earliest times, the Fathers praised virginity in terms that appear almost extravagant. They were certainly unmistakable. "Virginity stands as far above marriage as the heavens above the earth," according to Chrysostom. And more plainly, "Virginity has a special reward hereafter," according to Augustine. But while extolling the celibate life, the Church never assumed it was easy. Above all it must be safeguarded with mortification and humility, and nourished by prayer and the sacraments. As far back as the year 100 A.D., Ignatius of Antioch wrote that "if anyone is able to persevere in chastity to the honor of the flesh of the Lord, let him do so *in all humility.*" More recently, the late Pius XII frankly admitted that "virginity is a difficult virtue." To preserve it are needed constant vigilance, self-denial and fidelity to all the means of sanctification consecrated by centuries of tradition and proved effective for thousands of Christians since Apostolic times. Protestants repudiate the only instrumentality which can possibly insure the practice of what is admittedly not natural to human instincts. Unfamiliar by experience with the power that comes through Catholic channels of grace, and lacking evidence from close observation in the lives of others, they assume that what they cannot do must be impossible for everyone else.

One aspect of the Protestant attitude toward celibacy that should be briefly touched upon is the support and promotion which churchmen and organizations give to professional agents of anti-Catholicism. There are two principal types: the secularist who has no respect for Christian ideals, whether Catholic or otherwise, and the "convert" who gave up his sacred calling for a mess of fleshly pottage. Not the least of Paul Blanshard's appeal to a reading public running into millions is the prurient undertone of his writing on Catholic chastity. "Freud's wisdom," he declares, "was not available to the Popes and theologians who first imposed celibacy upon a reluctant clergy, and they could scarcely be responsible for failing to appreciate the gravity of the effects upon human nature of suppressing the basic human instincts."[34] Blanshard, who is not a Christian, might be excused for identifying celibacy with masochism. But how explain the fact that his books have been so well received in Protestant circles and described in church magazines as necessary reading for anyone to understand the Catholic Church? In the same way, the handful of human derelicts who found celibacy too hard are being used by denominational leaders to discredit the Church's authority and malign her discipline, especially on sexual morality. When national agencies like the Southern Baptists endorse the defamation, its effect far exceeds what might be expected from the number engaged in this sordid business.

There is a brighter side, however, to the general apathy or even hostility to Catholic ideas of evangelical chastity. For almost a century, the Protestant Episcopal Church in the United States has actively promoted the religious life for men and women who wish to dedicate themselves to a life of celibacy. Apologists for this striking departure from Reformation policy explain it was a mistake for continental Protestantism to repudiate the religious life and set marital devotion above the old vows of obedience and chastity. "Free from the passions of controversy, we can now see, as the Church did in its early centuries, that these things are not exclusive," that while praising the dignity of monasticism, the Church by no means depreciates the dignity of marriage. By 1930, the Anglican Communion took official cognizance of religious orders under its jurisdiction, and prescribed the general norms that govern this "Catholic" nucleus in Protestant Anglicanism. In 1958 the Lambeth Conference of the Episcopalian hierarchy went on record to say how greatly it valued "the special form of vocation evident in Religious Orders and Communities," and "hopes that this form of vocation may find its expression in a wide range of ecclesiastical tradition within the Anglican Communion."[35] Nothing comparable to this venture has been tried by other Protestant bodies, although recently an important segment of the Lutheran Church in America (the Augustana Synod) organized a community of religious to follow the Rule of St. Augustine, as did Luther, and become "a symbol of the life of faith in Christ our Lord" so badly needed in the modern world.

V

MARITAL MORALITY

IN A RECENT study of current ethical patterns, the author observed that Protestantism labors under a grave handicap in dealing with moral and social problems. Lacking the absolute principles of Catholicism, its morality becomes more passive than active. Having a limited cultural tradition, the Protestant more easily identifies himself with the given structures, with the moral environment in which he finds himself. If it happens to be Christian he tends to be conservative; if it is secularist, he readily accommodates his conduct to the prevailing norm.[1]

The moral issues arising from marital relations illustrate this principle of conformity. With the growth of secularism and its consequent demoralization of family life, Protestant churchmen and their communicants find themselves defending positions that a few generations ago their ancestors had repudiated as utterly unchristian. Within the surrendered territory the most serious loss is a clear concept of the primary function of marriage, the procreation and education of children, which the pagans had always subordinated to selfish interests but which now religious leaders eliminate from the teaching of Christ.

Reformation Responsibility

As in so many other cases, here, too, the Reformation prepared its adherents for what sociologists consider the most serious threat to family security in the western world. The right of private interpretation, or more correctly, the claim of private inspiration, exposed the Protestant conscience to the dangers of illuminism and allowed each person the option of setting up his own standards of marital conduct. Marriage itself was removed from the category of sacred institutions on the pretense of saving it from papistical control. In line with the Lutheran theology of concupiscence, the people were told that "no conjugal act takes place without sin," yet "God covers up the sin without which the married cannot live."[2] Thus all marital actions, whether licit or otherwise, were reduced to the same level of culpability. By denying the power of moral choice and stressing the force of human passion, the Reformers practically made self-control impossible. Luther's statements on the urgency of the sexual impulse and its imperious demands are impossible to quote except in paraphrase. In one of his milder moods, he says that neither nature nor the law, the Bible nor even God and His commandments can restrain the desires of the flesh.[3]

However the most radical factor which led to the acceptance of birth control among Protestants derives from their rejection of the Church's authority in the moral order. Artificial contraception is indeed against the natural law, but the generality of men need revelation to arrive at a correct knowledge of ideas beyond the crude elements of morality. To recognize interference with conception as gravely culpable demands clarity of vision that may be had only with difficulty by those who either repudiate the assistance of revelation or refuse to accept its divinely appointed interpreter. In either case, the mind becomes prey to the emotions and easily convinces a man that what he prefers to be false is really not true or at least not certain and morally binding.

Ecclesiastical Approval

The idea of preventing conception is not new and was already known among the ancient primitives. Among savage peoples a great variety of contraceptive methods, some magical and superstitious and others more effective, were employed along with infanticide and abortion to restrict the population because of a limited food supply. In the United States the organized effort to popularize contraceptive methods was started during the period 1828–1832 by Robert Dale Owen and Charles Knowlton. Owen was the son of the British Socialist, Robert Owen, who influenced the writings of Karl Marx and whose thesis that "man's character is the product of his social and economic environment" has become the mainstay of Marxian sociology. Owen Jr. popularized his father's ideas in several books, especially *Moral Philosophy*, in which he advocated artificial contraception. By the time of his death in 1877, seventy-five thousand copies had been sold. In 1832, Knowlton, a Massachusetts physician, brought out anonymously *Fruits of Philosophy*, to give the people the medical side of what Owen promoted on economic grounds.

Until the beginning of the twentieth century, however, contraceptive methods were mostly learned through person-to-person communication and generally discredited by religious leaders and even civil laws. As late as 1873, the United States Congress passed the Comstock Law which forbade the dissemination of contraceptive knowledge. "Every obscene, lewd, or lascivious, and every filthy book, painting, picture, paper, letter, writing or print, or other publication of an indecent character . . . and every article or thing designed for preventing conception or producing abortion, or the giving of information directly or indirectly, where or how or from whom or by what means any of these articles can be obtained is a crime."[4] Except for occasional and minor complaints about legal restriction, the matter rested until Margaret Sanger began her crusade before the first World War and in 1914 organized the American Birth Control League with the avowed purpose of legalizing contraceptive information and obtaining public aid for birth-control clinics. Yet all her efforts and incredible zeal were quite secondary to the parallel movement in Protestant circles which first became indifferent and then favorable to family limitation and now considers planned parenthood one of the doctrines of the Christian creed.

The earliest denominational statement on birth control came from the Lambeth Conference in 1920, and affected the whole Anglican Communion, including the Protestant Episcopal Church in the States:

We utter an emphatic warning against the use of unnatural means of avoidance of conception, together with the grave dangers—physical, moral and religious—thereby incurred. In opposition to the teaching which, under the name of science and religion, encourages married people in the deliberate cultivation of sexual union as an end in itself, we steadfastly uphold what must be regarded as the governing consideration of Christian marriage. One is the primary purpose for which marriage exists—namely, the continuation of the race through the gift and heritage of children; the other is the paramount importance in married life of deliberate and thoughtful self-control.[5]

Ten years later the 1930 Lambeth Conference modified its position to say that, "If there is a good moral reason why the way of abstinence should not be followed, we cannot condemn the use of scientific methods for preventing conception which are thoughtfully and conscientiously adopted."[6] In 1958, the Conference raised the practice to the dignity of a Christian virtue, since "the responsibility for deciding upon the number and frequency of children has been laid by God upon the consciences of parents everywhere."[7] While reprobating abortion and infanticide, the Anglican hierarchy formally approved those "methods of control (which) are medically endorsed and morally acceptable"—the latter phrase being added to satisfy a conservative fraction of church members.

Official declarations of national church bodies follow the same pattern. In 1931 the Federal Council of Churches, with a membership of twenty-eight American denominations, led the way. It published with approval a resolution that "the careful and restrained use of contraceptives by married people is valid and moral. They take this position because they believe that it is important to provide for the proper spacing of children, the control of the size of the family, and the protection of mothers and children; and because intercourse between the mates, when an expression of their spiritual union and affection, is right in itself. They are of the opinion that abstinence within marriage, except for the few, cannot be relied upon to meet these problems, and under ordinary conditions is not desirable in itself."[8] Since the Federal Council became the National Council of Churches in 1950, there has been no change in policy. But now the roster includes 72 religious bodies with constitutive or affiliated membership, and much of the Council's literature expatiates on the ethical propriety of judicious birth control.

In view of the Federal and National Council's attitude,

there would be no point in rehearsing the teaching of individual churches and Protestant leaders except when they elaborate on the motives or offer specific measures for implementing the practice of contraception.

A year following the Federal Council's statements, the Congregational Christian Churches came out officially in favor of birth control and since then have pioneered in the field. Their Commission on Devotional Life recently expressed its "Christian conviction that there is no reason why only the procreative aspect of the marital relationship should be recognized." They look for the day "when the techniques of planned parenthood should have emerged completely from the shadowy realm of the underground, and some absurdly antiquated attempts at legal prohibition, into the open light of approved scientific and social education."[9] They hasten to add, however, that "this advocacy of birth control" should not be misunderstood as minimizing the fundamental role that children must have in assuring a happy marriage.

Another early promoter was the Methodist Church. Concurrent with the Federal Council, Methodist churchmen meeting in New York recommended legislation that would permit a physician to render medical information on contraceptive methods. They argued that a bill of this kind would give "greater freedom to physicians, hospitals and clinics in extending to needy persons such information as would be in accord with the highest principles of eugenics and the best health of the individual."[10] While not alone, their recommendation contributed to the New York state law which declares that a contraceptive device prescribed by a doctor "is not an article of indecent or immoral nature or use . . . if in his opinion, the health or condition of the patient requires it."

The Protestant Episcopal Church did not wait long to put into effect the 1930 Lambeth concession. Meeting in General Convention four years later, it passed a resolution called (to prevent criticism) "On Principles of Eugenics," to the effect that "We endorse the efforts now being made to procure for licensed physicians, hospitals and medical clinics, freedom to convey such information as is in accord with the highest principles of eugenics and a more wholesome family life, wherein parenthood may be undertaken with due respect for the health of mothers and the welfare of their children."[11] Though worded with characteristic Anglican diplomacy, Episcopalians commonly recognized this as *carte blanche* to use artificial contraception and more recently admitted that "birth control is general among members of the Episcopal Church." The proof of this fact, if needed, is the small size of Church families.[12]

Perhaps the most surprising attitude is the Lutheran. In spite of his secular concept of marriage, or because of it, Luther advocated large families, seems never to have sanctioned onanism and, in fact, urged women to bear children, if need be, even to sickness and death. "That is what they are for!"[13] Until very recently, at least one large denomination, the Missouri Synod, denounced "the frustration of conception by the use of artificial means, by drugs or unnatural practices (as) a sin that has become widespread in modern civilization."[14] But now even this stronghold of Lutheran conservatism has surrendered to the prevalent trend and no longer requires its pastors to teach that contraception is sinful. Other Lutheran bodies were never concerned about the morality involved and either permitted or approved what, after all, "countless Lutherans" were doing. Thus, according to the American Lutheran Conference, the means which a married couple uses to determine the number and spacing of births are for them to decide with their own consciences, on the basis of competent medical authority. No moral significance should be attached to any of the approved methods for controlling the number of children. "Whether the means used are those labeled 'natural' or 'artificial' is of far less importance than the spirit in which these means are used." Indeed, continence in the marital relationship becomes just as sinful as the use of contraception if the motive is a selfish avoidance of pregnancy.[15] So that the sin of contraception has nothing to do with the abuse of a faculty, but should be judged solely on the refusal to have children.

Moral Rationalization

Inevitably churchmen have defended the adoption of a practice that conflicts with their own religious traditions and which Catholic writers plainly tell them is a form of pagan degeneracy. Protestant apologetics in this area has been steadily growing in volume and intensity, suggestive of a need to answer, if not the reproaches of conscience, at least the criticism of Catholics and some Protestant communicants who still hesitate to accept the teaching of the churches. Writers follow two main lines of argument, depending on their church's emphasis in theology and, to a certain extent, conditioned by the circumstances of defense. As a rule conservative writers appeal to the Scriptures and revelation while more liberal theologians pass over the religious phase and concentrate on the "scientific" evidence from eugenics and sociology.

The crudest approach simply ignores the problem on the score that the Bible does not treat of birth control. Thus, for the Disciples of Christ, "where the Scriptures speak, we speak; where they are silent, we are silent." Or, less delicately, "Presbyterians do not believe this precept— 'Be fruitful and multiply'—is relevant today." However, most churchmen and moralists who still respect the inspiration of the Bible are at pains to show their people how contraception may be reconciled with the Scriptures.

They begin by postulating a new moral situation that was unknown to the ancients and, consequently, demands a reappraisal of standard principles in the light of modern conditions. The two reputedly new factors which enter the picture are that children, at least here in America, are economic liabilities, and increased knowledge of physiology and chemistry makes means for preventing conception readily available and (some of them) highly reliable. Hence the choice that faces a responsible Christian couple, either to go along with the current movement without moral guidance, or pause to reflect and, if possible, square the practice of family limitation with the teaching of the Gospel.

The people are told to re-examine the Christian concept of marriage. As described in the Epistles of St. Paul, marriage seeks to imitate the two primary attributes of God: His creative power and unbounded love. In Christian marriage, the two spouses receive a share in the divine creativity. True fatherhood was in God before it was in man, and our own human fatherhood is only a faint image of His creative fecundity. True motherhood must also be in God. After all, did He not make woman, and did He not give her mother-love? Thus through human parenthood, the Maker of the universe allows us to participate in His own creativeness, and Matrimony has been elevated to the dignity of a spiritual collaboration with the Creator of mankind.

But marriage has a more important quality. Married Christians are called upon to imitate the infinite love of

God. So exalted is their duty that, according to the ritual, "Holy Matrimony signifies the mystical union betwixt Christ and His Church," meaning that "the natural affection between husband and wife has been raised to a real likeness of the 'uniting agape' between the Persons in God and the 'uniting agape' between our Lord Jesus Christ and His faithful people. In the Epistle to the Ephesians, when it is said: 'Husbands love your wives even as Christ loved the Church,' the same word 'agape' is used both for the love of husband toward wife and for the love of Christ toward His Church."[16]

These two functions of marriage are related to each other by subordination. "Creativity is not the whole of marriage, any more than it is the whole life of God. Love not only creates; it also, *and primarily* seeks the deepest possible union with the beloved." Accordingly, if we would measure or balance one against the other, the fostering of mutual affection between the spouses takes precedence over the begetting of children, and the procreation of offspring is secondary to cultivation of love between the married partners. Some may wonder how this agrees with the traditional claim that procreation is the primary end of marriage. They will not be surprised, however, after making an unusual distinction. The generation of children is primary if we take marriage as a purely "natural" or "material" institution in which biological mating is necessary to bring human life into being. But on the higher "spiritual" level, as should obtain among Christians, carnal generation has been subordinated to the promotion of marital love.

But the problem has not been solved. "The question is still: does mutual devotion justify physical union even when conception is prevented?" Protestant theology, reputedly based on the Scriptures, answers in the affirmative by adroitly evading the real issue, whether the marital act may be deliberately frustrated in its natural power to generate life, and concentrating on the admitted superiority of spiritual love over carnal intercourse. The theory is ingenious. No Catholic would deny that promoting Christian charity deserves to be praised, nor that sexual relations may be sacrificed in the interests of a higher, moral good. In fact, celibacy and virginity carry this very principle into effect. Without questioning the holiness of the married state, those who embrace a life of the counsels offer to God, by abstention, the use of a natural function to which they have a perfect right but which they may freely restrain for the love of God and the greater service to their fellowmen. Sacrifice and abstinence, however, are not interference and deliberate frustration. If two persons wish to foster their mutual affection, they may do so to their hearts' content, provided they keep within the precepts of the natural law and obey the dictates of right reason. Here the two philosophies, Protestant and Catholic, clash head on. Protestant moralists admit that "the physical expression of the mutual devotion of Christian husband and wife is no substitute for the primary (in the carnal sense) use of that act for procreation." Then they add what the Catholic Church reprobates as contrary to reason and revelation. "But when Christian parents have fulfilled or are fulfilling that primary 'material' function (by having *some* children), the rational and spiritual use of that bodily union for the expression of their total union does provide the moral justification for sometimes excluding the possibility of conception."[17] In other words, since the primary "rational" end of marriage is the good pleasure of the spouses, the primary "material" (euphemistic for "unrational") end may be not only sacrificed but positively hindered by a mutual abuse of the sexual faculties.

Comparatively few Protestant writers undertake to defend birth control on scriptural grounds. Their normal defense is either eugenic or sociological, either concerned to produce better children of healthier mothers, or to stem the "suffocating tide of humanity" which threatens to make the earth unlivable through overcrowding. Among church leaders arguing from a eugenic bias the most representative and outspoken has been G. Bromley Oxnam. Currently bishop of the Methodist Church, formerly president of the Federal Council, and for one term a president of the World Council of Churches, his aggressive support of birth control had much to do with raising the dignity of the movement from sexual conspiracy to a religious crusade. His opinions on the subject are now incorporated into standard textbooks and quoted as source material in the social sciences. "It was but yesterday," he said, in speaking for the Federal Council of Churches, "that some persons, in the name of religion, condemned the use of anesthesia in childbirth, arguing suffering was the just lot of women because of the sin of Eve." So now there are those who condone planned parenthood if instruments are not used but condemn it if scientific means are employed.

They miss the religious reason which rests on the respect for personality. Planning for our children so that the mother's health may be preserved and healthy children born should be our real interest. When we make available to mothers sound scientific information which is used for the high moral objective of bringing to our families healthy happy children, we are wisely using scientific means for moral ends. Religious leaders are awake to the dangers to family life which planned parenthood can help to correct. Communities which fail to provide marriage counseling, sex education and child-space service are recreant in their trust. Fundamentally, the family rests upon the acceptance and the practice of the law of love as revealed in the prophets and Jesus.[18]

Oxnam has written extensively in favor of planned parenthood, promoting family limitation not only as a private practice but as public policy. His position, which is generally accepted by liberal Protestants, claims that too many parents bring children into the world that lower the national vitality, become a financial burden to the state, and out of proportion to their numbers create all sorts of social problems. Consequently, as the meaning of human inheritance becomes clearer, the obligation of society to protect itself grows more imperative. Meantime, the churches should second the efforts of the state to improve the quality of its citizens by encouraging a voluntary limitation of offspring, especially among the lower economic classes which by eugenic standards are a social liability. One effect of this propaganda, however, was not expected. The "higher" levels of society have become notoriously self-arresting, while the lower groups are still very prolific. And, as more than one Protestant commentator has warned, Catholics will "take over America" by sheer propagation if they remain faithful to their Church's teaching on birth control.

In recent years the sociological approach has become more common. The basic pattern still follows the Malthusian theory that population increases faster than the means of support, unless checked by famine, pestilence, war or other calamities. But where Malthus encouraged sexual restraint, church leaders recommend contraception; and where Malthus proposed only a theory, they assume an established fact. Their most authoritative statement was voiced at the Evanston Assembly of the World Council of Churches in 1954, where they suggested two remedies for the problem of adequate resources for all nations. "Redistribution of population," along with "family planning and birth control," were offered to the 170 million members of the Council, "to be courageously examined" and put into effect under ecclesiastical guidance.[19]

The more popular religious press follows the same lines, with dramatic overtones to rationalize a practice whose real motivation could not be further removed from the reasons that are alleged. Describing the situation as a "demographic explosion," church editors face the readers with an array of impressive facts. In 1830 the world population finally reached one billion persons. It had taken the world 50 centuries of economic and social development to reach that stage of population. By 1930 the world figure was two billion people. And the acceleration continues. The third billion should be passed by 1965, the fourth in 1980, and by the year 2000 the earth will be bulging with 6 to 7 billion persons. "Thus is man's most intimate creativity suddenly becoming his grossest problem. This is the situation that has to be talked about by churches, scientists, governments; it cannot be talked around or talked away. Facts are facts and the discomfiture they bring to a church or a scientist or a government has less than nothing to do with their ineluctability." What to do? There are palliatives, of course. Shifting population density by immigration, stepping up production of natural resources, more equitably distributing the raw materials needed for human consumption—are all possibilities. The United Nations Bureau of Social Affairs points out that vegetable substance in the sea can be compressed into food, that solar and nuclear energy can be released for power, and scientists will no doubt discover still unimagined means of helping an over-prolific world make better use of what is available. But no accumulation of new methods or discoveries will solve the problem. "Unless the breakneck population increase is itself brought under some control even while all possible adjustments to a jam-packed world are being made, the dreadful end will overwhelm all stop-gap efforts."[20] In a word, the only hope of averting the threatening disaster is scientific birth limitation.

To a Catholic reading these terrible forebodings of the future and the fixed idea that only one way can save the earth from destruction, they sound unreal, quite apart from the heavy coating of emotion or accusing Rome of celibate articulations of the natural law with no relevance to present reality. The world population has been growing steadily for over a century, yet no Protestant concern for the fate of mankind was manifest until the past few years, in fact not until the birth control movement got fairly under way in the late '20's. Strange, too, that religious spokesmen in the most prosperous nation on earth (and one of the least popu-lated) should be so zealous to ward off impending doom by resorting to contraception. Political leaders in densely popu-lated countries like India have thought otherwise. Mahatma Gandhi was no Christian, but he was a shrewd observer. "Contraceptives," he declared, "are an insult to woman-hood." The greatest harm done by the propaganda for birth control "lies in its rejection of the old ideal and substitution of one which, if carried out, must spell the moral and physical extinction of the race. Contraceptives of a kind there were before and there will be hereafter, but the use of them was formerly regarded as sinful. It was reserved for our generation to glorify vice by calling it virtue." He admitted that "millions in this world eat for the satisfac-tion of their palate; similarly millions of husbands and wives

[97]

indulge in the sex act for their carnal satisfaction and will continue to do so and pay the inexorable penalty in the shape of numberless ills with which nature visits all violations of its order."[21] One of the tragedies of the present time is the approval that Christian missionaries have given the practice of birth control in India, Japan and elsewhere, ostensibly teaching the doctrines of Christ yet promoting a species of moral decadence that even traditional pagans had to be taught to understand.

If the real motives for birth control are transparent to Catholics who understand the struggles of the flesh in conflict with the laws of God, only a few scattered voices among Protestants have been raised against the unanimous teaching of their churches. Some high-minded churchmen place the matter on the level of faith. "God knows when the coming of a certain child by a certain conception would be a blessing, perhaps not only to the family but to society, perhaps to a world waiting for leadership. And God knows what the parents' income will be when the child arrives, and how its coming will affect the mother's health. God knows all this and we don't; and the doctors don't. All this He can order and we can't."[22] Others are more brutally frank. "The real reason underlying birth control no doubt in most cases is the desire to be unrestricted in the gratification of the sexual urge without suffering the inconvenience of pregnancy and childbirth and the care of children, which care to a large extent confines the mother to her home."[23] But these sentiments are exceptional. Rarely does a churchman of any rank or a Protestant journalist recognize the pleasure basis of the arrested family; that a determined policy to inhibit conception normally rises from a craving for personal advantage or the seeking of pleasure. What even social scientists with no religious bias are willing to admit is obscured to the point of denial by sectarian framers of thought; that while ambition, professional or social, tempts some people to contraception rather than risk success by assuming the liability of children—for most people the arrested family issues from a desire to have the pleasures of comradeship and sex without assuming the duties which nature may place on those who enjoy the intimacy of marriage.

Criticism of Catholic Doctrine

It can be assumed that wherever birth control is defended, the Catholic Church will be abused for its uncompromising attitude and appeal to the natural law against the hedonism which other Christian churches are promoting. Much of the criticism is shapeless and hard to analyze. Catholics are said to be devotees of a modern fertility cult; their Church is oblivious to the sufferings of mankind and the great benefits that birth control would bring; her authorities indulge in pious inanities while thousands of infants are brought into the world to die shortly without any chance of life. But running through the welter of hostility are certain estimates of Catholicism which underlie the whole opposition movement. Still somewhat hazy, they are being clarified in a desperate effort to make theological sense of a situation that was not born of doctrinal reasoning but crept into the churches unawares and now its presence has to be justified.

The most specious argument credits the Church with a naïve syllogism: children have souls, souls are destined for heaven to glorify God forever, therefore the greater glory of God requires the greatest possible multiplication of souls to praise Him. Besides standing at variance with the facts, since the Church has never taught that as many children as possible should be conceived, the argument betrays a callous notion of Providence that seems unbelievable. As though the mystery of generation was a kind of mathematics or the creation of souls not in the hands of God.

A more intelligent approach takes issue with Catholic doctrine on the primary end of marriage. This is still the favorite target for evangelical contraceptionists. Where "the Roman maintains that marriage and sex have as their primary purpose the procreation of children; we must dare to redefine their purpose as the expression of love and loyalty, that others might come to see through our married lives the love and loyalty of God who was in Christ Jesus." According to this thesis the Catholic Church was so preoccupied with the materiality of sex that she lost sight of what the modern Protestant discovered, that by enjoying the pleasures of marriage minus their onerous consequences, married love grows in a way that is impossible under Catholic standards. A student of history may find here a touch of Manicheism, whose distaste for the material things of life was mostly speculative; in practice the Manichees were so fleshly that, as French Albigenses, they threatened the moral order of a whole nation. And even without theological argument, divorce statistics show the highest index of instability among childless couples, with family security guaranteed in direct proportion to the number of children.

A recent import from Europe bases the practice of contraception on the universal "law" of sexual urgency. Since the demands of the flesh are not controllable, any theology like the Catholic which preaches marital restraint hinders the demands of nature and opposes nature's God. "If we are ever to master the rebellious uprising of all those natural instincts which have so long been repressed, we must resist this dangerous perversion of truth with all our might. This view is indeed all the more dangerous because it enforces its appeal by the claim to represent all that is most serious and most sacred in the Christian faith."[24] Taking their stand on the Reformation ethic that man's will is impotent against concupiscence, and adding now the Freudian thesis that sex control is psychotically harmful, modern Reformers are as hostile to Catholic morality in marriage as their ancestors were against the Church's teaching on faith.

However, the ultimate disagreement with Catholic principles calls into question more than dogmatic creeds. It denies the whole structure of the moral order founded on the natural law. Over twenty years ago, the late Cardinal Hayes of New York located this root of the problem. In the fall of 1935, he preached a sermon in St. Patrick's Cathedral in which he answered the speakers at a Carnegie Hall meeting, whom he accused of having "misrepresented the Catholic position on birth control." Immediately eleven prominent ministers (joined by two rabbis) challenged the Cardinal in the public press. "Birth control," they asserted, "is not to be dealt with from the postulates of Roman Catholic theology or metaphysics." The Cardinal replied in a lengthy statement that showed remarkable insight into the spirit of a movement whose basic principles are still unrecognized by too many people. "Fundamentally," said the Cardinal, "it is not a question of advocating or condemning birth prevention. It is a question of the existence or non-existence of an objective code or standard of morality. I, and all those who think with me, be they Catholics, Protestants or Jews, hold that there is a moral law and that contraception is an offense against it. The clergymen, on the other hand, have abrogated belief in a moral law."[25]

Twenty-five years ago this indictment might have seemed overdrawn, especially when so many Protestants joined with Catholics in protesting against their own liberalizing churchmen. But now there can be no doubt. The philosophy of planned parenthood implicitly denies the natural law by allowing every man to be his own judge of what is ethical with no reference to an objective norm. What aggravates the situation is the defense by Protestant leaders of moral subjectivism which, though inherent in Reformation theology, required an issue like contraception to bring it into the open. Thus when leading ministers were asked in a national survey what their denomination held on birth control, they said the practice was sanctioned because the churches have no right to intrude on the moral judgments of an individual. For example, no ecclesiastical convention of Baptists has ever by resolution expressed disapproval of planned parenthood. "Even if it had, such resolution would not be binding on any Baptist. Most Baptists would resent and repudiate any such resolution as an unwarranted intrusion into the private life of husband and wife."[26] If they think birth control is all right, it becomes moral for them, anyone to the contrary notwithstanding.

The ethical relativism of birth control and opposition to the Catholic Church for opposing it were dramatically illustrated in the recent controversy provoked by the Protestant Council of Churches in New York City. In the summer of 1958, Dr. Louis Hellman, a Kings County Hospital physician, had failed to provide a contraceptive device for a Protestant diabetic woman for whom pregnancy (according to the doctor) would have been fatal. Promptly the Council of Churches demanded redress and published a formal statement condemning not the action of Hellman but the orders of Dr. Morris A. Jacobs, Commissioner of Hospitals, who forbade Hellman to fit the device. Jacobs defended himself on the basis of policy and was supported by the Catholic Physicians Guild of New York. Meantime, the Protestant Council (now assisted by other groups) pressed for a decisive settlement of the problem on the score that New York city hospitals forbade contraceptive therapy out of deference to the Roman Church, whose view on this question Protestants consider immoral. "In fact," said the Council's executive director, "birth control or planned parenthood practiced in Christian conscience fulfills rather than violates the will of God." Two months after the incident made national headlines, New York City's Board of Hospitals reversed the Commissioner's decision. Voting 8 to 2, the board directed that municipal hospitals henceforth provide "medical advice, preventive measures and devices for females under their care whose life and health in the opinion of the medical staff may be jeopardized by pregnancy and who wish to avail themselves of such health services."

The Archdiocese of New York and the Diocese of Brooklyn issued a joint statement which repeated their previous condemnation of birth control. By sanctioning the practice under pressure from the churches, the Board of Hospitals "departed from a long-established and accepted moral standard. It rejected traditional morality, the teaching of all Christian and Jewish belief until recent times. Catholics are rightfully distressed at this decision of the board. It is a deterioration of moral life in that such a policy introduces an immoral practice in our hospitals that perverts the nature and the dignity of man."[27] Catholic doctors and nurses were reminded of their duty not to cooperate actively in a practice which contravenes the laws of God.

By contrast, the Protestants were jubilant. They interpreted the event as a victory for freedom and removal of another barrier in the path of Roman imperialism. Liberal commentators asked for a definition of the natural law and opposed the Church's right to define that law absolutely. Some merely questioned its existence. The evangelicals, on the other hand, directly challenged the fact that contraception is against the moral law.

We are heirs of the Reformation. We cannot acknowledge "natural law," for both "nature" and "law" have been redefined by the act of justifying love of God in Christ—and "sin" is the very allegiance to "natural law" which denies the work of Christ. Rome starts from the point that "grace does not destroy nature but fulfills it," and defines marriage and sex consistently therefrom. We Evangelicals need to cast away our population statistics and spend our energy defining the meaning of marriage and sex from the starting point of the freely justifying grace of God.[28]

Not even Luther could improve on this nihilism. It was axiomatic with the Reformers that nature had been thoroughly corrupted by the fall. Since man is incapable of any ethical good, whether rationally to know the truth or morally to practice virtue, any pretense of obedience to a natural law becomes blasphemy. The only law for Christians is confidence in Christ, that the sins we inevitably commit have been cleansed in His blood and not imputed to us by reason of His mercy. Four centuries ago Luther preached that "We must reject the law when it seeks to affright the conscience," that "when we have in hand the righteousness that justifies before God, we cannot too much disdain or despise the law."[29] The lesson has not been lost on his followers.

Protestant churchmen are fully aware of the difference between their own and the Catholic position on birth control. In fact, this is one of the main arguments in discouraging their people from entering into mixed marriages with Catholics. Other reasons are also given, notably the Church's demand that children be brought up in the Catholic religion, thereby putting the other member into a domestic strait-jacket and making him a stranger to his own family. But the real irritant is birth control. For suasive purposes, the Church is described as cruelly indifferent to health or human life, with no suggestion of the pleasure motive behind contraception. "The question of family planning," Protestants are told, "is one of the difficult issues in mixed marriages. If a mother already has several children and medical science says she will die if she becomes pregnant again, even then the Roman Church does not permit her to use contraceptive means considered adequate or sound by the medical profession. The same is true if she has tuberculosis or some other grave illness from which she ought to be cured before undertaking to bear another child." In the face of such tyranny, it is only proper to urge young people to "stand firm against the requirements of a church which would handicap them in their family relationships."[30] Presumably this recommendation of the National Council of Churches to "stand on their rights" applies equally to persons contemplating marriage and to those already married.

Chesterton once remarked on the satisfaction that Christians might take at seeing the effects of agnosticism on those who began by rejecting the articles of faith and ended by questioning the principles of reason. "We did not ourselves think that the mere denial of our dogmas could end in such dehumanized anarchy" The same, with reservation, might be said of the sectarian acceptance of birth control. Until modern times the logic of the Reformation was still obscure. The obscurity has been clearing up to reveal what Catholics can easily recognize and what they hope Protestants will see before it is too late, that self-indulgence is being blessed and defended in the name of Christianity.

V I

CHURCH AND STATE RELATIONS

THIRTY YEARS ago, John Dewey argued a brilliant case in favor of political secularism by tracing its genesis in America to the Protestant Reformation. When the founding fathers were laying the groundwork of the Constitution, said Dewey, they had "the lesson of the two and a half centuries lying between the Protestant revolt and the formation of the nation," to warn them on "the necessity of maintaining the integrity of the state against all divisive ecclesiastical divisions." No doubt, "many of our ancestors would have been somewhat shocked to realize the full logic of their own attitude with respect to the subordination of churches to the state—falsely termed the separation of church and state."[1] Dewey's thesis was that Reformation theology laid the principles for a concept of Church and State in which the latter becomes progressively dominant in every phase of human activity, including the religious and ecclesiastical.

While Dewey's theory is a biased simplification, it has the merit of drawing attention to what Catholics may easily overlook, that the current propaganda on separation of Church and State is not a passing fancy but has theological roots imbedded in the soil of four centuries of Protestantism. Its ultimate purpose is state control.

Political Ideals of the Reformers

Among the changes in religious thought introduced by the Reformation, few have been more radical than the idea of a universal priesthood of the laity and the corresponding denial of a real distinction between the secular and ecclesiastical state. Luther's theories have been rightly considered the watershed which divides church and state principles into two antithetical positions, the Catholic and the Protestant; so that many of the current problems arising in this sphere, at least in America, can be traced to his innovation. He laid the groundwork for the secular state.

Luther first proposed his thesis in the appeal he made to the Emperor Charles V and the German nobility in 1520, three years after his separation from Rome. It has since become the stock-in-trade of non-Catholic political philosophy. Directing his attack on the Church whom he charged with responsibility for the social distress in Germany, he pleaded for the tearing down of three walls which the Romanists had drawn around themselves, "so that no one could reform them, whereby all Christendom has suffered terribly." The second and third of these walls (the claim that only the pope can summon a general council) do not concern us here and were quite incidental to Luther's main argument. His principal accusation was that, "if pressed by the temporal power, the Romanists have affirmed and maintained that the temporal power has no jurisdiction over them, but, on the contrary, that the spiritual is above the temporal."

What should be made of the claim? The very idea of two classes is a fable. "It is a fiction by which the pope, bishops, priests and monks are called the 'spiritual estate,' while the princes, lords, artisans and peasants are the 'temporal estate.' An artful lie and hypocritical invention, but let no one be afraid of it, because all Christians are truly of the spiritual estate, and there is no difference among them, save of office. For we are all consecrated priests by baptism. Since we are all priests alike, no man can put himself forward, or take upon himself without our consent and election to do that which we all have alike power to do. Therefore, a priest should be nothing in Christendom but a functionary; as long as he holds his office, he has precedence; if he is deprived of it, he is a peasant or a citizen like the rest. But now they have invented 'indelible characters' and even imagine that a priest can never become a layman; which is all nothing but mere talk and human conjecture."

As a logical consequence to equating the secular and priestly state, the Church cannot be superior to the State. "What kind of Christian doctrine is this, that the 'temporal power' is not above the 'spiritual,' and therefore cannot punish it?" And if the temporal is superior, "it has been ordained by God for the punishment of the bad and the protection of the good. So that we must let it do its duty throughout the whole Christian body, without respect of persons, whether it strikes popes, bishops, priests, monks, nuns, or whatever it may be. Whatever the ecclesiastical law has said in opposition to this is merely the invention of Romanist arrogance."[2]

Behind Luther's denial of a real distinction between the temporal and ecclesiastical domain lay the disclaimer that Christ established a visible Church, vested with His authority and delegated by Him as a perfect society with divine rights to prosecute its spiritual aims. His motives, we know, were dictated by the pressing need for help from the secular rulers of Germany. The price he paid was to deny any superiority of Church over State. In return he received the political assistance required to propagate the new evangel by catering to the instincts of envy and lust for power. It was no accident that the formula proved successful or that its impact was so far-reaching.

The full implication of Lutheran theology touched every aspect of Church and State relationship. Only civil laws have binding power on the citizens, since the State has a right to pass judgment on ecclesiastical legislation, but not vice versa. Civil officials may determine if churchmen are serving the common interest, and punish or depose as they please; but the Church has no rights except those conceded by the State. Indeed, civil coercion can deprive any ecclesiastic, even the pope, of his ministry and if need be, of the very title he pretends to have received from God.

Historians of the Reformation soften the harshness of this doctrine by comparing it with the "milder" position of John Calvin. The Geneva Reformer also fused the civil and ecclesiastical powers, but his approach was more constructive. He was less concerned with decrying the pretensions of Rome than with building up a system of Church and State relations of his own. Theoretically, Calvin assumed that every member of the State was under the Church's discipline and demanded high virtue of those entrusted with civil authority. "What an ardent pursuit of integrity, prudence, clemency, moderation, and innocence ought they to prescribe to themselves, who are conscious of having been constituted ministers of the divine justice."[3] In a sense, therefore, political officials were subordinate to the Church, but to the Church invisible, from whom they derived their principles of moral equity as found in the Scriptures. But in the practical order the Church depended on the State to implement and direct its purely spiritual interests. "Civil government," wrote Calvin, "is designed, as long as we live in this world, to cherish and support the external worship of God, to preserve the pure doctrine of religion, to defend the constitution of the Church, to regulate our lives in a manner requisite for the society of men, to form our manners to civil justice, to promote our concord with each other, and to establish general peace and tranquillity." In a word, the whole gamut of external action comes under civil authority, whose comprehensive function is "to provide a public form of religion among Christians and insure that humanity be maintained among men."[4]

Calvin did not stop with theory. He put his ideas into practice by setting up a theocratic state modeled on the ancient Israel. His preachers supplied the inspiration and the civil arm the sanctions for making Geneva a byword for moral rigorism. Penalties were imposed for consulting fortune tellers, for laughing during preaching, for passing tobacco during service, for settling a bet on Sunday, for inability to recite one's prayers. Other regulations were directed against the remnants of Catholic practices. A goldsmith was punished for making a chalice for Mass, a barber for tonsuring a priest, another for saying the pope was a good man. The Genevan Council even forbade the baptizing of children with the names of Catholic saints.

Both Reformation attitudes, the Lutheran and Calvinist, have deeply affected the prevalent American mind on the relations of Church and State. One stream of influence has been linear, the tradition which almost identified the civil and ecclesiastical domain and gave to the State authority even in religious matters. The other influence came by way of reaction against the political establishment of churches in territories that adopted the Reformation; among the Protestant nobility in Germany, in Sweden, Norway and

Denmark, and most pertinent for the United States, in Tudor and Hanoverian England.

Protestant Nationalism in America

The dean of American church historians, Kirsopp Lake, felt that Protestantism lost something when the Reformers separated from Rome. For all her tyranny, he confessed, Rome is supra-national, while those who leave her tend to make their religion nationalistic. "When the English, Dutch, German and other North-European nations broke away from the Catholic Church, they adopted the principle that each nation had independent sovereignty in ecclesiastical as well as secular matters."[5] Though more relevant to countries like England and Scandinavia, the observation also applies to America.

It is true that Protestantism in the colonies and later in the States broke with the European custom of churches established by law. This factor played an important role in shaping Reformation polity along distinctively American lines. But the original principle was not substantially changed. Luther and Calvin on the continent, and Cranmer and Cromwell in England had too deeply implanted the idea that civil rulers have authority in the religious sphere.

We have already seen the drastic consequences of this theory in the field of marital legislation. Every phase of the contract, its conditions for validity and concessions for dissolution are woven into the fabric of American law, with the State assuming on principle that the government has final jurisdiction over the marriage of its citizens. According to Protestant standards, nothing else was possible. No institution as complex and intimately concerned with human welfare as marriage could have been left to fend for itself.

But where to find the authority to command obedience, once the Reformers had broken with Rome? Catholic authority was rejected, the Protestant was weak and divided. That left only the State which, in Calvin's words, is divinely appointed to "cherish and support the external worship of God" in all things, including marriage, that pertain to the public weal.

Marriage is not the only evidence of Protestant nationalism in American history. For more than a century the churches have successfully influenced the government to advance their own interests and to pass legislation which affected the whole country. They established in the process a tradition for which Catholics may properly be grateful: the idea that Church and State are not to be indifferent or hostile to each other but should cooperate for the common good. Christopher Dawson and others trace the commendable elements in Protestant nationalism to John Calvin rather than Luther. While Calvin went far along with Luther in coalescing the civil and ecclesiastical authority, he conceived the latter as more active than passive and consequently paved the way for the American concept of religious collaboration with the civil government. Hence though Calvinism has always been considered more opposed to Catholic ideals than Lutheranism, yet "it stands much nearer to Catholicism in its conception of the relation of Church and State and in its assertion of the independence and supremacy of the spiritual power. In this respect, it carries on the tradition of medieval Catholicism."[6] Though liable to sectarian exploitation, the cooperative principle (in which the government defers to religious interests) has been the mainstay of American Church and State policy.

The outstanding example of this theory in practice was the abolition of slavery, through the concerted action of a dozen denominations during the first half of the nineteenth century.

As early as 1787 the Presbyterian Synods of New York and Philadelphia recommended to all their people, "to use the most prudent measures in the counties where they live, to procure eventually the final abolition of slavery in America."⁷ The American Anti-Slavery Society was organized in 1833 by representative Presbyterians, Congregationalists, Methodists and Baptists, with the avowed purpose of "influencing Congress" to abolish slavery. In 1835 the Quakers petitioned Congress to outlaw the domestic slave trade, which prompted Senator Calhoun to complain that petitions "do not come as heretofore, simply and far apart, but in vast numbers from soured and agitated communities."⁸ About the same time a memorial was presented to Congress bearing the names of three thousand New England clergymen and begging, "In the name of Almighty God," that slavery be done away with. In a few months 125 distinct remonstrances were sent by the ministers of New England alone. When a House committee reacted against this clerical pressure, John Quincy Adams denounced the House measure as a "direct violation of the Constitution of the United States." His judgment prevailed.

Nine days before the first Emancipation Proclamation, Abraham Lincoln received a delegation of Chicago clergymen who believed that "the country is now suffering under Divine Judgments for the sin of oppression," and favored the adoption of a memorial to the President of the United States, urging him to issue a decree of emancipation. In the light of its background, it is not surprising that the final proclamation was couched in religious terms, invoking "the considerate judgment of mankind and the gracious favor of Almighty God."

On a more distinctly Protestant level, the national campaign against public gambling began with opposition to the Louisiana lottery, chartered by the state legislature in 1869 for twenty-five years. Church forces succeeded in preventing a renewal of the franchise in 1893; but the lottery forces were so powerful and widespread that nothing short of a national law was considered adequate to curb this "dangerous socially entrenched activity." Spearheaded by the clergy of Boston, the anti-lottery crusade enlisted the cooperation of the highest church officials in the country, including thirty-eight bishops of the Episcopal Church. Passed by the Senate, the bill was held up in the House until an intensive propaganda in the religious press succeeded in having the Anti-Lottery Act passed by Congress in 1895. The opening clause forbids "any paper, purporting to be a ticket, dependent upon the event of lottery, offering prizes dependent on lot or chance, to be brought into the United States, or carried by the mails of the United States, or transferred from one State to another," under heavy penalties of fine and imprisonment.[9] It is said that no event in our history has more effectively shown the influence of the churches and their clergy in the interests of wise social legislation. In 1903 the United States Supreme Court upheld the constitutionality of the Act and thus laid the basis for later legislation which excludes obscene literature from interstate commerce.

More openly sectarian and consequential for the whole nation was the Protestant opposition to alcoholic beverages, which goes back to John Wesley, the founder of Methodism, who forbade his followers to drink, sell or even to handle that "liquid fire." Led by the Methodists, American churchmen promoted the organization of a National Temperance Society (1865), and the National Prohibition Party, committed to "the total prohibition of the manufacturing, importation and traffic of intoxicating beverages." Five years before the Volstead Act, the liquor dealers of the country publicly identified their chief opponents. "It is only necessary," they said, "to read the list of those persons who are active in the present propaganda for legislative prohibition to realize that it is the Methodist Church which is obsessed with the ambition to gain control of the government."[10] After prohibition was repealed, the Methodist Episcopal Church declared "it has accepted no discharge in the war for a saloonless nation free from the domination of legalized liquor." In its current official statement of doctrine, the Methodist Church (membership 10 million) "reasserts its long established conviction that intoxicating liquor cannot be legalized without sin. Therefore to be true to itself the Church must be militant in opposition to the liquor traffic."[11] Heavily subsidized, the Methodist effort to reinstate prohibition is seconded by most evangelical bodies. How many more years, they ask, before the American people understand that repealing the 18th Amendment has brought about social and moral bankruptcy?

In much the same category is the legal status of conscientious objectors to military service. The Quakers were pioneers in American pacifism. In 1865 they secured the inclusion of a clause into the National Mandatory Enrollment Act, which seems to have been the first recognition by the federal government of a religious scruple against war. Section 17 of the Act provided that "members of religious denominations who should by oath declare that they are conscientiously opposed to the bearing of arms, and who are prohibited from doing so by the rules and articles of faith and practice of said religious denominations, should when drafted into the military service, be considered noncombatants."[12]

After the Civil War, conscription was not considered necessary until America's entrance into World War I in 1917. Congress exempted "the members of any well-recognized sect or organization whose existing creed or principles forbid its members to participate in war in any form." While this clause was liberally interpreted, there had to be a limit to its extension; and, consequently, those who refused to engage in non-combatant services were court-martialed.

Between the two World Wars, Baptists, Methodists and others successfully promoted a modification of the existing law. As it now reads, military conscription does not "require any person to be subject to combatant training and service in the land or naval forces of the United States who, by reason of religious training and belief, is conscientiously opposed to participation in war in any form."[13] An unsavory corollary to this generous concession is the broad use of it made by radical sects like the Jehovah's Witnesses, who have fought their way to the Supreme Court in defending universal exemption from military service.

One final sample may illustrate the general thesis that Protestant churches promote their religion as a national concept and use the civil government to protect (or advance) their special beliefs. Since the example concerns Christian Scientists, and both parties might otherwise take umbrage, it should be noted that according to an official declaration of the Mother Church in Boston, "Christian Science is a truly Protestant religion," claiming spiritual lineage from the Reformation.[14]

The legislative debate over Christian Science began shortly after Mrs. Mary Baker Eddy published her textbook, *Science and Health with a Key to the Scriptures*, in 1875. According to Mrs. Eddy, sickness is unreal, and healing should be done by spiritual understanding without medicine and surgery. Doctors opposed the doctrine as harmful to their profession and a danger to society. The Scientists defended themselves by appealing to the law. Depending on the juridical stand of their opponents, the followers of Mrs. Eddy introduced a variety of bills in the legislature to avoid prosecution for rejecting medical treatment and relying only on healing through the mind. Their efforts have been remarkably successful. By 1949 all the states had legalized the public practice of Christian Science as a healing art.

A typical federal law for the District of Columbia (1928), regulating the practice of medicine, declares "The provisions of this Act should not be construed to apply to persons treating human ailments by prayer or spiritual means, as an exercise of enjoyment of religious freedom."[15] The Ohio statute (1949) takes a different approach. "Treatment of human ills through prayer alone by a practitioner of the Christian Science Church, in accordance with the tenets and creed of such church, should not be regarded as the practice of medicine."[16] Other privileged recognitions of Christian Science are scattered through the state laws, notably exemption from jury duty for Science "readers" and "practitioners." A new issue is the question of certain health features of social security legislation, where the Scientists object to paying for disability benefits because they do not believe in the reality of sickness or disease.

Separation of Church and State

Parallel with a bias to use the civil government for promoting religious interests runs another tendency which practically characterizes American Protestantism. It came into existence as a reaction to the state churches in Europe, especially in England, and drew its inspiration more from political leaders in the Protestant tradition than from professional churchmen.

Before the American Revolution, ten of the original thirteen colonies had established churches, or religious bodies that were legally supported and promoted by the civil authorities, by way of monopoly and to the exclusion or at least non-recognition of rival churches. Thus the Church of England was established in New York, New Jersey, Maryland, Virginia, North and South Massachusetts (including Maine), New Hampshire (including Vermont) and Connecticut. While there was no established church in Rhode Island, Pennsylvania and Delaware, the Protestant religion had special privileges even in these territories. As a result of the Revolution, five of the States disestablished Anglicanism; which left five with and eight without a legally established church at the time of the Constitutional Convention in 1787. However, all the States had religious tests and in varying degrees excluded from office Jews, Catholics, Quakers, Unitarians and Atheists. Protestantism in one form or another had privileged status in the first American colonies; and, consequently, in that sense there was no principle of "separation" of Church and State among the Founding Fathers.

Nevertheless, separation was introduced, via the First Amendment, by the liberal Protestant element among the congressional leaders. Chief promoter of disestablishment and author of the First Amendment was James Madison, later fourth President of the United States. His theological studies at Princeton drew him into the stream of Presbyterian opposition to an Episcopal establishment. His pronounced sympathy with John Locke and the English Deists made him severely critical of any tie-up between church authorities and the political powers. Madison's judgment on

Anglicanism was outspoken. "If the Church of England," he wrote to a friend, "had been the established and general religion in all the northern colonies as it has been among us here (in Virginia), and uninterrupted tranquillity had prevailed throughout the continent, it is clear to me that slavery and subjection might and would have been gradually insinuated among us."[17] Even more severe were his sentiments on establishment which he interpreted to cover the whole period from the time of Constantine (313 A.D.) to the close of the eighteenth century. "Experience witnesseth," he stated in his famous Remonstrance, "that ecclesiastical establishments, instead of maintaining the purity and efficacy of Religion, have had a contrary operation. During almost fifteen centuries, has the legal establishment of Christianity been on trial. What have been its fruits? More or less in all places, pride and indolence in the Clergy; ignorance and servility in the laity, in both, superstition, bigotry and persecution."[18]

All the extant records indicate that Madison prescinded from this negative attitude when proposing the First Amendment for adoption by Congress. His unique appeal was to the positive benefit of religious liberty. Where the "no religious test" in the body of the Constitution precluded discrimination towards prospective holders of federal office, the amendment amplified this freedom to include any discriminatory practice by the federal authority. In effect, the First Amendment forbade the national government to establish, in the sense of set-up, any one church in preference to others. It also forbade the disability of any person by reason of his religious convictions and practices. It was, in a word, a charter of religious liberty as regards the federal government, though without laying the same restriction on the individual States. Thus Massachusetts did not disestablish

[120]

the Congregational Church until 1833, and New Hampshire by its Constitution to this day may legislate against any religious body not traceable to the Reformation. Adopted in 1912, the law authorizes municipalities "to make adequate provision at their own expense for the support and maintenance of public Protestant teachers of piety, religion and morality."[19]

If we would know the full intent of the First Amendment we should inquire of its author, who proposed no less than five versions to Congress before the sixth and present draft was adopted. In his own words, as reported in the third person, the amendment "had been required by some of the State Conventions, who seemed to entertain an opinion that the clause of the Constitution, and the laws made under it, which gave Congress power to make all laws necessary and proper to carry into execution the Constitution, enabled them to make laws of such a nature as might infringe the rights of conscience and establish a national religion; to prevent these effects he presumed the amendment was intended and he thought it as well expressed as the nature of language would admit."[20] During the ensuing debate, Madison made his mind still clearer. In reply to one Congressman who feared that the proposed amendment might favor those who had no religion, unless the word "national" were inserted before "religion," he said the adjective would be redundant. The whole context shows what meaning is intended by the statement, "Congress should make no law respecting an establishment of religion, or prohibiting the free exercise thereof." Hence the term "national" was not added to the First Amendment because, after Madison's explanation, the delegates considered the adjective unnecessary. Religious interests, they felt, were duly protected.

In view of Madison's unquestioned debt to Presbyterian

theology at Princeton, it is more than coincidental that Presbyterians are the only religious body whose stand on Church and State relations corresponds almost literally with the wording of the First Amendment and became part of their church law in the very year that the American Constitution was being drafted. First drawn up by the Synod of New York and Philadelphia and published by that body in 1788, it still remains in force as the clearest expression of Protestant theory on the subject. "They are unanimously of opinion," the members of the Synod declared:

That God alone is Lord of the conscience and hath left it free from the doctrine and commandments of men, which are in anything contrary to his word, or beside it in matters of faith or worship. Therefore they consider the rights of private judgment, in all matters that respect religion, as universal and unalienable: they do not even wish to see any religious constitution aided by the civil power, further than may be necessary for protection and security and, at the same time, be equal and common to all others.[21]

No other constitution of a Protestant church in America is more explicit or sweeping in its declaration of independence of civil authority.

The Episcopalians were faced with a different problem. Even after America became independent of England, the 37th of their Thirty-Nine Articles acknowledged that "The Queen's Majesty (and her successors) hath the chief power in this Realm of England, and other her Dominions, unto whom the chief government of all Estates of this Realm, whether they be Ecclesiastical or Civil, in all causes doth pertain." Clearly a change was in order, which the convention of 1801 effected by deleting the English version of the 37th Article and substituting what is still the official mind of American Episcopalians on the relation of Church and State.

The Power of the Civil Magistrate extendeth to all men, as well Clergy as Laity, in all things temporal; but hath no authority in things purely spiritual. As we hold it to be the duty of all men who are professors of the Gospel, to pay respectful obedience to the Civil authority, regularly and legitimately constituted.[22]

In its historical setting, this limitation of allegiance to civil authority in temporal matters broke the bond of juridical unity between English and American Anglicanism. It also symbolized, with great clarity, the true meaning of the First Amendment as disestablishment of a national religious body.

Among the major denominations, only the Presbyterians and Episcopalians have an authoritative doctrine on Church and State relations embodied in their respective constitution or articles of faith. Other churches were satisfied with accepting the status quo in the United States and perhaps adding, as among the Methodists, an exhortation on obedience to the civil authority; or warning, as the conservative Lutherans, that "we may not as faithful stewards approve of any legislation which tends towards a confusion of spiritual and secular affairs and endangers our religious liberty."

The Lutherans are almost unique in expressing concern over possible encroachments of the State on ecclesiastical rights, especially in the field of education. Two examples in which they cooperated with Catholics, and vice versa, are milestones in the history of religious liberty. Lutherans and Catholics successfully campaigned in 1890 against the Bennett Law, which would have placed all schools—including parochial institutions—under state supervision. A more celebrated instance was the *Meyer v. Nebraska* case in 1923 when the U. S. Supreme Court for the first time in constitutional history guaranteed the rights of religious freedom on the basis of the Fourteenth Amendment. In pursuance of a Nebraska law forbidding instruction in a foreign language to a child before finishing the eighth grade, the state supreme court convicted Robert T. Meyer, teacher in a school maintained by the Zion Evangelical Lutheran congregation. Meyer was successfully defended before the national judiciary by a Roman Catholic counsel and supported by Catholic as well as Lutheran interests.

Tolerance and Opposition

There is still another stream of Protestant thought on the relations of Church and State. The concept of a national church stems from the historical exigencies of the Reformation, modified in America by looking to the State for implementation of religious and sectarian ideas. Disestablishment was inevitable, given the War of Independence and the multiplication of discordant sects in post-colonial United States. But what to make of Roman Catholicism? It was impossible not to develop a *modus vivendi* and eventually some sort of theory on Church and State principles as relating to the Catholic Church.

The most sympathetic attitude goes back to Revolutionary days, when Roman Catholics became almost to a man supporters of the cause of independence. This fact is the more remarkable in view of the anti-Catholic feeling which had always been latent and which had been lashed into fury by the Quebec Act. In a letter attributed to John Carroll, first Bishop of the United States, four reasons are given why the Continental Congress showed a generous tolerance towards Catholic interest.[28] The basic reason was the character of the men who formed the congressional assembly. They were opposed on principle to "everything like vexation on the score of religion," and consequently saw the injustice of persecuting Catholics for adhering to their faith. Catholics proved just as eager as Protestants to be freed of English rule, recognizing that if they exposed themselves to the common danger they would also be entitled to a participation in the common blessings of independence. Also, France was negotiating an alliance with the United Provinces, and nothing could have retarded its progress more surely than any sign of ill will against the religion which France professed. Finally, the aid, or at least the neutrality of Canada, was judged necessary to defeat England, and by placing Catholics on a level of equality with other Christians, it was felt the Canadians would be favorably disposed to the revolution.

Symbolic of this feeling of friendliness is the wish expressed by George Washington, in writing to John Carroll as Catholic archbishop, that "the members of your society in America, animated alone by the pure spirit of Christianity, and still conducting themselves as the faithful subjects of our free government, may enjoy every temporal and spiritual felicity."[24] Writers are impressed by the spirit of toleration shown in these sentiments, that were typical of the new republic and scarcely possible in colonial times.

Political tolerance of the Catholic Church and recognition of her spiritual rights naturally affected a large segment of Protestant thought. Churchmen and religious leaders, even whole denominations have testified their acceptance of Roman Catholics as fellow citizens and more than once have defended Catholic liberties. Most recently, and effectively, the *Protestants United Against Taxing Schools* successfully opposed a concerted effort by California radicals to place in the state constitution a provision denying property tax exemption to all nonprofit, nonpublic schools from kindergarten to grade 12, except those for the handicapped.

Protestants who upheld tax-free schools stressed the fallacy of defining principles of social justice by statistics. "That 89 per cent of the nonpublic school enrollment is Roman Catholic has no relevance one way or other to the basic question of taxing education. We might as well tax churches, since a greater proportion of Roman Catholics than Protestants is reputed to be in their respective pews on Sunday. . . . These days of mounting tensions call for an autonomous and authentic Protestant strategy that issues from the deep places of its soul. The development and pursuit of such a strategy demand both courage and objectivity. Thus we would serve our God far better by thinking more about justice and less about Rome."[25] To the credit of California voters, the proposed amendment was defeated by a large margin in the 1958 elections. It is a standing tribute to the sense of equity among Protestant leaders who favored tax exemption.

Unfortunately there is a darker side to the picture. The more prevalent and vocal judgment of American Protestants has opposed the Catholic Church in her relation to the civil government. Some have traced this attitude to the writings of John Locke, the prophet of Madison, Adams and Jefferson among the founding fathers. Locke could be very tolerant of religious freedom and more than one of his ideas is imbedded in documents like the Declaration of Independence. But his blind spot was Rome. So when people like Samuel Adams projected Church and State relations in America they were tempted to follow the Englishman's bias. "Mr. Locke," Adams wrote in a formal statement, "has asserted and proved that such toleration (as he proposed) ought to be extended to all whose doctrines are not subversive of society. The Roman Catholics or Papists are excluded by reason of such doctrines as these: that princes excommunicated may be deposed, and those that they call heretics may be destroyed without mercy; besides their recognizing the Pope in so absolute a manner, in subversion of government, by introducing, as far as possible into the states under whose protection they enjoy life, liberty, and property, that solecism in politics, *imperium in imperio,* leading directly to the worst anarchy and confusion, civil discord, war and bloodshed."[26] Adams was an orthodox Puritan, bred in Calvinism, whose greatest fear was that Popery, the idolatry of Christians, would ever gain a foothold in America. His principles have remained the standard of anti-Catholic prejudice to the present day.

Between Adams and the current agitation against the Church by agencies like the P.O.A.U. is a history of misunderstanding and misrepresentation that can best be described by the title of Ray Billington's classic work on *The Protestant Crusade.* For generations most of the Protestant churches united in a wave of opposition to everything Catholic, often resulting in disgraceful scenes and reaching its climax in the nativist riots and persecution of the last century. Although the crusade has since tapered off, it is still active and needs only a provocation like the Smith campaign in the twenties or the Vatican representative under Truman to prove that "the psychological basis of much of American Protestantism lies in a negative rejection of Roman Catholicism."[27] The rejection is quite intrinsic to the genius of Protestantism.

In order properly to evaluate anti-Catholicism on the Church and State level we must distinguish between the permanent theories which underlay the antagonism and the contingent circumstances which put the ideas into action. The theoretical basis never substantially changed. With varying emphasis the Catholic Church was opposed for its divisive tendencies and clannish mentality especially in education, its past history in the Inquisition and future plans for "taking over" the country, the divided allegiance it required to a foreign potentate and, more recently, its conservative position on marital morality.

Two factors in the history of the country brought this prejudice to the surface: in the nineteenth century and early twentieth, the heavy Catholic immigration from Europe; and latterly, the growing population and influence of American Catholics.

While calculations differ, about sixty per cent of the 30 million immigrants to the United States from 1820 to 1920 were practicing Catholics. Typical of other large cities, in Boston between 1850 and 1855 the native-born voters (mostly Protestant) increased 14.72 per cent; those of foreign birth (mostly Catholic) 194.64 per cent. Although Catholics in Boston were accumulating at a more rapid rate than elsewhere, the same story could be told to a lesser degree of every city and state in the north, and many Americans agreed with a nativistic speaker when he prophesied that "in fifteen years the foreign population will exceed the native."

Protestant reaction to the growing tide of Catholic immigrants was spontaneous. Billington lists 44 professedly anti-Catholic newspapers and periodicals that started publication between 1830 and 1854, ranging from the daily *Native American* to the weekly *Anti-Romanist* and monthly *American Protestant.*

Under the force of this propaganda, societies were organized to consolidate Protestant fear into protective action against the rising Catholic tide. Two of these left a permanent mark on the nation's history. *The American Society to Promote the Principles of the Protestant Reformation* was founded, so the charter read, because "the principles of the court of Rome are totally irreconcilable with the gospel of Christ; liberty of conscience; the rights of man; and with the constitution and laws of the United States of America." Its purpose was to check "the influence of Romanism rapidly extending throughout this republic, endangering the peace and freedom of our country."[28] The *American Protestant Association* also believed "the system of Popery to be subversive of civil and religious liberty." Hence the call to "unite for the purpose of defending our Protestant interests against the great exertions now being made to propagate that system in the United States."[29]

Publications and societies were abetted by street preachers and pulpit orators, exhorting the people to save America from Rome. As a result a dozen Catholic churches were burned during the middle 1850's; countless more were pillaged, their altars violated, and their furnishings and windows broken. At Sidney, Ohio, and at Dorchester, Massachusetts, Catholic houses of worship were blown to pieces by gunpowder. In New York City a mob laid siege to the cathedral and only the arrival of the police saved the building. In Maine Catholics who had one church destroyed were prevented from laying the cornerstone of a new one by hostile Protestants. In New Orleans, Galveston, and Charleston, mobs stormed convents, shouted insults at the nuns, and were only prevented from doing serious damage by police intervention. As early as 1864, the Ursuline convent at Charlestown, Massachusetts, was burned to the ground. The Sisters of Mercy in Chicago were dragged into court by overzealous Protestants who sought to secure their release by legal means. So general were these attacks that

Gilmary Shea, writing many years later, believed there existed "a general conspiracy to destroy the church property of Catholics."

The theoretical basis behind this opposition seldom varied. Whatever real or imaginary grievance native Americans had against the immigrants—illiteracy, pauperism, charges of crime, lowering wage scale, increased taxation, political demagoguery—were summarized by Protestant leaders in the one felony of being subjects of a foreign power whose intention was to reduce "our country to the control of the Pope of Rome and his adherents." Time and again the Catholic hierarchy protested against the calumny. "We owe no religious allegiance to any State in this Union, nor to its general government," they declared in 1837 and repeated into the twentieth century. Our fellow citizens and we "by our constitutional principles, are free to give this ecclesiastical supremacy to whom we please, or to refuse it to everyone, if we so think proper. But they and we owe civil and political allegiance to the several States in which we reside and also to our general government." When, therefore, in perfect justice, "we acknowledge the spiritual and ecclesiastical supremacy of the chief bishop of our universal Church, the Pope or Bishop of Rome, we do not thereby forfeit our claim to the civil and political protection of the commonwealth."[30]

American nativism, aroused by the influx of Catholic immigration, reached its peak in the second half of the last century. Protestant hostility abated as Catholics proved themselves responsible citizens with a genuine love for their adopted country. However, and this must be added, the issue is still alive in our own day. While other and laudable motives were also operative, one factor contributing to the restriction of immigration in the 1920's was the attitude towards certain predominantly Catholic cultures in Europe. Anticipating the prospective legislation, Catholic bishops appealed to the civil authorities, through the National Catholic Welfare Conference. The Director of its Bureau of Immigration, "adverting to H.R. 101, the new Immigration Bill proposed by Chairman Johnson of the House Immigration Committee, *protests* certain phases of the Bill—embodying restriction of immigration quotas, and apparent discrimination against Eastern and Southern Europe."[31] When the Bill became law on May 26, 1924, the "apparent discrimination" became more patent. Three years before, the annual Polish quota of immigrants had been 31,000; it now dropped to 6,000. The Italian was reduced from 42,000 to 3,800; Austrian from 7,300 to 785. On the other hand, the United Kingdom and Germany remained constant, and the Scandinavians were reduced only by half. Viewed against the background of six million entrees from Italy and Austria-Hungary alone between 1900 and 1920, the restriction quotas take on additional meaning.

In fairness to the Protestants and others concerned, it should be added that Catholics were not always aware of the impression they made by retaining, beyond measure, those aspects of their culture which stigmatized them as aliens and, for propaganda purposes, as agents of a foreign power. Writing to clerics before the immigrant restriction Act was passed, the *Ecclesiastical Review* noted that "whatever may be the bigoted motive that inspires agitators to urge against immigration from Catholic countries, it is not answered by a general reference to the teaching and catholicity of the Church. It must be demonstrated by facts." Non-Catholics must see that the foreign clergy, while under the necessity of using their mother tongue for the time being, are actively bent on leading, and qualified to lead, their fellow-countrymen to the adoption of the American language, customs affecting public harmony, and ideals whose acceptance leads to cooperation in the upbuilding and sustaining of the national welfare.[32] It would be tragic if Catholics had not learned the moral taught by the immigration experience in dealing with the more serious crisis in Church and State relations which they currently face.

In the past thirty years a new element has entered to provoke Protestant suspicions of the Catholic Church in America The Roman threat from immigration is under control. Now the vexing problem is growth in Catholic population and influence to a point where Protestant writers are asking their readers, "Can Catholicism win America?" and answering with a foreboding, "Yes." They point out that during the American Revolution there were about 18,000 Catholics in all the colonies. Today they number 40 million. In less than 200 years the Roman Church has grown from the smallest denomination in the country to the largest. A population of this size proves that, in the foreseeable future, the Catholic faith may become dominant in the United States and attain political and cultural control. The process, they add, is signally aided by a curious theology which makes intelligent family limitation a sin. If the hierarchy ever gains the ascendancy, a country once overwhelmingly Protestant will have turned in another direction. Such a development would have consequences of the utmost importance, which Protestants must at all costs seek to avoid.[33]

As with immigration, so here the concern is not unreal. Apart from the numerical increase in a ratio above the national average, Catholics are making their presence felt and exercising influence in the country at large on a scale that even a generation ago would have looked impossible. A single institution, Georgetown University, in one election

(November 4, 1958) had twenty alumni chosen for major public office: 6 U. S. senators, 11 members of the House of Representatives, 3 state governors and the territorial governor of Guam. No wonder that Protestants without a trace of bigotry are anxious about the future which seems to be heading towards Catholic predominance.

In meeting this new threat to their interests, Protestants have allied themselves with persons and agencies that are not professedly Christian or even religious. Thus although the founders of the currently active P.O.A.U. were all Protestant leaders, including a Methodist Bishop and the President of Princeton Theological Seminary, the roster of the organization includes many who are not Protestants. Its broader appeal illustrates a corresponding change of approach to the problem. The issue has been raised to the level of political philosophy and cast in the form of a legal principle. Both are symbolized in a phrase that, like "liberty," can mean almost anything; but when used in the present context has only one connotation. "Separation of Church and State" is now the slogan used to check the advance of a rampant American Catholicism.

Perhaps the clearest definition of the term from the Protestant viewpoint is that of Dr. Charles C. Morrison, former editor of the *Christian Century* and co-founder of P.O.A.U. "By separation of church and state is meant the constitutional provision which forbids the making of any law, and therefore the taking of any executive action, that involves the interlocking of the official functions of the state with the official or institutional functions of any church."[34]

Apparently innocuous, this generally accepted definition means separation of the Catholic Church from the American civil government. Except for a handful of conservative sects, most Protestant churches are too fragmented ever to speak officially or function institutionally on more than a local basis. Even in a small community, they are too divided to present a united religious front that could legitimately be contraposed to the civil authority. This coupled with the spirit of their writing on the subject, allows us to say that when Protestants exclude the interlocking of state and church functions, the church they have in mind is Catholic.

They conceive the "interlocking" in two ways: as the separation of distinctly Catholic principles from exercising their influence on the State, and the separation of State benefits or even equities from the Catholic Church and her members, just because they are Catholic.

Protestants are not alone in reading this meaning into what can be a legitimate proposition, that Church and State are separate because each has its proper end or goal, the one spiritual and the other temporal, and each a corresponding sphere of activity which should harmonize for the common good of the nation. Secularists, agnostics, and the millions of unchurched Americans are tempted by the logic of their position and the evidence of a rising Catholic influence to adopt the Protestant attitude. In the degree to which their philosophy of life differs from the Catholic, they will seek to prevent Catholic principles from penetrating into state policy, which affects all the citizens, Catholic and non-Catholic alike, and try to keep Catholic institutions from sharing in community benefits which are at the disposal of state authority. However, though Protestants are not the only ones who hold this concept, they have given the idea its present momentum by over two centuries of "protesting" against Catholicism and are still the most organized force in the country animated by the same spirit.

Most familiar expressions of this theory have been the efforts to keep professed Catholics from election to public office and the parallel intransigence about Catholic schools participating in certain common facilities. Each has a long and checkered history.

A recent dramatic attempt to save the country from Catholic domination occurred in the presidential campaign of 1928. Scores of Protestant clergymen and lay leaders denounced the appeal to a religious issue against the Democratic candidate. "My Protestantism," wrote Dr. Van Dyke of Princeton, "is obedient to him who said, 'Render to Caesar the things that are Caesar's and to God the things that are God's.' My Americanism tells me that to vote against a man because of his church membership is to be untrue in act to the central faith of the Republic."[35] But the avalanche of inflammatory speeches, handbills and articles was too effective. In the opinion of an impartial Protestant observer, Smith's overwhelming defeat even in the areas of the "Solid South"—largely on the grounds of his Catholic faith—proved once more that few prejudices have struck more deeply into American life.

In the field of education, the heaviest barrage of opposition to Catholics securing their share of community benefits was occasioned by the Everson decision of the Supreme Court in 1947. The national judiciary upheld the right of children to share equally in such welfare benefits as bus transportation to and from the school of their choice, regardless of their religious belief.

Within weeks of the Court's decision, the Protestant religious press uniformly criticized the ruling and demanded its early reversal. A resolution of the Methodist bishops called it "a departure from the American principles of the separation of church and state (which) carries with it a

[135]

serious threat to our public educational system which is a bulwark of democracy."[36] A statement of the three major Baptist conventions in the country deplored the majority opinion for "turning back the hands of the clock as far as religious liberty and the separation of church and state are concerned."[37] The Seventh-Day Adventists, who operate schools of their own, protested against the concession and voted not to accept free transportation for children to and from their church-affiliated institutions.

By the end of 1947 plans had matured for the founding of a national society of Protestants and Other Americans United for Separation of Church and State. As previously seen, the organization was Protestant sponsored and is still so dominated, while leaving its membership open to other like-minded persons.

In a published manifesto, the society has spelled out its immediate purpose and ultimate objectives The financial and moral support it received from sympathetic sources in the past decade allow us to accept these principles as representing a large section of the Protestant mind in the United States.

Viewing with alarm the growing influence of American Catholicism, the organization seeks "to resist every attempt by law or the administration of law further to widen the breach in the wall of separation of church and state." Specifically, this means "to work for the repeal of any law on the statute books of any state which sanctions the granting of aid to church schools from the public treasury," .and "secure a reconsideration of the two decisions of the Supreme Court upholding the use of tax funds for providing the pupils of parochial schools with free textbooks, and for the transportation of pupils to parochial schools."[38] More positive aims are to unite as many citizens as possible to join in the crusade and give aid to every community or state which resists the present assault on the principle of separation of Church and State.

Following the statement of objectives is an apologia on motives, disclaiming any bigotry in the prosecution of these ends. "As Protestants we can be called anti-Catholic only in the sense in which every Roman Catholic is anti-Protestant." To a Catholic this explanation is less than satisfactory. Certainly profound differences separate the two cultures in the area of Christian belief. But Catholics respect the sincerity of those who differ from them in religious conviction and show their respect by corresponding deeds. They do not seek legislation against Protestants sharing in the common blessings of the nation, and much less do they try to remove benefits already secured by having the existing legislation changed.

VII

RELIGIOUS EDUCATION

AMERICAN PUBLIC EDUCATION is undergoing its most serious crisis in the history of the country. The issue at stake is the character of tax-supported schools in a democratic society. Opposing sides are both appealing to the Constitution to promote their own concept of education. Religionists argue that every citizen has a right to the knowledge of God and the moral law, which the schools along with the churches and the home should supply. Secularists appeal to liberty of conscience, which they claim is violated whenever civil authority presumes to teach religion. The conflict runs deep into the national culture and goes back to the early days of America. Its past history and present critical status embody the main theories and policy of the Protestant churches in the field of education. In this framework they offer a striking contrast with the principles of the Catholic Church on all levels of the educative process, from kindergarten to the university.

American Beginnings

Two qualities characterized education when the republic was born in 1776. The schools were normally religious in temper and purpose, usually linked with some church organization, and they were locally controlled. When Congress organized the lands west of the Atlantic seaboard in

1787, it legislated that "religion, morality and education being necessary to good government and the happiness of mankind, schools and the means of education shall forever be encouraged."[1] In expressing these sentiments, we know that Congress was not indulging in platitudes but reflecting the mind of most Americans, who were then mostly Protestants and whose emphasis on religion in education is recognized by all historians. A research collection of seven thousand old schoolbooks assembled at the University of Pittsburgh is only one sample of supporting evidence. School primers regularly included condensations of a Protestant catechism, like the Westminster Presbyterian; standard textbooks quoted freely from the Bible and religious writers, manuals of Christian doctrine were prescribed for use by the pupils and teachers. According to one authority, the average schoolboy in colonial times had only a catechism or primer, a Psalter, and a Testament or Bible. For Latin students the list was extended, but ordinarily these items covered all that a boy ever used as long as he went to school.

During the half century after the American Revolution, a gradual change took place. Religion continued to be featured in the elementary grades, but the emphasis was modified. Formal instruction in Christian doctrine become less frequent. In other classes the treatment was more about religion than the teaching of religious values to affect the students' lives. Still, even the secular subjects showed a preponderance of religious content, almost half of which could be defined as doctrinal or at least moral and ethical in character. Among the factors held responsible for the shifting attitude, the most prominent seem to have been a growing interest in secular literature, economic motivation because of trade and commerce, and especially jealousies and quarrels among rival sectarian groups who either owned the schools or exercised controlling influence in their operation. This period of flux has been overlooked in appraising the modern public school. Too often the blame for secularizing public education has been laid at the door of anti-sectarians like Horace Mann, when actually the process began two generations before his time as a phenomenon that grew, in large measure, from a combination of sectarian rivalry and the decline of dogmatic Christianity among the Protestant churches.

Consequently, if we are to consider Horace Mann the father of the American public schools, this can only be in a qualified sense. In 1837 a bill was passed by the Massachusetts legislature which established a state board of education and appointed the lawyer Mann, who sponsored the bill, as its first secretary. A product of the Calvinist tradition against which he revolted, Mann's lifetime agitation was for secular schools directed by the State. He believed that efficiently organized schools were impossible under existing sectarian conditions; he was even more convinced that Christianity, in the form which he knew, had nothing to contribute to the purpose of education. Though personally religious in the Deistic sense of admitting the existence and providence of God, he was unfriendly to the point of hostility towards sectarian or, as he called them, "orthodox" forms of belief. One incident illustrates how his early training brought on this anti-sectarianism. When Horace was fourteen, his elder brother Stephen was drowned on a Sunday, while absent from services at the local Congregational Church. All the young people who were in church for the funeral heard the minister preach a terrifying ser-

mon on "the lake which burneth with fire and brimstone,"
which left no doubt as to the future fate of Stephen Mann.
As reported by a later witness, "In the stunned silence
which followed the minister's final words, Horace heard his
mother groan." The effect on him was permanent. He
identified Christianity with a merciless Calvinism.

Mann's crusading spirit aroused violent opposition from
churchmen who accused him of "working with a resolution
to force sectarianism into common schools." Once he confessed that "the orthodox have hunted me this winter as
though they were bloodhounds, and I a poor rabbit." Yet
the substantial backing he received from like-minded persons among the clergy and educators finally crowned his
efforts with success. In less than fifty years American elementary education was profoundly changed. From institutions that were avowedly Christian, a system of free schools
maintained by state taxes was established, first in the East
and gradually throughout the country. Education was dis-
sociated from religion and school attendance became compulsory. Churchmen encouraged this silent revolution.

Conscious of the altered principles of American education, the Catholic bishops first advised and finally, in 1884,
decreed the erection of parochial schools in every diocese
of the country. Catholic parents were "bound to send their
children to the parochial schools, unless either at home or
in other Catholic schools they may sufficiently and evi-
dently provide for the Christian education of their children."[2] The faithful responded with great generosity.

Protestant Christians made sporadic attempts to build
confessional schools of their own. One Episcopalian report
on a meeting of bishops in 1839 stated that "the duty of
the Church to provide her own institutions for the Christian

education of her children—not of her candidates for the ministry only, but of all within her people—was a sentiment which was expressed with a degree of unanimity and feeling seldom witnessed."[3] For a while the project of an Episcopalian parochial school system was actively debated in the House of Bishops. But the people's lethargy slowly undermined the idealism of zealous churchmen. A major difficulty was finding teachers. For several years the Episcopal *Journal of Christian Education* earnestly campaigned for parochial schools and happily conceded that a number of such schools had been started. With few exceptions, however, they had to be closed, and from a common cause, the want of teachers. "The pupils have been promised, money has been furnished, rooms have been rented, but all to no purpose, because instructors could not be found."[4] Other religious bodies fared little better, and by the end of the nineteenth century practically all the churches became reconciled to state control of education.

Their adoption of the public schools was variously motivated. Experience with the bickering rivalries of the past no doubt had much to do with the new policy; financial inability to maintain separate schools for each denomination; and a lack of competent and dedicated teachers, were all significant factors, but quite secondary. The real cause was twofold, a growing secularization of the churches themselves and a concept of civil authority borrowed from the Reformation, that placed the state above the churches in every phase of human life dealing with external activity. At various times in the past century the churches took a stand towards the philosophy of public education, partly to defend the abandonment of church-affiliated schools, and also to answer the Catholic complaint about Protestant Bibles with comment being used in tax-supported institutions. A typical statement was issued by the General Conference of the Methodist Bishops in 1872.

Whereas, we have always, as a Church, accepted the work of education as a duty enjoined by our commission to "teach all nations"; and whereas, the system of Common Schools is an indispensable safeguard to republican institutions; and whereas, the combined and persistent assaults of the Romanists and others endanger the very existence of our Common Schools; therefore:

Resolved that we would cooperate in every effort which is fitted to make our Common Schools more efficient and permanent.

Resolved that it is our firm conviction that to divide the common school funds among religious denominations is wrong in principle and hostile to our free institutions and the cause of education.

Resolved that we would resist all means which may be employed to exclude from the Common Schools the Bible, which is the charter of our liberties and the inspiration of our civilization.[5]

The sentiments expressed in this manifesto are still in effect. In 1952 and 1956 the General Conference repeated the declaration of its predecessor by affirming that "The Methodist Church is committed to the public school as the most effective means of providing common education for all our children." But, after seventy-five years, there is no longer any reference to the Bible. Other major bodies like the Episcopalians, Baptists and Congregationalists have followed the Methodist lead with minor modifications.

Secularization in the Public Schools

While describing public education as their "gift to the nation," Protestant churchmen are deeply concerned over the extent and depth to which secularism has invaded tax-supported institutions of learning. They frankly confess that conflict over principles was resolved "by the steady secularization of the schools, which has brought its own problems and for which no satisfactory solution has been found."[6] In view of the frequent charge that Catholics are hypercritical, it is instructive to see how candidly denominations face up to the religious crisis that public schools have reached in the United States.

As a rule they admit that responsibility for the education of their children belongs to the parents. "God entrusts children to parents, not to the nation." However the parents collectively, acting under the civil laws, may establish public schools which provide formal educational facilities for their children. In the past century thousands of parents have freely established these common schools which, by and large, are responsible to the interests and needs of the communities they serve. Yet the system is defective. "Its chief defect has been its non-recognition of God as Creator, Sustainer, Ruler and Judge of His universe, although many teachers individually exert a profound influence through the impact of their Christian personalities."[7] As a statement of the American Lutheran Church with only minimal interest in promoting its own parochial school system, this declaration may be taken as a cross-section of American Protestantism. The Methodist Church has also expressed its "unalterable opposition to the purposes of the small minority of aggressive humanists and others who seek complete secularization of public education."[8] Even the liberal Evangelical and Reformed body, recently fused with the Congregationalists, is disturbed over the situation:

Not since the days of Constantine has there been such a complete absence of a Christian background in our culture. We can no longer depend on that culture to reinforce the religious nurture and teaching of the church. Our society in general, and public education and religion in particular, have been deprived of their spiritual rootage. It is this crisis which arouses our basic concern.[9]

Running through these and similar statements is a new awareness of the religious vacuum which public education has generated in the past century. Protestant churchmen are remarkably clear on what this vacuum means. They see it as an implicit denial of what our highest judiciary declared, that "we are a religious people whose institutions presuppose a Supreme Being." Instead of a confessional school system, operative in countries like Germany and Canada, or even the hybrid Unitarianism advocated by Horace Mann, the philosophy of public education in America has followed the line of least resistance. Except where the principles of a teacher break through the official barrier, public schools have come more and more to reflect the secular attitude of the times. While still attempting to develop a code of ethics in the pupils, they have done so without relation to any historic religion. Though dealing with everything from civics to family problems, religion was made conspicuous by its absence. Consequently the net impression on the pupil was, "what the school does not teach, does not matter," and instead of being assisted in their efforts to Christianize the child, the home and church were hindered and contradicted by the religious apathy created in the classroom.

One danger which the churches fear is the rise of a mystical nationalism. Denied the right to direct pupils' thoughts upward in reverence to God, the public schools may fill the void by making "democracy" or "the American way" an idolatrous substitute for religious belief. "Man craves a religion, even if it be the false worship of man and his accomplishments." Indeed the consequences are already being felt among the denominations. More than once in private conversation with ministers or in committee meetings with Protestant churchmen, the writer was told of the devastating effect on active church membership resulting from the silence of public schools on the subject of religion. Occasionally the complaints appear in print. "Silence creates the impression in the minds of the young that religion is unimportant and has nothing to contribute to the solution of the perennial and ultimate problems of human life. Therefore it is vitally important that the public school deal with religion."[10] But more significant than verbal comment, the churches have undertaken to prevent what has happened in other countries, where state-supported education has been turned against the home and religion, as under Communism.

Religion and Public Education

Faced with the reality of having nurtured an agency that was oblivious to Christian principles, the Protestant churches looked around for solutions. The dilemma that lay before them was either to reform the basic philosophy on which public education is built, or abandon the system as inadequate for raising religious literacy.

Outstanding among the bodies that followed the Catholic lead and made the more difficult choice was the Lutheran Missouri Synod, which now has the largest Protestant school system in America, operating twelve hundred institutions with an average enrollment of one hundred students. "It is not correct," they say, "to divide education into a religious and non-religious category, to separate the one from the other, and to set up a dual education offered by institutions which differ in their nature and philosophy."[11] As explained by their administrators, Lutheran schools have the manifold purpose of indoctrinating children in the word of God, of giving them social contact with teachers and pupils of the same religious faith, of laying the groundwork for a conservative ministry in the Church, and, in general, of preparing the students for a lifetime of Christian citizenship.

Relatively few other denominations have undertaken a confessional school system of their own. The reasons are plain. Their ecclesiastical structure and authority are too weak, and their doctrinal content too vague and discordant to make denominational schools either a creedal necessity or even a practical possibility. High Church Episcopalians are an apparent exception. But their academies and finishing schools, about a hundred, are normally directed by the most "Catholic" members of the clergy and laity who have the highest interest in preserving distinctly religious values.

The bulk of American Protestants, therefore, are dedicated to the public schools and look for solutions to the religion problem within the existing structure. For generations they have organized Sunday schools, attached to the church, where the local minister or zealous lay people instruct the children in the rudiments of Christian doctrine. Though widespread and well organized, Sunday schools are insufficient. They cater mostly to young children, attendance is irregular and in one hour they can hardly correct the non-religious impressions received during the week in the public school. A more serious difficulty is the lack of competent teachers, who may be excellent pedagogues but unable to teach religion in the formal sense of Christian doctrine. A domestic examination of the materials used in one popular Sunday school series revealed that they contain "very little of the Church's official teachings as expressed in the Bible and Prayer Book, and a great deal of emphasis on the problems, interests and concerns of the children." This emphasis on morals instead of doctrine reflects the attitude of the churches themselves. So many opinions are tolerated that writers have no choice between general moralizing and offending someone's convictions.

More recently the program of released time was developed, which allows pupils to receive instruction from their respective ministers of religion for one hour a week during school time. In 1948 the Supreme Court declared the practice unconstitutional unless instruction were given off the school grounds. Though released time was first promoted by the Protestant churches, they are becoming critical of its deficiencies, especially the need of suitable teachers. Among published criticisms, perhaps the most influential is from the pen of a leading Baptist theologian and church historian, Conrad H. Moehlman. He opposes the plan on the grounds that it unduly favors Roman Catholics, whose centralized teaching system makes them more effective in cooperating; that it destroys unity and democracy in the classroom through magnifying the differences between Protestants, Catholics and Jews; that it encourages the breach between fundamentalists and liberals in religious education; that it creates conflict between Sunday school and weekday class standards, and reaches only a small proportion of the pupils. Moehlman expresses the mind of most liberal Protestants in the country, as indicated by the small headway that released time has made on the legal front. Only thirteen out of forty-eight States allow the practice, and even then not always by law but only by court decision, as in Illinois.

Since 1948 when the Supreme Court outlawed religious instruction on school property, many Protestants have felt that a more positive strategy should be adopted to meet the critical need of spiritual values in public education. Their efforts in this direction can only be described as phenomenal, considering the magnitude of the problem and the opposition of secularists in the government and education. Several volumes have been published on the subject in the last decade, and the prospects are at least encouraging.

In 1955 the National Council of Churches sponsored a three-day conference, attended by the writer as an observer, dealing with the general topic of "Religion and Public Education." Agenda for the conference were five years in the making, and the conference itself was composed of invited delegates from all the major denominations in America. This was the first time in our history that the Protestant bodies took corporate action to check the growing secularization of the public schools. Out of the mass of reports and resolutions passed by the conference, certain features and the lines of opposition stand out. Two principal methods were proposed for integrating religion with the public school curriculum. One calls for the actual teaching of moral and spiritual values based on a "common core" of fundamental truths that should be admitted by all religious creeds. The second method wants to avoid indoctrination and recommends a factual teaching about religion with no imposition of theistic principles. Underlying the common core method is an assumption that if ministers and educators agree on the minimum essentials of every religion, teachers can be given legal sanction for interpreting the subjects of a curriculum in the light of religious ideals.

When the Council of Churches, through one of its study groups, spelled out the basis on which "to solve the problems of how public schools should deal with religion" it listed five principles which may encourage Catholics in their estimate of Protestantism. The child or educand was declared to be a creature of God, loved by God and responsible to God for his actions. By virtue of his divine creation, he has a right to the fullest development of his faculties, which places a joint responsibility on home, church *and community* to see that adequate facilities are provided for educating every child according to his capacities. Accordingly, the school should respect the child's individual conscience and faith, and cultivate his belief in the community, not only in the sense of common loyalties as citizens, but as being brothers, children of God, and as such, having inalienable rights which transcend our differences of race, nation and creed. Finally, "since religious truth is a part of our heritage of truth, it should be included in the child's education wherever relevant to the subject matter of education."[12] Unfortunately, these noble sentiments were contradicted by a powerful minority that would compromise by advocating instruction in moral and spiritual values with no essential relation to God. While protesting that "the public schools are not god-less," advocates of this theory require that "they do not teach God because to teach God is to define and interpret God, and this becomes sectarian." Moral and spiritual ideas, therefore, may be communicated to the students provided the schools "respect the religion of each child, and his belief *or disbelief in God* as taught by the home." This straddling effort to reconcile theism and atheism was said to have been endorsed by all the superintendents of school systems in cities with more than 200,000 population. In most cases the endorsement was purely nominal.

As an alternative or complement to the teaching of a "common core," educators have coined a new phrase. teach-

[151]

ing about religion. The National Council of Churches has strongly advocated this method, to have the teacher take cognizance of religious events, principles and personalities whenever intrinsic to the subject matter of the regular curriculum. No subject would be exempt from the integration. Thus when studying history, the pupils are told about the evangelization of America by Spanish and French missionaries, in literature about the religious poetry of John Milton and in the social sciences about the function of moral principles in the shaping of human conduct. However, to do this effectively requires dedicated persons who will translate their religious convictions into value judgments for the pupils, without infringing on the rights of conscience or stepping into the forbidden zone of sectarianism. Such masters, the churches lament, are sadly wanting. Hence the urgent need to have ministers stress public school teaching as "a Christian vocation worthy of our finest young people" Without instructors of this calibre, teaching about religion can be worse than useless. It may become an instrument of pagan indoctrination.

Attitude Toward Catholic Schools

A standing tribute to the judgment of many Protestant leaders is their recognition of Catholic schools as an integral part of American society. "We need the privately supported school and college," they say, "in order to provide the kind of educational opportunity the parent wants for his child. This is certainly consistent with the American ideal of free choice."[13] Because they see the benefits of training in a Christian philosophy of life, churchmen and religious writers are sometimes lavish in their praise of Catholic education and regret their inability to duplicate the achievement.

Normally the willingness to accept church-affiliated schools on a basis of equality with tax-supported institutions is most common among professional educators. Through years of experience and contact with Catholic teachers and administrators, they have lost much of the prejudice of former days when people were told that parochial school children "cannot breathe day by day teachings like this, without becoming dwarfed citizens and having their thoughts poisoned against our common country."[14] Catholic participation in educational associations and even a limited cooperation with the National Council of Churches have further contributed to remove bias and misunderstanding. Also, many Protestants are attending Catholic schools, especially colleges and universities, where in some cases they represent one third of the student body.

But this is not the whole picture. On closer study we find that Catholic education is still an object of distrust, and sometimes hostility, among the denominations. Their opposition to any kind of tax support of parochial schools, even for the least auxiliary aids like health benefits and transportation, is only the surface manifestation of a deeper conflict.

Theologians and serious writers on the subject isolate four elements of tension between the Catholic and Protestant concept of education. In their view, Catholic schools are committed to an authoritarian philosophy of education, their very existence in competition with public schools is a divisive factor in American society, they indoctrinate values that contradict our democratic way of life and, for some evangelicals, their religious principles are against the teaching of the Bible.

The charge of authoritarianism merely repeats the stock accusation against the Church's claim to speak in the name of Christ and direct the faithful on the road to salvation. When parochial schools came on the scene, Catholic teachers were said to be untrained for independent thinking, "being taught to teach and do what the Church demands. Their high character is therefore to be balanced against a tendency to narrowness and subserviency." Though loyal enough to the republic, their teaching becomes "so dominated by theological and ecclesiastical authoritarianism as not to fit pupils adequately to discuss impartially and independently in the classroom the great social and political problems which face the country."[15] Catholics find it hard to take this indictment seriously. They would point to the alumni of their schools who can think as independently on the "problems which face the country" as any product of public education; or they demand proof for the accusation, which never comes. The real irritant, they know, is the unspoken denial that the Church teaches divine truth. Unrestrained freedom of thought means chaos, which Protestants as anyone else understand. They have no complaint with authority if it confirms their own prepossessions; but if not, it becomes authoritarian.

The Catholic Church has been called divisive since the dawn of her existence. One reason for the Roman persecutions was the calumny that Christians threatened the unity of the Empire. Much the same criticism is leveled against the Church and her institutions in America. Protestants are told "the proliferation of Catholic parochial schools," along with other Church agencies, "means that an effort is under way to create a separate social order which will exist side by side with the rest of American society in the same political unit, but will as far as possible limit its contact with that society to the market place." Such pluralism is intolerable. "A plural society nullifies the unifying function of education by splitting up among its constituent units the responsibility for providing education, rather than allow the state to provide a common education for all children."[16] Thus with complete fidelity to Reformation principles the State becomes molder of the ideology of its citizens in the creed of American Protestantism.

However, the most popular polemic against Catholic schools is their reputedly undemocratic character. This, according to the critics, goes beyond the mere isolation of one religious group from the others and keeping them out of touch with the main stream of community life. It involves an irreducible conflict between the ideals of American democracy and the principles of Catholic separatism. "We believe," they say, "in democracy as a form of government. In what manner can a free people deal with successive oncoming generations so as to fit them for the competent exercise of their citizenship and win their allegiance to common good? The only procedure likely to accomplish these ends is a system of free schools, open to all, financed by all, conducted by officials in the name of all, and promoted by a high regard for the good of all." Are there no other ways? Could these ends not be achieved, say, through private schools run by individuals or a corporation from a desire for profit or a motive of benevolence? "Scarcely. The result would be pure chaos." Or, might the same purpose be attained "through parochial schools operated by a congregation or a communion to render service and promote its own special interests?" Hardly. "The most likely result would be an almost equal degree of chaos."[17] Only public education can serve the needs of democracy.

Catholics are mistaken if they believe this attitude is limited to secularists like Glenn Archer or progressivists in the late John Dewey Society. It represents the considered opinion of a large, perhaps the majority, segment of Protestant religious leaders. They explain their own scattered parochial schools as an exception not sufficient to disprove the rule that, "both on principle and in practice, Protestantism stands committed to our American public schools," and looks upon confessional institutions as something to be tolerated but not encouraged by the churches.

Relatively few bodies, either officially or through individual spokesmen, oppose Catholic education on the grounds of teaching heresy. No doubt their own obscurity of doctrine keeps them from favoring or opposing any position assumed by the Church. In some sectors of Lutheranism, however, and among certain evangelicals, the Church and her system of education are roundly condemned for apostacy. Thus, "in the Papacy we have the most pronounced and greatest imaginable 'falling away' from the Christian religion. What the air is for the natural life of man, the doctrine of justification by faith without any merit of man *is* for his spiritual life. But this doctrine is officially anathematized by the Papacy, and the entire machinery of the papal Church is geared to oppose and destroy this doctrine."[18] Therefore, Romanist schools are antichristian because they perpetuate the error, once for all exposed by Luther, that man contributes anything to his final salvation, that his will is neither seized by divine mercy and grace lifts him into heaven nor enslaved by concupiscence which drags him into hell. In both cases the credit belongs only to God. The instructive feature of the criticism is that students for the ministry are given this view of Catholicism to carry into the classroom of their own parochial schools.

The grounds of tension in the Protestant mind when faced with Catholic education have a common origin which reflective thinkers in all denominations are willing to admit.

They see Protestantism today as the anomaly of a strong majority group with a growing minority consciousness. Fear of the Catholic Church is the most powerful motive for protective action in American Protestantism. "The one emotional loyalty that of a certainty binds us together is the battle against Rome."[19] For more than a decade, the Protestant religious press has been discussing its affairs under the shadow of "the Catholic problem," with an awareness and concern that Catholics would scarcely believe. The problem is more than numerical since the growth in both religious cultures has been almost the same. The issue is qualitative and psychological. American Catholicism has been acquiring a social status in every walk of life which belies the tradition that America is Protestant and her blessings are derived from the Reformation. Hence the logical distrust of the one instrument which Catholics consider most responsible for their solidarity as a religious body and for their influence in contemporary society.

VIII

SOCIAL IDEAS AND PRACTICES

IF WE HAD only Reformation theology to analyze, it would be a discouraging task. Its core as a religious system is independence of judgment to the point of regarding any doctrine imposed by authority as enslavement of the free intellect and imprisonment in the walls of tradition.

But Protestants are not only individuals who, in Milton's phrase, have made a fetish of human liberty "to know, to utter, and to argue freely according to conscience, above all liberties." They are also members of a society which they are constantly shaping and in which their distinctive principles are often more faithfully mirrored than in theological tracts or popular journals. The modern preoccupation with social problems and their solution makes this area a safe index of the Protestant character, whether in the realm of theory or in the practical order. Take, for example, the current attitude on the race question, which might better illustrate the Protestant mind on obedience to the will of God than a learned treatise on *The Divine Imperative*. The latter may be only one man's opinion; the former can be shared by millions.

Capitalism and Communism

So much has been written on the tie-in between the Protestant spirit and capitalism that most people take it for granted and argue from the theory as an established fact. Dean Inge, in one of his cynical moods, observed that the successful money-maker of today is either a child of the Ghetto or a grandchild of John Calvin. No system, he felt, was ever so effectual as Calvinism in promoting that kind of progress which is measured by statistics. If you can convince a nation that steady industry in profitable enterprise is eminently pleasing to God, but that almost all ways of spending money unproductively are wrong, that nation is likely to become rich.

Less critically and more professionally, the German Max Weber defended as a proved thesis that Western capitalism originated in the Reformation and derives from its religious spirit. He argued that Protestantism gave immense ethical value to the vocation of labor as a sacred duty and averted man from the purely ascetical ideal to more worldly but religious aims. It also inspired honest money-making as a sinless activity, compared with traditional Catholic prejudice against usury. Weber reasoned from the fact that since the Reformation economically leading countries like England, Holland and the States, have been predominantly Protestant, while Catholic countries have generally lagged behind.

Sociologists, whether Catholic or otherwise, have challenged this theory on several counts. The term "capitalism" covers such a variety of meanings that a general equation with the Protestant spirit shades into ambiguous jargon. If the concept of free enterprise is capitalistic, then capitalism existed long before the Reformation. Moreover, to identify economic progress with Protestantism is an oversimplification. Too many other factors are involved and enough exceptions present to weaken the basic argument.

Still we may find a legitimate sense in which Protestant

theology encouraged the negative phase of capitalism by denying or obscuring the relation between man's earthly actions and their eternal recompense. From this point of view, the Lutheran and Calvinistic currents are quite similar. Where Calvin linked salvation to arbitrary divine election, Luther made it depend on faith alone. In neither case are the earthly works that a man does, or fails to do, consequential for eternity. Given a moral code which divorces secular activity from religious consequences, economic criteria tend to take over in all but the purely spiritual pursuits of human life. If an action is to have no other reward or punishment than its temporal effect, the rationalizing principle of conduct in business affairs becomes that of maximum tangible success

Respected Protestant authorities see here the seed-bed of eighteenth and nineteenth century liberalism which shattered the brakes of moral considerations out of its orbit, while driving the mechanism of production and trade over all competitors. As Tawney has pointed out, the early and medieval Christians did not acknowledge an unconditional right to private property. The Catholic Church branded "avarice" as one of the capital sins, prohibited "usury" or interest on loans, and tried to force a "just price" on merchants. There was certainly a gulf between the ideal and actuality in the Middle Ages; but the ideal was that economic activities should be controlled by religious principles and subordinated to spiritual ends.

Luther, and especially Calvin, did not directly question the norms set up by the Church in the economic sphere. But their tampering with the inner drives of motivation by questioning responsibility for secular conduct fostered in later Puritanism the spirit of economic individualism. "The

Puritans spoke of the blessing of wealth and regarded it as ordained by God." While insisting strongly that business should be guided by ethical standards, "they put the responsibility upon each Christian to apply these principles for himself and repudiated the economic restraints imposed by Church and State. As long as they subordinated their worldly interests to the attainment of eternal life, their moral scruples imposed a check upon their economic ambitions. But they tended increasingly to seek the riches of this world and to regard prosperity as a sign that they were among the elect. Businessmen could make the best of both worlds, reaping the rewards of success here as well as being assured of heavenly blessing hereafter."[1] Thus the later Puritans, through John Calvin, prepared the way for the future triumph of secular virtues.

This background has more than historical interest. The reaction against laissez-faire individualism has been widespread and profound. Men of all religious persuasions and of none sensed the intrinsic contradiction of a theory which made unrestrained competition the ruling principle of the economic world. If proof were needed, it was found in the consequences that followed from the free rein given to this rampant individualism.

Among religious leaders who denounced these aberrations, two especially are relevant to our purpose. The Roman Pontiffs were unsparing in their criticism of those who claimed that free competition, open markets and economic supremacy, with no dependence on social justice and charity, should direct the conduct of business and industry. But the Popes did not repudiate capitalism as such. They considered "free competition, within certain limits, just and productive of good results"; and economic supremacy as not intrinsically evil but being "a headstrong and vehement power, if it is to prove beneficial to mankind, needs to be curbed strongly and ruled with prudence."[2]

The World Council of Churches, on the other hand, was less discriminating. At the Amsterdam Assembly in 1948, the Council passed judgment on capitalism for conflicting with Christianity on the following grounds: Capitalism tends to subordinate what should be the primary task of any economy, the meeting of human needs, to the economic advantage of those who have the most power over its institutions. It tends to produce serious inequalities. It has developed a practical form of materialism in western nations in spite of their Christian background, for it has placed the greatest emphasis upon success in making money. It has also kept the people of capitalist countries subject to a kind of fate which has taken the form of such social catastrophes as mass unemployment.[3]

However nobly conceived, this manifesto lent itself to serious misgivings even in the ranks of the World Council. These were further accentuated by the imprecision with which Communism was condemned by the Assembly, leaving the impression that Amsterdam had equated communism and capitalism as twin perils to a society satisfying Christian demands and had appraised their achievements as equally negative, without making a decisive judgment between them.

Six years later, the Evanston Assembly supplied a healthy corrective. Capitalism was given a measure of praise: "At its best the business system has provided incentives for the responsible initiative and hard work which produce economic progress, and has embodied the wisdom of decentralized decisions and widely distributed power."[4] Along with this nod of approval to private enterprise, the Council repeated its condemnation of Communism as materialistic and deterministic, and therefore "incompatible with belief in God and with the Christian view of man as a person, made in God's image and responsible to him."

Unfortunately, while censuring Communism, the Council of Churches refrained from spelling out the terms as definitely as it might. Communism was too closely identified with the political system and its abuse in certain countries; less clearly with a historic ideology which transcends the limitations of space and time, and may infect all peoples anywhere. Indeed, the Council in its final report declared there are worse evils to fear than Communism, such as the injury to civil liberty under the spell of a Red phobia. "Preoccupation with the real dangers of subversion in many situations has led to a less widely recognized and more subtle danger to society from those who identify as subversive any unpopular opinions or associations."[5] This critique was more than a passing gesture since shortly before Evanston one of the presidents of the World Council had been subject to a widely publicized inquiry before a Congressional Sub-Committee.

One episode at the Evanston Assembly served to highlight the difficult problem which faces the Council on the subject of Communism. It also illustrates how truly "inclusive" is Protestant Christianity. Bishop Johann Peter, of the Reformed Church of Hungary, attended the Assembly as an Accredited Visitor, having been personally invited by the Secretary General to address the delegates on "The Witness of the Church" in his country. The substance of his speech was a glowing tribute to the development of Christianity in Hungary in recent years.

Bishop Peter was admitted to the United States on a restricted visa. He was limited to the Evanston area and forbidden to attend any press conferences of the General

Assembly. So at the request of the Press Committee of the General Assembly he answered 32 questions put to him by the Committee. Many of them dealt with the relation of Communism to Christianity:[6]

Question. Can one be a Communist and a Christian at the same time?

Answer. Yes, in a certain sense of the word.

Question. Can Christianity co-exist successfully with Communism?

Answer. Yes.

Question. What restrictions, if any, are put upon the churches of Hungary?

Answer. None, from the point of view of the churches.

Question. Is Communism taught in the public schools and is attendance at public schools compulsory?

Answer. Yes, in a certain sense of the word and in a certain measure, but there are religious instructions as well.

Question. Is the church free to evangelize?

Answer. Yes.

Question. To what extent if any is religion being used by the state for the furtherance of its own purpose?

Answer. The churches have their freedom to support solutions which may improve the living conditions of the people. They are free to withdraw from any common action and to oppose those instructions upon which they do not agree.

Question. Are Hungarian Christians satisfied and contented under Communist government? Do they feel that it is compatible with their religion and that it provides a reasonable atmosphere in which it can flourish?

Answer. Yes.

Question. If Communism, in its basic dogma, teaches

Christianity is an opiate, and if the government, through newspapers, radio and school teaches Communist tenets, is this not a menace to the future of Christianity?

Answer. It is not.

To the credit of the World Council, the existence within its body of churches which had compromised with Communism did not prevent the Assembly from officially reprobating the Communist philosophy of life. However, Catholics find it hard to understand how Communist sympathizers can remain in good standing and even become leaders in the Christian ecumenical movement.

In the United States, Protestants are divided as much on the theory of Communism as on the practical way of dealing with Russia and her satellite countries. The latter is less surprising, yet can prove highly embarrassing in the absence of a uniform and consistent policy. Meeting at Cleveland in 1958, the National Council of Churches issued a formal message to its constituent members, urging the immediate recognition of Red China as "part of a much wider relationship between our peoples." A blast of protest from many churches that were supposedly represented at Cleveland suggested that the message was not unanimous. As reported by one news agency, "Definitive evidence was forthcoming to shatter the pretense that 'Protestantism', as embodied in the leftist National Council of Churches, favors the admission of Red China to the United Nations."[7] While the Communist *Daily Worker* triumphantly proclaimed that 38 million Protestants finally saw the light on the Red regime, an independent Committee of One Million sent questionnaires to 45,000 Protestant ministers across the country to get their reaction. Out of 9,000 answers received, the majority were against American recognition of Red China and her membership in the United Nations.

Regarding Marxist theory, there is no question where the rank and file of American Protestantism stands: unalterably opposed to the principles of Communist ideology. But the picture is less clear among theologians.

Writing in the mid and late thirties, Reinhold Niebuhr spoke with foreboding of the early demise of capitalism. There was no middle way. The only hope was the socialization of the economy along Marxist lines as an essentially correct analysis of the economic realities of modern society, correct in its theory of class conflict, correct in regarding private ownership of the means of production as the basic cause of economic crisis and international war, correct in insisting that "communal ownership of the productive process is a basic condition of social health in a technical age."[8] Even after the postwar triumph of Russian communism, Niebuhr still clung to the optimism of considering Marx only quantitatively removed from the program of Jesus Christ. "Communism," he felt, "does not glorify race or nation. It does not worship power for its own sake. It believes in a universal rule of justice. It may be provisionally cynical but not in the ultimate sense. It still belongs to civilization."[9] Since then Niebuhr's admiration for Marxism has been greatly chastened. He now believes "the deepest tragedy of our age is that the alternative to capitalism has turned out to be worse than the disease which it was meant to cure."[10] He found this failure to be a natural consequence of Marxist illusions and not a corruption of Marx by Stalinism. It results from ascribing all human virtue to a single class, the proletariat, and all human evil to a single institution, private property.

But if Niebuhr revised his estimate of Communism, his confrere in the Evangelical and Reformed ministry, Paul Tillich, appears not to have substantially changed. For more than two decades, he has been exploring the relation between the inner meaning of Protestantism and the essence of Socialism, and finds them so closely related that the one cannot be understood without the other. Both, he affirms, conceive man's nature as essentially perverted. But, where in Protestantism the perversion refers to the individual person, in Socialism it concerns the whole of human society. "The perversion of human existence is real in social, just as strongly as in individual distortions and with even more primitive force; and collective guilt is just as real and perceptible as individual guilt; neither can be separated from the other." Concretely, this becomes manifest in the "inner contradiction of a society that permits such a thing to exist as a proletarian situation and the breaking-up of society into classes." Accordingly, "in this negative moral judgment about man's actual existence, the socialistic evaluation of the proletarian situation and the Protestant understanding of the universal human situation agree." Where Protestantism declares that men are individually corrupted, Socialism identifies this corruption with the existence of divergent classes in the human family, notably the exploiters and their victims, engaged in perpetual and deadly conflict for ultimate mastery.

Tillich does not stop with an accolade to Socialism. "Religious Socialists," like himself, "have accepted many of the scientific results of the Marxian analysis of society, especially of economics, because they have found them to be true." By its stress on existential thinking, Marxism protects us against any pretense to possessing timeless categories or abstract formulas for solving every problem. In the same way, without subscribing to any system of mechanistic economics, it must be acknowledged that "Marx is right in emphasizing material reproduction as the foundation of the whole historical process." Also the dialectical method which describes the movements of life as a process of tensions and contradictions tending towards "more embracing unities" sheds light on the whole panorama of human history. In a word, "religious socialism, with the tool of the Marxian analysis of society brought up to date, is able to give a meaning to the present world situation," which Christianity can profitably employ.[11]

It would be unfair to leave the impression that Niebuhr and Tillich are representative of the American Protestant mind. They are both *sui generis* and speak only for themselves whether on this subject or any other. A more typical judgment sees Communism as "a crystallized philosophy *that denies the existence of God,* and ruthlessly attempts to destroy faith in God on the part of all who come under its control." Therefore, "the Christian's concern must be one of honest evaluation and right reaction. And the material advances made in backward countries that are Communist dominated *should not becloud the basic issue.*"[12] When writers allow themselves to be misled by appearances and dally, however speculatively, with Marxist theory, they are not sympathetically received. To their credit, American Protestants have not been plagued with such eminent radicals as the Hungarian Bishop Peter or the Red Dean of Canterbury, whose unnatural devotion to Communism is the scandal of European Protestants. Even the liberal *Christian Century* retaliated when the most prominent theologian in world Protestantism, the German Karl Barth, presented the American way of life as a greater danger than Communism and urged Christians suffering under Red oppression not to ask God for deliverance. "Should you not fear that He may grant your prayer in the frightful fashion of letting you awake one morning among the fleshpots of Egypt as a man bounded to the American way of life."[13] The fatalism implicit in Barth's plea for non-resistance to communist policies also made a "dolorous impression" on his European admirers.

Race Relations

Modern race-feeling as understood in Western society has been traced by historians to the religious background of certain nations, especially the English, who are of the Protestant persuasion.

The Protestant movement in our Western history started immediately before the movement of overseas settlement; and in the eighteenth century the competition among the peoples of Western Europe for the command of the overseas world ended in a victory of the English-speaking Protestants. They secured for themselves the lion's share of those countries, inhabited by primitive peoples, that were suitable for settlement by Europeans, as well as the lion's share of the lands inhabited by non-Western civilizations that were incapable of resisting Western conquest and domination. The outcome of the Seven Years' War decided that the whole of North America, from the Arctic Circle to the Rio Grande, should be populated by new nations of English Protestant lineage, and that a government instituted by English Protestants and informed with their ideas should become paramount over the whole of Continental India. Thus the race-feeling engendered by the English Protestant version of our Western culture became the determining fac-

tor in the development of race-feeling in Western society
as a whole.

Toynbee considers this a misfortune, for the Protestant
temper and conduct in regard to race, as in many other
vital issues, draws heavily from the spirit of the Old Testament. And in matters of race "the promptings of this old-
fashioned Syriac oracle are very clear and very savage. The
'Bible-Christian' of European origin and race who has settled among peoples of non-European race overseas has
inevitably identified himself with Israel obeying the will of
Jehovah and doing the Lord's work by taking possession of
the Promised Land, while he has identified the non-Euro-
peans who have crossed his path with the Canaanites whom
the Lord has delivered into the hand of his chosen people
to be delivered or subjugated. Under this inspiration, the
English-speaking Protestant settlers in the New World ex-
terminated the North American Indian, as well as the bison,
from coast to coast of the Continent."[14] By contrast Spanish
Catholics in South America were content to step into the
shoes of the Aztecs and the Incas, sparing the conquered
people to rule them as subject populations, converting them
to their own faith and inter-marrying with their converts.
Modern Bolivia is a fair example. Fifty-three per cent of its
four million inhabitants are Indian, thirty-two per cent
mestizo, and only fifteen of Spanish ancestry. Brazil has an
estimated seventeen million mulattoes, and in Colombia
sixty-eight per cent of the population are of mixed Indian,
Negro and Spanish blood.

The English Protestants also took up the trade in Negro
slaves from Africa to the New World, and by the end of the
seventeenth century obtained a virtual monopoly as one of
the conditions of the Peace Settlement at Utrecht in 1713.

[171]

Thus Spain conceded to England the right to import into America forty-eight hundred Negroes a year for thirty years. "The Spanish and Portuguese Catholic settlers," says Toynbee, "bought the human merchandise which the Protestant slave-traders offered them; but the Spanish and Portuguese Empires and the 'successor-states' which eventually took their place as independent states-members of the Western Society were not the field in which the institution of plantation slavery, which had thus been introduced into the New World, struck deepest root and grew to the most formidable proportions. The stage on which the tragedy of Negro slavery in the New World was played out on the grand scale was an English-speaking country; the United States." What confirms this judgment is the evidence of other countries under British domination. Unlike Spanish America, only a negligible number of the "natives" were converted to the religion of the ruling race or physically assimilated by interbreeding.[15]

Some might quarrel with Toynbee's analysis because it rests on a plausible theory, that Protestants identified themselves with the chosen people of the Old Law and acted accordingly in their dealing with subjugated colonies. The fact is that Protestant theology made an intrinsic contribution to the race problem as currently understood in the United States. By severing their dependence on ecclesiastical authority not only in matters of faith but in social morals, the Reformers left their followers without the control which human society needs to observe the natural law.

While Protestant colonizers were left to their own devices, Catholic rulers and their people had the bridle of a constant restraint placed upon their slave-trading propensities. In 1462, Pius II castigated the adventurers who were stealing African Negroes for enforced labor in Europe. He branded slavery a great crime (*magnum scelus*), which disgraces the Christian name.

Six months after the discovery of America, Alexander VI issued a bull commanding the colonists, "with God's grace, to bring the natives to the Catholic faith." When this proved ineffective, Pope Paul III intervened with a celebrated Brief, dated May 29, 1537, forbidding the enslavement of the Indians and threatening the severest penalties against those who disobeyed. "These Indians," wrote the Pontiff, "although they live outside the bosom of the Church, nevertheless have not been, nor are they to be deprived of their freedom or of ownership of their possessions, since they are human beings, capable of faith and salvation. They are not to be destroyed by slavery, but invited to life by preaching and example." Anyone of whatever rank who would dare to bring the Indians into slavery, incurred automatic excommunication, "from which they can be absolved only by Ourselves or the Roman Pontiff reigning at that time, except if they are at the point of death and have previously made amends."[16] Urban VIII repeated the prohibition in 1639 and Benedict XIV in 1740. Pope Pius VII demanded of the Congress of Vienna in 1815 the suppression of the slave-trade, and Gregory XVI condemned it in 1839.

Behind these and similar condemnations was something deeper than merely outlawing slavery as an institution. St. Paul did not praise the system but in the circumstances of his day he exhorted slaves to obey their masters, according to the flesh, in the sincerity of their heart from the supernatural motive of pleasing Christ. Long before she condemned the cruelty of Spanish and Portuguese traders in human cargo, the Church recognized the Christian citizenship of enslaved men and women, as far back as apostolic times. What St. Paul urged on Philemon, to receive the runaway Onesimus, "no longer as a slave but as a brother, both in the flesh and in the Lord," became the lodestar of the Church's policy in dealing with those who were victims of a primitive state of human culture. From the beginning of the Church's history, slaves enjoyed all the rights and privileges of freedmen, participating without discrimination in the liturgical assemblies and, once freed, were eligible for the priesthood and even the episcopacy. Their marriages were protected by canon law and their masters forbidden, under penalty, to interfere with the rights of conscience or the spiritual duties of the persons whom they legally held in servitude.

Hence the painful contrast between the dealing of the generality of Protestant colonizers and their Catholic contemporaries. The latter were quite as human as the former and, therefore, prone to the same inhumanity when profit or ambition were at stake. But where Catholics had the faith, and under the impact of the Church's sanctions (and we may add, with the help of her sacraments) might yield in favor of Christian justice, Protestants were practically a law to themselves and, as history so graphically records, too often acted as their feelings and not as their conscience dictated. If we compare the two mentalities on the level of missionary zeal, the difference is abysmal. "Between this Protestant method of conversion by extermination," as among the Indians of North America, "and the methods of the Jesuit missionaries in Canada and Paraguay there is indeed a great gulf fixed"—separating, in fact, two philosophies of human nature, the one Catholic and the other not.

As time went on, the original ferocity of that race-feeling considerably abated, some would say as Protestantism evolved through Rationalism and Agnosticism, but more correctly as the traditional principles of Christianity gradually affected the policies of those who were not members of the Catholic Church. Yet the abatement was only relative.

In South Africa today there stand facing each other two conflicting theologies, the Catholic and Calvinistic, divided over the present government's pressure of total racial segregation (*apartheid*) between the Negroes and the whites. Protagonist in the conflict is the dominant Dutch Reformed Church of South Africa, Calvinist to the core, and representing the purest and most traditional form of Protestantism still surviving. For Calvinism religion is something primarily spiritual, a relationship between the soul and God, with no pretended human mediation, whether ritual or ecclesiastical, required to bridge the gap. Man's primal sin, say the Calvinists, is that of paganism, which consists in man's attempting to save himself. God's way of salvation goes just the opposite and saves man without his cooperation. All intrusion of human initiative and cooperation in the work of salvation is a pagan threat to Christianity that must be firmly resisted.

The same, in due proportion, obtains in the social and cultural spheres. To cut across barriers established by God is to go contrary to the divine will and spells disaster. Nations, languages and races must be kept separate. The ideal would be for each divinely formed group, like the Afrikaner people and the Africans in South Africa, to maintain its own identity, while conceding the same to others. If this proves impossible where they live together, territorial and political segregation becomes a workable compromise. Sincere Calvinists in South Africa look forward to a complete territorial separation as the only true answer, while accepting the present partial segregation as a temporary expedient.

Fundamentally opposed to this concept is the teaching of the Catholic Church, courageously voiced by the South

African hierarchy. Instead of conceiving religion as purely spiritual and individualistic, they proclaim it to be material and social as well. The material element is embodied in a visible authority with divine mandate to preach the word of God and direct the moral destinies of men; the social element sees the Church as an organic union of all nations and climes, joined together in the Mystical Body of Christ. Catholicism, so the bishops say, tends not merely to transcend racial divisions, but to destroy them, as soon as life brings people into a common human society.

Superficially, the Dutch Reformed churches seem to be supporting *apartheid* as a political measure, and are backing the Nationalists to keep the black man in his place only as a passing phase. Hence the fear that "unless that Church changes its views, Protestantism will become, in the eyes of the native population, a religion which preaches that the black man is doomed, by the will and word of God, to be forever inferior and subservient to the white."[17] But really the issue lies deeper. It involves the awful choice of admitting or denying that everything that is must be. To a Catholic the differences among the races are opportunities for the practice of justice and charity, which seek to unite what is naturally disparate into Christian unity; to the Calvinist, these differences are providential dispositions that are not to be tampered with or changed.

The American situation offers a more pleasant scene. True the Negro in the States has been only legally emancipated since the Civil War. His social and economic status has been much improved, but only as a matter of degree. In a volume published fifteen years ago on the question of *What the Negro Wants*, the first of ten top-ranking leaders of their people began by saying that "the Negro problem is our number one domestic failure and our number one international handicap. Common sense, devotion to our democratic ideals, and the imperatives of our national security and our moral leadership in world affairs demand its immediate improvement and ultimate solution."[18] That was in 1944. Since then the Supreme Court has outlawed racial segregation in the public schools to precipitate a crisis in American Protestantism which the churches are painfully but unmistakably solving.

For a number of reasons, desegregation in the public schools is mainly a Protestant problem. Tax-supported education has become the right arm of the Protestant churches, who prefer not to operate parochial schools of their own. With denominations almost completely segregated, a school system that reflects the contrary policy will be a liability, by creating all sorts of tensions. Less than four per cent of the American Negro population is Catholic; the rest is at least nominally Protestant. Finally, until recent years, sectarian churchmen let well enough alone. Periodic statements on racial justice were more in the nature of ferverinos than realistic confrontations of a grave moral problem, and always they lacked the power to command in the name of God. The decision of the Supreme Court, therefore, has made the clergy face the issue as they had never done before. To a Catholic their reaction is one of the most sanguine features of American Protestantism. On all levels of the dogmatic scale they are examining their conscience, offering the people motives and inspiration and admitting their inability to heal the wounds of three centures of prejudice without the divine assistance.

In anticipation of Race Relations Sunday in 1958 the Protestant churches published a list of their latest official statements on racial justice as affecting the American Negro in the country.[19] In the words of the editor, they prove that evangelical Christianity in America is deeply cognizant of its obligation to offer to the nation Christian answers to its major problem in human relations. They show that the churches, working independently, have achieved remarkable unanimity since the Supreme Court handed down its historic decision on May 17, 1954.

Among Northern bodies, the National Baptist Convention declared that "according to Christ and Paul there can be no question of race relations, because there is only one race, the human race. Man himself has divided the race on the basis of color. Segregation in the church of God is the ugliest thing in the religious world, and a disgrace to a Christian nation." The American Lutheran Church condemned stratification as "the evil fruit of natural man's pride and his arrogant assumption of superiority over those who appear to be different from him." Disciples and Christians called upon their people to "re-examine themselves in the light of the Christ's gospel," and the Presbyterians received "with humility and thanksgiving the recent decision of our Supreme Court," while urging all Christians "to assist in preparing their communities psychologically and spiritually for carrying out" its full implications.

More cautious were statements by the Methodist Church, which has labored for years under the burden of a racial conflict. Conscious of the need for making "far-reaching and often difficult adjustments," it pleaded for "good faith, with brotherliness and patience, lest the cause of Christ suffer at our hands." Southern denominations and church councils freely commended the wisdom of the nation's highest judiciary as "consistent with the teachings of Jesus Christ" (New Orleans), "in accord with Christian principles" (Virginia) and, therefore, demanding, "as fully as possible, in the Spirit of Christ, to realize an integrated school system" (North Carolina).

However, the most detailed and outspoken message came from the National Council of Churches. Its thoroughly Christian sentiments offer great promise for the future and belie any suspicion that American Protestantism is spiritually moribund.

All men, created alike in the image of God, are inseparably bound together. This is at the very heart of the Christian gospel. This is clearly expressed in Paul's declaration on Mars Hill, that "God who made the world and everything in it, being Lord of heaven and earth, made from one nation of men to live on all the face of the earth."

Again it is expressed in the affirmation, "There is neither Jew nor Greek, there is neither slave nor free, there is neither male nor female; for you are all one in Christ Jesus." The climax of this universality is expressed in the fact that Christ died for all mankind. This broad universality standing at the center of the Gospel makes brotherhood morally inescapable. Racial segregation is a blatant denial of the unity which we all have in Christ.

The churches themselves have largely failed to purge their own bodies of discriminatory practices. This evil persists in most of the local churches, church schools, church hospitals, and other church institutions. Emotions must not run wild, and the motives of love, patience and understanding goodwill must dominate all of our actions.[20]

Any discussion of segregation in America, the National Council admits, emphasizes the urgent need of prophetic voices. These are slowly emerging and appeal to motives that draw profoundly on the wealth of Christian tradition.

Perhaps for the first time in American history, Protestant writers are speaking of a "theology of race relations," which even thirty years ago would have sounded strange to any but the most evangelical ears. Racial prejudice and exploitation are no longer denounced in generalities, but analyzed from the viewpoint of revelation and on this ground shown to be incompatible with Christianity.

In their approach to the race question, theologians stress the importance of two factors that sociologists and others had largely overlooked. The origin of race prejudice must be sought primarily in man himself, in his fallen nature and tendency to sin; and the remedy for the problem must be found, along with human effort, in the saving grace of God.

Men like Waldo Beach of Duke University and H. Richard Niebuhr of Yale have no quarrel with social scientists who boldly affirm their moral bias and defend a departure from strict scientific neutrality as necessary and good. In fact the very preoccupation of social science in America for the past quarter century with the racial problem shows it is prompted by a deep moral compunction. "Social science's interest in ethnic tensions as a form of social pathology is a mark of its concern for social health. Its assumption that the reduction of prejudice is desirable is not in any sense derived from the facts, but is an ethical dogma, taken for granted."[21] All well and good. But everything depends on whence this ethical dogma is derived. Throughout the literature on race there appears a wide disparity on the grounds of social harmony. Some authors make the religion of democracy, resting on its own bottom, the justification of moral value. With others, "adjustment of life to life" becomes the ultimate motive. At other points, science (without explanation) is taken as the basis of ethical duty. For the most part, such theories cluster about a vapid kind of religion which has a constellation of purely human and this-worldly ends. Here the Christian theologian must step in to offer a healthy corrective and furnish the principles that sociology by itself cannot provide.

[180]

At the head of these principles stands the belief that racial prejudice is not one of a catalog of sins but a facet or expression of the single sin of pride, the rejection of the Infinite Sovereign Source of life and the attempt to set up as final some substitute sovereignty lower than God. Because of his fallen nature, man tends to make for himself or some projection of himself the center of love and value. Thence follows a distortion of value judgments, whereby the neighbor is regarded not in the universal family of creation as a 'Thou,' but by reference to the partial principle of color or external features, as an 'It,' with the result that the community of persons is broken and divided. Instead of concentrating on the essential unity of human nature, racism looks upon other people not only as different but as inferior and thereby denies the basic equality founded by the Creator. In the words of the Evanston Assembly, the Bible teaches us that God made the world to be united, "but man by his sin, by his disobedience and pride and the lifting of his arm against his brother, has filled it with division and distrust."[22]

But if this were all that theology could offer, we should have only diagnosis without cure. The Christian faith has another and more valuable contribution to make. Why, theologians ask, does sociology consider integration of the races the morally normative form? Or even if black and white should live together in harmony, how can the integration be achieved? Though expressed in Protestant language, the answer is highly congruent with Catholic thought.

The norm of community where men regard each other as persons in mutual love, the integrated community, is not of human making, but is set there by divine hand, both as a principle of judgment and as a principle of grace and forgiveness whereby men are turned from their prejudice. To account adequately, in short, for the presence and power of the norm of human brotherhood in history, one must go beyond humanity and history and say that the norm is grounded in the revelation of God's grace. Theologically, of course, this is a primer point, but it is precisely where sociology must be "born again" in its premises in order to understand fully its own enterprise.[23]

What is most hopeful about these sentiments is the certainty they are not born of idle speculation but arise to meet a grave and pressing need. Faced with the dilemma of solving a problem that historically was of their own making, or repudiating the Christianity which they still profess, American Protestants are finding in that Christianity principles which happen to be Catholic and promise the solution which they want.

I X

DOCTRINAL VARIATIONS

CENTURIES before the Reformation, doctrinal differences among Christians were regarded as a mark of error and inconsistency. Faith, it was argued, speaks with simplicity. The Holy Spirit does not contradict Himself, and the truth which He teaches has a language that remains uniform. On this ground the ancient doctors condemned the Arians, who were always making new confessions of faith in a futile effort to reach some kind of agreement. "You are like amateur architects," St. Hilary told them, "who are never satisfied with their work. You keep building up and pulling down, whereas the Catholic Church raised an immortal edifice the first time it assembled. To condemn Arianism for ever, nothing more is needed than a repetition of the Nicene creed."[1] The same principle was applied in sequence to all heretical systems before the Protestant revolt.

Within less than a generation of Wittenberg, Catholic apologists found such a medley of Protestant opinion on fundamental Christian doctrines that the Reformers themselves, in the words of Melanchthon, feared "the utter destruction of religion from all these dissensions." Yet Protestantism on the continent and in Europe generally remained fairly consistent. At least the initial differences did not proliferate beyond control. But in America the dissonant tendency has run riot. Every possible form of discord is apparent and frankly admitted. On the broadest level, the churches differ in their official statements of doctrine; within denominations of the same family are further varieties; periodically the churches change their professions of faith and repudiate what previously had been required belief; most vacillating are the teachings of churchmen and theologians, normally at variance among themselves and opposed to what their churches profess, while remaining in good standing in the ministry or representing the very institutions they oppose.

Trinity and the Incarnation

In their confessions of faith, Protestants still profess to believe in the Trinity and the Incarnation of the Son of God. With rare exception, they include among their symbolical writing the Apostles' and Nicene Creeds, although the Athanasian formula is usually dropped for being "too woodenly orthodox." Nominally, therefore, they would accept a distinction of Persons in the Godhead and the fact that Christ was in some sense divine. But beyond this verbal agreement the variety of interpretations is infinite.

A minority of churchmen explains the Trinity and Christ's divinity with complete deference to Christian tradition. Seminarians are taught that "God is absolutely one, and that He is also three persons, absolutely distinct; that when Scripture calls Christ 'God' and 'the Son of God,' it uses these terms in their proper and metaphysical sense."[2] Evangelists of the Billy Graham type and fundamentalists generally subscribe to the same doctrine.

At the other extreme are liberals in every denomination who claim the Trinity is the product of reflection and not a *kerygma* or message originally found in the Gospels. Reinhold Niebuhr reduces the divinity of Christ to the symbol of a God-man which makes "the doctrine that Jesus was both human and divine religiously and morally meaningful and dispenses with the necessity of making the doctrine metaphysically plausible." When heretics in the early Church were refuted by successive councils, it was only at the price of committing "absurdities." Not only should we say that Christ was not God, but the Incarnation is objectively impossible. "Since the essence of the divine consists in its unconditioned character, and since the essence of the human lies in its conditioned and contingent nature, it is not logically possible to assert both qualities of the same person."[3] What makes these judgments significant is the stature of their author. Among his followers, Niebuhr ranks as "the most important living American theologian," whose impact on the Protestant mind has been immense. His position as clergyman in the Evangelical and Reformed Church (now the United Church of Christ) was enhanced, if anything, by thirty years of writing in the liberal tradition. As the closing speaker at the World Council of Churches in 1954, his creedal iconoclasm may be fairly attributed to a large section of American Protestantism.

Between the two extremes of fundamentalist orthodoxy and open rationalism is a nebulous concept of Christ whose relationship with God is said to be unique in human history. Modern psychology is called in to explain how Jesus could be both human and divine. Two people who live together in love and harmony come to believe alike, act alike, and sometimes even look alike. They are united in ideals and therefore in action. Thus "the union of Christ and God may be thought of as a union of *will*, so that all that Christ did, God did in him." When thinking of human friendship, we speak of having one will with a friend. But Christ's friendship with His Father was immeasurably closer. "His motives, his attitudes, and his whole personal life did move according to the will of God, and therefore we know him to be the 'Son of God' even as the Scriptures saw."[4] This sample of Arianism is part of an instruction manual for Christian youth, sponsored by the Methodist Church and offered to adolescents as "a source of strength and guidance in Christian living." Ironically, the same religious body which approves these opinions, still includes among its official *Articles of Religion* a statement that "the Son of God, who is the Word of the Father, the very and eternal God, of one substance with the Father, took man's nature in the womb of the blessed Virgin." How reconcile the two positions? By the device of "inclusive Christianity" which tolerates contradictions in the spirit of John Wesley, who was only mildly interested in what a man believed, provided his heart was "in the right place."

The Unitarian urge in large bodies like the Methodists and Baptists partly accounts for the frequent split in their ranks when enterprising ministers demand a return to the religion of the Bible. If they get no satisfaction, they organize a new church or whole denomination, depending on the number of their followers. Though successful in some areas, these splinter groups run into difficulties when they try to formulate their own beliefs and thus become the seed-bed of further schisms along doctrinal lines.

Baptismal Controversy

Protestant differences over baptism go back to Reformation times. Luther and Calvin rejected the Catholic doctrine on the sacraments which confer grace *ex opere operato*, that is, whenever the rite is performed and no obstacle stands in the way. But when the Anabaptists came along and condemned infant baptism, their doctrine was branded "impious" though it followed the Lutheran principle to its logical conclusion. More commonly, however, even churches in the main stream of Protestantism were torn between rejecting baptism entirely, as they should have done on a theory of justification by faith alone, or keeping baptism and compromising on their novel theology. The tension born of this dilemma remains unchanged and better than almost anything else points up the disunity among the denominations.

Most churches agree with Calvin that baptism is a sacrament only as the sign of admission into the society of the Church. Nothing really happens in the soul of the person baptized to suspect the removal of sin. Congregationalists describe the rite as "the sacrament of Christian dedication in which we dedicate ourselves or our children to God." Disciples call it the effort of a true Christian to honor Christ by the white flower of a stainless life, and in this promissory sense baptism may be said to "remit" moral guilt. The Methodist *Discipline* offers three elaborate rituals of baptism, one each for infants, youths and adults, but never a suggestion that sin is being removed. Lutheran churches of the "orthodox" school teach the opposite. Their manualists protest that "Zwingli and his co-laborers invented the Reformed teaching of baptism, and Calvin propagated it. For the Reformed doctrine that baptism is merely a symbol, image or emblem of the remission of sins there is not a shred of proof in Scripture."[5] In the same way, the Episcopalians favor Luther against Calvin. The twenty-seventh of the *Articles of Religion* expressly defines baptism as "not only a sign of profession, and mark of difference, whereby Christian men are discerned from others that be not christened, but the promises of the forgiveness of sin, and of our adoption to be the sons of God by the Holy Ghost, are visibly signed and sealed." Again, as with Christ's divinity, between the purely symbolic and the "sacramental" concept of baptism is a plethora of theories, often expressed by creedal documents in such terms as to satisfy both parties.

The same for the necessity of baptism. Some churches believe it, others do not. A minority takes seriously what Luther said in his *Large Catechism* that "We must be baptized or we cannot be saved." However, most Protestants deny the necessity of baptism for salvation. Faith alone justifies. Some like the Baptists and *Disciples of Christ* take the principle so literally they will not recognize the validity of infant baptisms, although their opposition to the practice is hard to rationalize. Those who baptize children defend the custom on the grounds that no supernatural change occurs in any case, whether in childhood or maturity; what matters is not baptism but personal acceptance of Christ as one's Saviour. What about children who die without baptism and before reaching the age of reason? Some Lutherans and Episcopalians hold that unbaptized children will not see the face of God, others distinguish between Christian and pagan offspring. The latter will not be saved, the former reach heaven on the faith of their parents. Staunch Presbyterians fall back on the divine election; if a child was predestined it is saved, otherwise not. But normally the question is either glossed over, or, when handled with some logic, not only baptism but even faith becomes unnecessary for salvation.

The churches which demand "believer's baptism" in adult life also require baptism by immersion. Learned treatises are written to prove that the word *baptizein* in classic Greek and therefore in the New Testament means to immerse. Baptists are told that "immersion in water, of a believer in Christ, is essential to baptism—so essential that there can be no baptism without it." Adventists, Mennonites and the Churches of Christ hold the same. More sophisticated bodies like the Presbyterians have no ritual prescriptions. The *Discipline* of the Methodist Church leaves the matter optional, directing the minister to "Let every adult person, and the parents of every child to be baptized, have the choice of sprinkling, pouring or immersion." So tenaciously do Baptists and Disciples hold to immersion that Protestant observers consider it one of the main obstacles to sectarian unity. They invest immersion with the high importance not only of New Testament authority but of explicit command of Christ. "Obviously we have here a really difficult problem as we strive to envisage a united Church." In pursuance of this theory, rigid immersionists excommunicate anyone who was baptized by ablution; others refuse the Lord's Supper to those who have not "resigned their old life by descending under water." As a rule, immersion characterizes the more primitive and undeveloped churches and at least two sects, the Mormons and Jehovah's Witnesses, on the borders of historic Protestantism. Once the practice becomes established its very queerness gives cohesion to a religious body, and a sense of solidarity. This, in turn, isolates the people from other denominations.

Most churches require the Trinitarian formula. Some do not. Lutherans allow baptism "in the name of Christ," on the argument that "Christ did not make the blessing of baptism dependent on certain letters, syllables or phrases." When aspersion is used, some churches make sure the water flows; others are satisfied if a wet cloth is touched to the body.

In view of the wide variance among Protestants on the meaning of baptism, converts to Catholicism are usually "rebaptized" conditionally, to insure valid reception of this indispensable sacrament. In some dioceses the practice is mandatory. However, when the Holy Office was asked in 1949 whether in adjudicating matrimonial cases, baptism conferred among the Disciples of Christ, Presbyterians, Congregationalists, and Methodists should be presumed invalid for want of a right intention on the part of the minister, Rome answered in the negative. Unless the contrary is proved in each particular case, the presumption favors valid baptism provided flowing water and the Trinitarian formula were used.

The Lord's Supper

Like baptism, the Lord's Supper was a bone of contention from the first days of the Reformation. Luther, Calvin, Zwingli and Cranmer each had their own theory about the Real Presence. They oscillated among four variables: whether the Eucharistic presence was real or only symbolic; if real, whether it was bodily or only spiritual; and whether bodily or spiritual, does it take place at the words of consecration or in the act of communion; and if the words of consecration effect a change, is it transubstantiation or only impanation—does the substance of bread and wine remain or is it converted into the Body and Blood of Christ?

These differences still remain, except that four centuries of rationalism have corroded much of the old Protestant belief in a Real Presence as understood by Martin Luther or even Cranmer. Zwingli's pure symbolism is practically common doctrine among the free churches in the Baptist and Congregational families. "When we eat the bread and drink the cup," say the latter, "we are to remember Jesus."

For the Baptists, "the Lord's Supper is plainly a commemorative institution. It commemorates chiefly and supremely the death of Christ." By indirection "in the Lord's Supper we also express our Christian fellowship for our fellow-communicants." But nothing else Calvin's theory of a spiritual presence has entered Presbyterian and Methodist theology. "The body of Christ," says the Methodist ritual, "is given, taken and eaten only after a heavenly and spiritual manner." If certain Methodists believe in a corporeal Eucharist, they do so on their own and quite against the church's official formulary. Confessional Lutherans "unanimously reject the doctrine that the bread and wine are only figures," and postulate a "sacramental union of the intransubstantiated essence of the bread and of the body of Christ." Episcopalians of the Anglo-Catholic variety go further. They believe in a real bodily presence under the Species, and explain the article of their creed which denies transubstantiation as "antiquated" and directed against certain Catholic abuses in the sixteenth century. Several congregations of cloistered Episcopalian religious give expression to this faith in their practice of adoration "before the Blessed Sacrament exposed" on the altar.

The consecration of the Eucharistic elements follows consistently from the concept of the sacerdotal office in the denominations. Lutherans and Episcopalians would never allow women and much less the laity to consecrate the bread and wine for distribution as Holy Communion. But Congregational and Methodist Churches make both concessions. Women are admitted to orders with consequent power to dispense Communion to the people. They also provide for the consecration of the Eucharist by the unordained laity, men or women, when actively engaged in preaching. "An unordained (Methodist) pastor, while serving as a regularly appointed pastor of a charge, may be authorized to administer the Sacraments of Baptism and the Lord's Supper." But where Methodists limit this privilege to students for the ministry, Congregationalists extend it to all preachers indiscriminately.

More extreme is the difference in the elements used for the Eucharistic rite. All the churches who believe in the Lord's Supper use leavened or unleavened bread. But they differ widely on the use of wine. Lutherans and others take wine. Adventists and Methodists require unfermented grape juice. Mormons use water. Behind the substitution lies their inveterate opposition to alcohol. The anomaly is emphasized by the contradiction between elements and prayer. In the Methodist ceremony, the minister refers to "receiving the bread and wine, according to thy Son, our Saviour Jesus Christ," yet the ritual absolutely forbids him to use anything but "the pure unfermented juice of the grape."

Grace and Sanctification

The original cleavage between evangelical and reformed churches stems from the contrary emphasis that Luther and Calvin placed on the mystery of predestination. In both systems the slogan was "to God alone the glory," with a corresponding denial or obscuration of man's effort on the road to salvation. But where Calvin stressed the divine transcendence and sovereign will, Luther favored sentiments of absolute trust in God's mercy. Reformed theology was little concerned with man's sinfulness as such; its theory of arbitrary consignment of some people to heaven and others to hell, irrespective of their deeds, looked upon sin as a mark of perdition and on sinners (defined by Calvinist standards) as predestined victims of divine justice. Evan-

gelists softened or ignored the Calvinist side of Luther and
built a system of grace in which the sinner must not despair
but trustfully hope that, in spite of his impotence to avoid
evil, God will finally save him through the imputed merits
of Christ.

Protestants in America and elsewhere have either followed one of these traditions, or combined the two in a
strange mixture, or departed from them in the direction of
Catholic principles. Depending on the orientation, we find
different religious bodies, sects within churches and schools
of theologians opposing each other on the basic issues of
man's relation to God.

On the broadest level, confessional Lutherans repudiate
the predestinarian theory of the reformed churches. A Lutheran theologian summarized the discord in a series of
propositions aimed at the Calvinists. We reject as unscrip-
tural, he said, "that God so created man that he had to sin,
that God's saving grace is not universal, but pertains only
to the elect, that the election of grace was an absolute act
of sovereign God, and was decreed without consideration
of Christ and His vicarious satisfaction for the sins of the
world, that the elect cannot altogether fall from grace or
wholly lose their faith in spite of the greatest sins, that the
wicked are lost not through their own sin and unbelief, but
because of the absolute decree of God, by which He with-
held from them His grace and mercy, and lastly, we reject
every doctrine of Calvinism which denies universal grace,
and every doctrine which denies salvation by grace alone."[6]
By adding the last phrase the author made sure that his
condemnation of reformed theology would not leave him
suspect of Catholic sympathies. But on the main point of
his critique there was no question that Lutheranism has no
love for the Calvinist deity.

Traditionally, Presbyterians have been the champions of absolute predestination, independently of merit or sin. Many still profess the doctrine, and their churches teach it officially. Under title of God's "Eternal Decree," the current *Westminster Confession of Faith* explicitly teaches that, "By the decree of God, for the manifestation of his glory, some men and angels are predestinated unto everlasting life, and others foreordained to everlasting death." To remove any ambiguity, the *Confession* explains that those predestined for heaven are chosen by God "without any foresight of faith or good works, or perseverance in either of them, or any other thing in the creature, but solely to the praise of his glorious grace."[7] With minor changes, American Presbyterians have subscribed to this doctrine since colonial times, though not without struggle and schism. At the turn of the century, the liberal Northern branch kept the confessional statements intact but added two sections on the Holy Spirit and the love of God in order to "lay greater emphasis on human freedom, and endeavor to repudiate the idea that the sinner's fate is fixed beforehand." Later on the more conservative Southern faction did the same. Encouraged by this success, an attempt was made twenty years ago to revise the *Confession of Faith* by eliminating the offensive sections on predestination. In order to make the change constitutional, 66 out of 87 presbyteries would have had to vote in favor of deletion. Only 64 wanted to remove the sections, so they were kept by a minority of less than one-third of the national representation. The conflict still remains, between the church's authorized creed and the faith of most of its members; also within the church between a liberal majority and the intransigence of those who wish to remain faithful to Calvin's straddling hesitation between Protestantism and Popery.

For fifty years Wesley wrestled to show that while he was a thoroughgoing Protestant, he did not believe in Calvin's theory of predestination. At one time he preached that "neither is salvation of the works we do when we believe: for it is then God that worketh in us: and therefore that he giveth us a reward for what he himself worketh, only commendeth the riches of His mercy, but leaveth us nothing whereof to glory." This was orthodox Protestantism. At other times, he urged the people to repentance and told them to work out their salvation with fear and trembling. "What is your choice?" he pleaded. "Let there be no delay: now take one or the other. I take heaven and earth to record this day, that I set before you life and death, blessing and cursing. Oh choose life! the life of peace and love now; the life of glory forever."[8] No Catholic could improve on this exhortation.

Those within the Methodist communion are divided in accepting one or the other side of the dilemma: either denying good works and favoring Calvinism, or believing in free will and rejecting what (on occasion) Wesley called the blasphemy which makes God more malicious than the devil. Others are simply confused. "Wesley has rendered man powerless and, in spite of that, requires him to respond freely to grace." So they become agnostic. If even Wesley "does not truly possess an understanding of how salvation is possible," how can they?[9]

Outside the structure of Methodism has grown a protest movement which disagrees with the main body of Wesley's followers. While giving lip-service to the Wesleyan theory of sanctification, Methodists are accused of ignoring the principle in practice. Verbally, as their *Discipline* prescribes, they believe "Sanctification is that renewal of our fallen nature by the Holy Ghost, whereby we are not only delivered from the guilt of sin but enabled, through grace, to love God with all our hearts and to walk in his holy commandments blameless." But this is not Protestant doctrine, and Methodists generally know it. Hence the "oversight" of something that contradicts the idea of total depravity. Holiness churches make an issue of the point by stressing man's ability with grace to arrive at Christian perfection. But they are divided on precisely what sanctification means, how it is recognized and, especially, how the state of holiness is achieved. Some believe the process must be gradual, others that the effect comes suddenly. Some indulge in wild orgies of emotionalism, others are satisfied with listening to the word of God and waiting for the coming of the Spirit. Until recent years they were practically ignored in professional circles. Today their number is estimated at twenty million, often disorganized and not even listed among religious bodies but having a profound influence on American culture.

So much for the churches and writers who still believe in the supernatural order. Confused and often contradictory, their creedal bias at least recognizes the existence of grace and the possibility of God's friendship which leads to beatitude. While the divergence from Catholic doctrine is extreme, it is not absolute. There remains something of a common ground. But among liberal Protestants the break is complete. Spokesmen for dominant bodies like the Methodist and Episcopalians defend positions that subvert the basis of Christianity. They may use Christian or Protestant terminology, but the concepts have been washed clean of traditional meaning. Paul Tillich of the Harvard Divinity School denies that God is personal except in a figurative sense as the ground of all being. Where Christianity speaks of man as elevated by grace, Tillich reduces the economy of salvation to the realm of symbolism, in which man reaches God as the projected hope of his anguish and despair. "How often we commit certain acts in perfect consciousness, yet with the shocking sense that we are being controlled by an alien power. That is the experience of separation of ourselves from ourselves, which is to say 'sin,' whether or not we like to use that word." If sin is the sense of control by an alien power, what is grace? "Do you know what it means to be struck by grace? It does not mean that we suddenly believe that God exists, or that Jesus is the Saviour, or that the Bible contains the truth. To believe that something *is*, is almost contrary to the meaning of grace." It must be experienced, and means, fundamentally, that we "accept ourselves" as we really are. "Sometimes it happens that we receive the power to say 'yes' to ourselves, that peace enters into us and makes us whole, that self-hate and self-contempt disappear, and that our self is reunited with itself. Then we can say that grace has come upon us."[10]

In Paul Tillich, the ancient terms have been suborned to serve a new purpose, "to break up the incrusted formulations of familiar modes of thought and thus to overcome the supernaturalism which is still widely held in religious circles."[11] Yet his reputation in Protestant circles has grown as a consequence. An ordained minister in the Evangelical and Reformed Church, his orthodoxy and affiliation were never questioned. Although the Constitution of this body demands recognition of the Holy Scriptures as the Word of God, Tillich's naturalism is considered a valid interpretation of their contents.

Life After Death

Belief in immortality is universal among the Protestant denominations. Except for extreme naturalists, death ushers in a new life whose happiness or misery depends on God's election and, in some churches, on man's cooperation with divine grace. But here the agreement ends. Biblical churches and tract societies generally believe in a supernatural reward, not unlike the Catholic concept of heaven, though seldom elaborating on the beatific vision. The final resurrection of the body is equally professed in the traditional creeds and also a final judgment. But as a church recedes from the Scriptures, faith in eternal happiness becomes more dim or is reduced to a natural instinct. "Cherish this immortal hope," members of the newly formed United Church of Christ are told. "You cannot and need not prove it. You are born with it. You are going somewhere, you are becoming something." In the same way, the bodily resurrection is still professed in the Apostolic and Nicene symbols but explained so etherially that Fundamentalists make this one of their tests of orthodoxy against Protestant "heretics."

Hell as a place or state of eternal punishment is freely admitted, denied or doubted, according as a church believes in the inspired Bible and tolerates no compromise on this difficult mystery. Judging by the religious journals, not many will admit the existence of hell as professed by the Catholic faith. Typical opinions are that "Baptists find it difficult to reconcile the fact of an all-merciful God with endless punishment for sins committed within the short span of a lifetime on earth." For the Episcopalians, "God does not alter His saving activity toward those who have died, but that, directly and through the fellowship of those who serve Him, He continues to seek those who have closed their lives against Him. It would seem, then, that the door to hell is locked only from the inside." Among Methodists, in a symbolic sense our lives are judged at death, "yet we believe that God is love, that He cares for every single person, however sinful, and that God's will must triumph. Since we hold these things to be true, we are confident that in the eternal life, under new conditions, God will call out men of sin until at last all men are won to his fellowship of love."[12]

Churches on the periphery of Protestantism simply deny eternal punishment. For the Mormons, hell is eternal as long as sin remains to be punished, Christian Scientists think of hell as terminating with this life, Jehovah's Witnesses and Adventists prefer annihilation, Unitarians who believe in immortality hold a theory of universal salvation. The thread of unity running through all these theories is the plea that God loves the world too much to allow anyone finally to be lost. Absolutely opposed to any compromise are evangelical groups like the Concordia Lutherans and churches in the Southern Bible belt. On the rare occasion when their doctrine appears in print, they point out that all objections to hell are "based on the false principle that it is proper and reasonable to make our human sentiments and judgments the measure of God's essence and activity." For the compromisers, not faith but feeling becomes the arbiter of divine truth.

American Protestants are almost unanimous in rejecting purgatory as an intermediate stage for souls who die in God's friendship but stained with some minor faults. But here, too, divergencies appear. In fact, where eternal punishment is denied, purgatory substitutes for hell. The familiar appeal to God's mercy that must "win out" over man's sinfulness is applied not only to venial guilt, as in Catholic theology, but to all sins indiscriminately.

The strains of opinion on the subject appear among the churches. Where perpetual estrangement from God is disclaimed and some retribution for sin allowed, purgatory (in concept if not in name) takes the place of hell. Where eternal punishment is admitted or not positively denied, the more confessional sects have no sympathy with the idea. "Some of the Church Fathers," they argue, "advocated the idea that the intermediate state is a state of purification. Augustine thought it not incredible"—which is a prize understatement.[13] Augustine had no doubt about purgatory, often described in his writing, from which he trusted his mother would soon be delivered through the Masses he offered for her soul. The true reasons for denying temporal purgation after death are historical and dogmatic. Luther and Calvin were adamant on the point, since the Reformation was practically born of this issue, that all sins are mortal and no suffrages are useful for the dead. Churches less committed to defend the Reformers are not so inflexible. "The Catholic doctrine on purgatory seems perfectly reasonable," a Presbyterian teacher of theology told the writer. The Protestant Episcopal Church has a strange situation. Its *Articles of Religion*, borrowed from England, still describe purgatory as "repugnant to the word of God." But "Masses" for the dead are sanctioned by the bishops, and since 1928 prayers for the dead are included in the Book of Common Prayer. Frequently, the motives behind this Catholic compromise are less doctrinal than instinctive; the natural desire to do something for a deceased relative or friend breaks through the inherited prejudice.

However, the real melange surrounds the second coming of Christ and the final judgment. Here the spirit of the Reformation has full rein. Even staid denominations like the Methodists and Presbyterians have been touched by the messianic complex that now characterizes most of the biblical sects, the so-called "third force" group of Holiness Bodies and much of the popular evangelism in missions and radio programs. Their common denominator is a sense of urgency. "Jesus is coming! Be prepared!" are familiar slogans. This divides into a variety of theories which first sever the American churches into two camps, fundamentalist and all other, and then separates the former into dozens of competing sects.

The term "fundamentalist" was coined by Dr. Curtis Lewis, a Baptist publisher who in 1920 rallied the conservative elements in his denomination "to do battle royal for the faith of our fathers." He outlined the five-point program which still identifies the movement: an infallible Bible, Virgin birth, Christ's divinity, atonement, and imminent second coming in the flesh. Calculations vary, but some place the number of fundamentalist sympathizers at more than twenty million. While the real issue between them and those whom they call "Modernists" is the acceptance or denial of revelation, the early parousia is a more distinctive label. It also furnishes a powerful stimulus in preaching and revivalism, which characterize this brand of Protestantism.

Fundamentalists take the early return of Christ so gravely that in practice this element accounts for most of their sectarian divisions. Some are strong believers in the millenium, or thousand years preceding the final cataclysm, which they find in the Apocalypse of St. John. Others ignore the millenium and say that the Son of Man will appear very soon. "There are apocalyptic trends, marked by the war, famine, pestilence and death that we know so well are riding around the world at this very moment. It may well be true now that 'this generation should not pass, till all these things be fulfilled.' "[14] Those who expect a millenium conceive it in different ways. For some, the last thousand years will be introduced by the personal appearance of Christ on earth. Premillenianism is the watchword of all Pentecostal bodies. Postmillenianists teach the opposite; according to them Christ will not come until after the thousand years are over. However, both groups are divided on whether the reign "with Christ a thousand years" will be in heaven or on earth. The majority favors a terrestrial reign; Adventists place it in heaven, not on earth, "which will remain a desolated, depopulated wilderness throughout this period." A final discordant note is the localization of heaven. As a rule, strong millenianists confuse beatitude with the "new earth" of St. John and literally make "heaven on earth, purified by fire and re-created at the command of Christ into the eternal home of His redeemed." Not only fringe sects like the Witnesses, but churches in the direct Protestant tradition have adopted the concept.

Vagueness and ambiguity about human destiny have created more than sectional differences among the churches. Their worst effect has been to obscure the purpose of life. In the degree to which the end of man, either personally or collectively, is darkened by contradictions, fidelity in God's service and the practice of virtue are correspondingly weakened. If the reality of hell is questioned and the existence of sanctions denied; if religious leaders disagree on almost every aspect of the future life, the results on the people are predictable. Educated Protestants are tempted to moral relativism, and the others to follow their feelings.

X

SECTARIANISM

THE MULTIPLICITY of separate and independent Protestant churches in the United States is something unique in the modern world. Scarcely a European commentator on the religious scene in America, or a domestic critic of American Protestantism, fails to note with shocked amusement the statistical exhibits which show that the United States has 255 sects, or whatever may be the number for that year. Not many examine the picture far enough to discover that two-thirds of the listed churches have practically no people in them. By actual count, fifty denominations have 50,000 or more members each and represent ninety per cent of all the Protestants in the country. But even fifty autonomous bodies is an embarrassing figure that no other country can duplicate.

In view of the current interest in the World Council of Churches, it will pay to study at close range the sectarian condition of American Protestantism, which may properly be called the testing ground of the world ecumenical movement. On the one hand, the problems facing ecumenism are magnified many times in America, so deep have been the ravages of religious liberalism outside the Catholic Church. On the other hand, in spite of these obstacles, if any measure of success is achieved in the United States, then the world ecumenical movement may take heart and not despair that unity is possible. As Protestants themselves have observed, the problem of achieving unity on a world scale will be solved more readily if many lesser units of world Christianity provide actual demonstration of church union. The most convenient and promising of these units is the church within a particular nation.

Our immediate purpose, therefore, is to inquire into the divided state of the Protestant churches from two viewpoints that should be of peculiar interest to Catholics: how did sectarianism become so prolific in the States, and how do Protestants estimate it? Both questions have profound implications for the Catholic Church whose unity is a constant rebuke to sectarian institutions and whose members should know the problems of those separated from Rome.

Why So Many Denominations?

Protestant scholars have undertaken to analyze the background of American sectarianism. They frankly admit that while Protestants have been divided into different sects from the beginning, the division has not been so rapid or radical as in the United States. The original Reformers founded different churches in Germany, England, Switzerland and France. They were not only geographically separated but doctrinally opposed to each other in many ways. Yet, for the most part, European Protestantism has followed the general pattern set by Luther, Cranmer, Zwingli and Calvin, with some, but relatively little, further fragmentation. How explain the abnormal situation in America?

The first explanation is that the principle of religious liberty granted by the American Constitution tended to be carried over from the political sphere to the field of religion, that is, from the state to the church. This psychological transference was more or less unconscious. Seeing the neutrality of the American state toward all forms of religion, Protestant people were subtly predisposed to assume that a new denomination was not only legally irreproachable but could be religiously approved. "This is a free country, isn't it?" became the colloquial justification for a disaffected group to withdraw and form a new church, and no one seemed to question the propriety of their action.

If an enterprising leader wanted political approval for starting another denomination, he could find it almost anywhere in the writings of the Founding Fathers, not excluding the highest authorities in constitutional history like James Madison, author of the religious freedom amendment and fourth President of the United States. "The more independent religious bodies," he said, "the more secure would be the government in its freedom from church influence." Protestants assumed that if the multiplication of sects were good for the government, it was also good for religion. Sectarian diversity was, therefore, accepted as an ecclesiastical virtue.

Unlike European Protestantism which has a pattern of stability behind its denominations, the American churches had no valid objection to make when a dissatisfied group wished to secede. In fact, secession was part of the American tradition since practically every sect which migrated to the States had broken away from the parent denomination in Europe. How could the parent now chide her children for doing what she herself had done a century or two before? The Baptists had originally been Anglicans who as Separatists were opposed to English ritualism. The Methodists had broken with England for much the same reason. Evangelical Lutherans escaped from Germany where the Emperor tried to amalgamate them with the hated rationalists. Quakers were an offshoot of Non-Conformism. Disciples and Christians were malcontents from the Baptists and Presbyterians. When they began to splinter into sects it was because this concept of liberty had been bred into them by their forebears. They had learned to express dissatisfaction by starting a new religious body.

Parallel with this inherited urge to secede were occasions for discord that were only mildly present in Europe until recent times. Two streams of thought were characteristic of American Protestantism in its formative years: a cold naturalism that came in from the Anglo-Saxon countries, and a stolid evangelical piety, found especially among the Germans and Scandinavians. For ethnic and cultural reasons, the evangelicals went into protective custody in the mid-western and lake areas; the liberalizing Separatists were concentrated on the Atlantic coast. In both cases fragmentation was partially the result of their self-imposed isolation. New England Congregationalism split in three directions; extreme liberals first chafed under creedal restraint and finally broke off to form the Unitarian and similar bodies, doctrinal conservatives seceded in favor of the more authoritative and tough-fibred Presbyterians, and the remnant continued in a mixed religious polity that caters to every shade of theology or unbelief. A comparable situation occurred with the Methodists and Baptists, with varying emphasis, in the direction of liberalism for the Methodists and of fundamentalism among the Baptist denominations.

The biblical churches from Germany and Scandinavia were less troubled with dogmatic problems, or at least their schisms were not only doctrinal but also racial and linguistic. Even today the multi-sectarian Lutheran family is basically divided according to European origins. While the original cause of proliferation was the absence of ecclesiastical authority, the two camps (liberal and evangelical) could have checked their sectarianism to some extent if they had cohabited from the beginning instead of avoiding each other. For example, the Lutherans might have shared some of their doctrinal stability with the free-wheeling Congregationalists, and the latter have Americanized the Lutherans to inhibit the rise of new churches along national lines.

Another factor explaining the wild growth of denominations on American soil may be found in the pioneer psychology of the nation. Until recent years the American people have been living on the frontier. New regions had to be explored, new territory cultivated, new homes and institutions established—among them also churches. Except for those who were traditionally Catholic and were blessed with the services of a priest to move along with them, the majority settled as small religious communities that were distinct from the original denomination, at first only geographically, but later also in doctrine and ritual discipline.

Add to this fact the size of the country, and the multiplication of sects becomes a logical corollary. Even in 1950, the per square mile population in the United States was only one-fourth that of Europe, excluding Russia. But in the mid 1880's, with only ten to fifteen persons to a square mile in the States, with intercommunication rare and unnecessary, it was no wonder that small groups first migrated and then separated completely from the parent denomination. It was perfectly consistent with Protestant theory.

Divisions have often been started by zealous preachers who might be traveling missionaries like the Methodist circuit riders or more stable evangelists like Jacob Albright for the Pennsylvania Lutherans and Mrs. Aimee McPherson of Four-Square-Gospel fame. Historians explain that revivals made the people aware of encasing formalities, ceremonies and institutions which long years of gradual retrogression had set up. They demanded essential changes. Either the customary religious forms were blamed for the slackening of fervor, or they seemed incapable of adaptation to the new spirit which the evangelists had bestirred. Another sect was organized as a promising channel of expression. Came a second revival, and the same reaction started again. While the phenomenon is not peculiar to American Protestantism, since the Reformation itself was a kind of revival, conditions in the United States favored starting a new church every time enough people had their religious feelings aroused. Legal sanction and financial means would be typical favoring elements.

The institution of slavery provoked a series of divisions in the Protestant churches, some of which have since been healed, but others are certainly permanent. Methodists, Baptists, Presbyterians and Lutherans split into rival organizations around the time of the Civil War, first over the inclusion of colored members, and later on a strictly racial basis, when all-Negro churches came into being. Protagonists in every case were the white churchmen and Protestant lay leaders. They were not lacking in zeal for the Negroes as repeated declarations by their various assemblies testify. Thus among the statements of the Southern Baptist Convention in 1866 was the resolution that "in our changed relations with the colored people, we recognize as heretofore, our solemn obligations to give religious instructions to them, by all those means which God has ordained for the salvation of men." Furthermore, "we suggest to the pastors of our churches, the duty of giving theological and other instruction to such colored brethren as are now prevailing, and to such as, in the judgment of the churches, may be called to this work."[1] But while zealous enough to have the Gospel preached to Negroes, the churches were less convinced that this preaching should be given together with the white members of the congregation. The result was an outcropping of new denominations, with some historical relation to the major religious bodies but completely independent in government and ecclesiastical authority.

Today out of approximately fifteen million Negroes in the United States, ten million are in the South, and about fifty per cent of the total population are church members. Their sectarian divisions are impossible to classify, but the majority follow the Methodist or Baptist tradition, preferably the latter, whose lack of formality and absence of set ritual are more appealing than the episcopal structure of the Methodists.

Liberal Complacency

Some years ago an illustrated volume, *Protestant Panorama*, fairly described the minority attitude toward American denominationalism. The United States was called "the largest and most virile Protestant nation on the face of the globe." Ever since the English dissenters reached America in 1620, men in search of religious liberty have been coming to a free land, "each fiercely determined to find sanctuary for his right to believe and worship as he saw fit, and as God seemed to lead." No doubt the mixture of different sects grew out of the variety of cultures among the European immigrants. Yet they had one thing in common, "their thirst for religious liberty." Consequently if America may be called a melting pot for diverse social and national customs, it is even more a crucible of denominational diversity.

But this is nothing of which to be ashamed. So far from

being something to carp at, diversity is Protestantism's glory. Only those who do not comprehend the patterns and processes of democracy can fail to appreciate our profusion of sects. "It conforms to the rich pattern of heterogeneity that characterizes so much of life in these United States. Americans glory in their system of economic free enterprise; American Protestants glory too in the spiritual free enterprise that is as much a part of the American idea as States' rights in individual initiative."[2]

Far from being unhealthy, diversity is said to be part of the original tradition of the American Republic. Did the Founders of our country look aghast at this religious coat of many colors? On the contrary, they helped design it. When James Madison laid down the principle that "all men are equally entitled to the free exercise of religion, according to the dictates of conscience," this political expedience "started us on our diversified way." According to Madison, freedom of religion in America is more closely bound to sectarianism than most people suspect. A multiplicity of churches first creates the demand for independence of worship and then becomes "the best and only security for religious liberty in any society. For where there is a variety of sects, there cannot be a majority of any one sect to oppress and persecute the rest."[3] Thomas Jefferson believed that denominations are as expedient to politics as beneficial to religion. "The several sects," he felt, "perform the office of a *censor morum* over each other." Is uniformity attainable? Not except through torture and imprisonment. And what has been the effect of coercion? "To make one half of the world fools, and the other half hypocrites. To support roguery and error all over the earth."[4] Clearly American denominationalism should not be deplored but encouraged. Its very existence is a tribute to the spirit of American democracy.

The most eloquent panegyrics come from those whose religious convictions have lost their grip on the Christian faith, while still speaking, ostensibly, in the name of Protestantism. Behind this complacency lurks the implicit feeling that churchmen are wasting their time in splitting hairs over doctrinal differences. The acid test of religion is not what a man believes but "Inasmuch as you have done it unto one of the least of these. . . ." Not creeds and ritual but the Social Gospel marks the essence of Christianity.

Evils of Sectarian Division

However, most Protestants are agreed that sectarianism is evil. They are ashamed and deeply concerned about their destiny. "We call the world," they confess, "burdened with its own tragic divisions of race and class and nationality, to find its unity in the one Father and the one Christ, and then we add other divisions to those with which it already struggles. 'Woe unto the world because of offenses.' The simple are confused and the sensitive are offended by the incongruity between the churches and the Church."[5] It is a strange spectacle when those who call the world to reconciliation are themselves unreconciled.

In appraising their discordant character, churchmen are brutally frank and willing to expose the consequences that follow on sectarianism. No critic from the Catholic Church could be more outspoken; at least he would not be as competent to pass judgment on the "scandal of this hostile diversity" which those who are part of it have simply called a sin.

Dissipation of Natural Resources. On the most tangible and practical level, denominationalism is said to be scandalously wasteful of Protestant resources. The prodigal waste of money applies to the support of local churches. Sixty million Protestants, most of whom are only occasional church-goers, operate a total of 270,000 church edifices, which means an average of two-hundred plus persons for each building. By comparison, the Catholic Church with forty million members has 21,000 parishes and mission stations, with an average membership of more than eighteen hundred.

This would be less serious if the Protestant churches were at least evenly distributed, which is not the case. Most of them exist side by side with other Protestant churches in the same community. Not only are funds wasted with too many churches, but the multiplicity of sects adds the further burden of multiplied overhead to run the separate organizations. If only the sects united, instead of spending their money in competition with other churches, they could use it "directly to the great enterprise of the Kingdom of God."

A more subtle aspect of this wastefulness is the psychological void that comes with division when faced with pressing responsibilities. Material facilities and manpower may be amply available but the motivation that comes from unity is missing. Delegates to the National Council of Churches were bluntly told, "It is a standing rebuke to the so-called 'old-line' Protestant churches in America that with such large resources of money, institutions, trained leadership, all the ingredients of effectiveness, they have so little expectancy. We do not look for any great work of God. As we face the mission of the Christian church in our time, we know that it requires the united resources and dedication of all the churches. We need this expression of our oneness in Christ not that our churches may be made *more* but that they may be made *new*. Not just more churches but new patterns of Christian community that are authentically the answer to the loneliness and fragmentation of man's life today."⁶ Thus without the courage that comes of cooperative effort, the grave problems that beset people will be evaded by religious leaders. Or if timorously undertaken they will not be solved when men see their own internal struggles reflected in the destiny of the churches that are supposed to help them.

Hindrance to Missionary Expansion. Beyond the home front, Protestants recognize that the missionary expansion of the Christian faith is seriously handicapped and misrepresented by their sectarianism. A divided church at home inevitably, and to a high degree, hinders the spread of the Gospel to the people of non-Christian lands. Missionaries writing back to the States report how shocked their converts are to find the Christian community for which they have sacrificed so much divided against itself. What can it possibly mean but confusion and distress of mind when a Hindu from North India joins the American Southern Baptists, thus adding a divisive heritage of the American Civil War to a country already burdened with a heavy caste system?

At the Evanston Assembly of the World Council of Churches in 1954, the delegates were told in unmistakable terms how their ecclesiastical divisions inhibit the advancement of Christ's kingdom. World-wide evangelism, the speaker said, cannot be divorced from the quest for Christian unity. For more than a century, the main stream of Protestant missionary expansion has taken place under the shadow of a denominationally divided Church. "The result has been the projection across the world of the historic divisions of Western Christendom. This is not a situation which we dare contemplate with easy complacency." Nor is it merely a question of tactical expediency, "Christ's Church is one. That we must surely believe. But the failure to express in visible form the unity given in Christ is a formidable obstacle to effective world evangelism."[7] How can pagans and infidels be asked to believe that Christianity is true unless the missionaries themselves witness to the truth by professing the same teaching of the Gospel and living in religious harmony with their fellow-laborers in the Gospel vineyard?

Frustration of Social Efforts. Even the most creedless churches feel the injury done to their cause by a separatism which keeps them from living up to the social teaching of Christ. A disunited church, they admit, is no match for the tremendous power of the social collectivities that have risen in modern America. "Great magnitudes of social organization have emerged, over against which our denominational churches present a picture of limp futility." Protestantism has been learning the painful lesson of the strength in unity, which it lacks.

The American mind is supposed to be collectivist in structure, molded by relatively few massive blocs of secular interest, each under the control of its own center of propaganda. This allows Protestants to make an invidious comparison between the relative strength of the Catholic Church and their own divided sects. The contacts of Protestantism with "government, labor unions, the movies and television, the press, industrial management, the educational system, scientific enterprise, even the family," are confessedly tenuous and unimpressive. By contrast, these blocs of collectivist power have ample reason to be respectfully conscious of Roman Catholicism. Though fewer in number, Catholics are united and therefore represent a standing threat to the enemies of personal liberty, which Protestants cannot duplicate unless they unite.

With all its enthusiasm, fellowship and emphasis on individual responsibility, sectarian religion finds it hard to cope with the massive problems of modern society. As long as the churches are disunited, their impact on the "organization man" will be minimal. They are no match for highly centralized political and economic institutions. Some feel that the bulk of American Protestants have already surrendered to more united agencies by moving out of the big cities and concentrating in smaller towns and less influential areas. In Cleveland, from 1920 to 1950 the membership of five Protestant denominations (American Baptists, Congregational Christian, Methodist, Presbyterian U.S.A., and Protestant Episcopal) declined by more than thirteen per cent, while the Catholic and total population of the city increased by twenty-four and fifteen per cent respectively. The statistics of one denomination's history in New York City show that during the past century in Manhattan and the Bronx it has dissolved fifty-four churches and another forty-two were lost to other congregations.

Unprejudiced observers have noted the almost natural association of a fragmented religious culture with the small community, to the point that "an anti-urban bias has become almost a point of dogma in American Protestantism. Many Protestants feel that a permanent and deadly hostility exists between urban man and those who are loyal to the Christian faith and ethic; that village ways are somehow more acceptable to God than city ways."[8] From their point of view they are right. Apart from economic reasons, the continued autonomy and even existence of a Protestant congregation may depend on its removal from the alien pressures of city life. Without the strength that comes from solidarity with other religious bodies in the same metropolitan area, relative isolation in a small community may be the only hope of survival. In the same way, Protestants in the cities are often left churchless in favor of new congregations being organized in the rural and suburban districts, out of all proportion to the objective needs of a shifting population. Ministers have learned from experience that a half dozen churches of their denomination soon become lost in a large city like Chicago or New York. Unless the preacher has a reputation like Harry Emerson Fosdick, membership may drop to the point of diminishing returns and foreclosure or absorption by another church may be the only choice.

Norman Vincent Peale's predecessor at the Marble Church in New York had been Dr. Daniel A. Poling, a highly respected religious leader. Marble Collegiate itself was a national monument as the oldest religious institution in the city, dating from 1628. Yet within three years of Poling's departure, under a succession of temporary pastors, the congregation had almost disappeared. By dint of hard labor and the attraction of writing a best-seller on *The Power of Positive Thinking*, Peale succeeded in keeping the church alive, although when he first received the New York appointment he hesitated about working in a city that was known as "the graveyard of ministers." The price of his becoming pastor, incidentally, was an act of anti-sectarianism. He changed denominations from Methodist to the Reformed Church in America.

Weakness in Competition with Catholicism. Protestant leaders without a trace of bigotry freely admit that denominationalism robs the churches of their inherent strength in competition with a formidable and aggressive Catholicism. They concede that Protestantism and the Catholic Church are both engaged in resisting the gradual secularization of American life. As a result, many Protestants have been led to believe that the two are therefore cooperating in a common cause. But they are mistaken. "This notion is not shared by Catholicism. The Catholic Church knows that itself and Protestantism represent two profoundly different kinds of religion, and it draws the line sharply between them. In the past, Protestants have always been clearheaded on this matter. It is only in our generation, under the influence of a sentimental and false conception of tolerance, that a considerable portion of the Protestant mind has been beguiled into the delusion that Protestantism and Catholicism are allies."[9] But they are not. They are competitors in the struggle for the soul of America, in which Catholicism has been rapidly overtaking Protestantism. The figures quoted are revealing. In the City of New York, Catholic Church membership outnumbers the Protestant five to one, in Chicago three to two. In Buffalo, Pittsburgh, St. Louis, Philadelphia, Cleveland, San Francisco, Washington, and Cincinnati, the ratio is about even, with a growing edge in each of these cities in favor of the "Roman Church." Boston, from Plymouth Rock to the beginnings of the twentieth century the proud capital of New England Protestantism, is now overwhelmingly Roman Catholic.

How to meet the challenge? It can never be met, the critics point out, and Protestantism is doomed to failure while it persists in spreading its efforts, dividing its interest and localizing its forces, when the Catholic Church strong in unity is aggressively out to win America to its side.

Injury to Spiritual Welfare. Unity-minded churchmen accuse the denominations of provincializing Protestant mentality by erecting barriers against the free flow of Christian thought. About half the Protestant churches in the country are congregational in character, without strong bonds to the past or to each other, without resources in liturgical tradition or theology to temper the lack of inspiration in their preachers. Because of the heavy sectarian demands, the clergy are often recruited from ill-suited and poorly educated subjects, with corresponding decline in respect from the people and influence on their lives. "The whole American development has largely transferred the religious and ethical vitality of Protestantism to religious and ethical groups outside the ecclesiastical structure. The bare bones of church institutions and authorities are often regarded as somehow necessary but antiquated and unlovely and still potentially dangerous. One might almost describe American Protestantism in its dominant patterns as an experiment in Christianity with a minimum of the church."[10] As strong as it seems, this self-accusation remains unchallenged. There are too many cross currents in the denominations to give church authorities a united judgment on pressing moral issues, and too little sense of community among the members to take the judgment as more than a counsel even when made. In more than one area of human relations, the fragmented religious bodies have ceded their right to teach the people in favor of trans-sectarian institutions whose membership is heavily Protestant. Some estimates place the percentage of American Methodist clergymen who are Freemasons as high as ninety per cent. In England, sixteen members of the Anglican hierarchy, including the Archbishop of Canterbury, are high ranking lodge members.

Denominationalism affects not only the teaching authority of the churches, it also injures their capacity of ministering to the spiritual needs of the people. A case in point is their administration of the Lord's Supper, which differs a great deal from one church to another, and within the same church from one denomination to another. Reportedly, the Lutherans are fairly homogeneous in doctrine and ritual, yet among their nineteen species in the United States are nineteen customs in vogue on the reception of Holy Communion. The *Una Sancta* publication recently illustrated the confusion by telling the story of a soldier boy from a sacramental parish who was in the city of Chicago on a Sunday morning in summer. "It was the first time he was away from home. Above all he wanted the Sacrament, believing that he would thus be united with loved ones who were also at the Altar at home. He called one church after another. In the great city of Chicago with its thousands of Lutherans and hundreds of parishes, only one parish was celebrating Holy Communion on this Sunday, and it was so far out that he could not make it in time."[11] Comparable situations exist in the other denominations, especially the more liturgically-inclined. Often the first grace which led a person into the Catholic Church was the experience of frustration in finding contrary practices in churches of the same Protestant tradition and even the same denominational name.

Encouragement of Dubious Loyalties. The most damaging criticism of sectarianism sees it as a cultivation of antiquated values, breeding a "subtle and perilous moral insincerity among Protestant Christians." Critics of their own churches find the denominations as hardly more than survivals of an era that is well on its way out. The principles on which they were founded have lost their vitality. "Yet the structure, the shell of the denomination persists." What happens? In order to maintain their positions as ministers of a distinct religious group, churchmen are accused of keeping obsolete issues alive and vesting them with a semblance of importance, thinking there is no better way to inspire and preserve denominational loyalty. Many of the clergy, especially those who have been "enlightened by the ecumenical ideal," recognize the situation as unreal. But they are victims of the system. A sectarian minister is "caught in it and cannot extricate himself from it. Protestantism provides him with no opportunity for a Christian ministry except one that is identified with and results in the strengthening and greatening of his denomination."[12] Thus instead of promoting the ideals which are or should be the common heritage of all Christians, the sectarians are dividedly preaching their own peculiar speciality. Adventists teach the imminent Second Coming, Baptists the necessity of baptism by immersion, Quakers the idolatry of church ritual, Methodists the sinfulness of traffic in liquor. They are constrained to defend their denominational bias by advocating doctrines and practices which are distinctive of their sect; yet, if they are at all familiar with religious history, they should recognize these differences as arbitrary innovations which originated in human caprice. To preach them as divinely sanctioned is called hypocritical and demoralizing in the extreme.

Although coming from Protestant sources that presumably know their own people, these sweeping accusations need to be qualified. We must first distinguish between the average lay Protestant who, even when highly educated, is woefully ignorant in religious matters, and professional church leaders in the ministry. Even among the clergy, it would be an over-simplification to reduce ecclesiastical differences to "absolute issues." Some of them may be trivial and out of date, but not all and, perhaps, not even the majority. Divergencies among the churches are often rooted in principles which have their measure of truth and on which contrary theological systems have been built. No doubt personal factors color the dogmatic antagonisms, but coloring is not substance.

In a professional study prepared for the World Council of Churches before the Evanston Assembly, the authors analyzed the non-theological-social and cultural-factors in church divisions among Protestants. Under the title *More than Doctrine,* they enumerated some twenty contributing elements: historic isolation, reaction against compulsion, habit, sentiment, vested interests, political pressures, institutional pride, mental limitations, indifference, property ownership, prejudices, doctored history, love of status quo, misrepresentations and personal ambition. The list was long and depressing, and the analysis of each factor humiliating. But in fairness to Protestant churchmen, the critics had overlooked what Catholics at least can appreciate: that in the spirit of sectarian divisiveness is an instinct to believe in Christian revelation and a jealousy that fears losing what is already possessed. Denominational differences continue, ultimately, because the churches wish to retain what they consider essentials of the Gospel message. They prefer to remain divided but faithful to their own convictions than united at the price of infidelity. The pity is they do not see the further alternative of finding the fullness of revelation under Catholic unity.

X I

DESIRE FOR UNITY

THE EVANSTON ASSEMBLY of the World Council of Churches in 1954 was reportedly the most highly publicized religious gathering in American history Yet for most Americans, including Catholics, it remained something of a mystery. Ostensibly it was only a huge convention at which twelve hundred men and women, representing one hundred and seventy million church members, came together to discuss the general subject of "Christ, the Hope of the World." In reality it was a public confession that the divisions which plague non-Catholic churches are opposed to the will of God, and that efforts must be made to heal the disunity if Christianity outside the Roman communion is not to disintegrate. As expressed by an official bulletin, "it is a sad thing that there needs to be a World Council of Churches. For the Council exists to bring together churches that are divided, separated from one another by differences of theology, worship, church culture, race and past history." This is contrary to the New Testament, which "knows no separated churches, but only the one Church, the Body of Christ, the colony of heaven."[1]

It would be easy to dismiss the World Council or (in America) the National Council of Churches as another vain effort to unite what lacks a principle of unity, and to regard as fantastic any comparison between Evanston and "the Council of Nicea and the other ecumenical conferences of

[223]

the early Church." But Catholics have a duty in charity to understand the anxiety which disturbs sincere non-Catholics, and to promote by study, prayer and action that union with the Vicar of Christ which alone can solve the differences in Protestant Christianity.

History of the Ecumenical Movement

On the international level, the ancestry of the World Council of Churches may be traced to two events, both occurring in 1910, when the modern ecumenical movement is said to have been born. In that year, the (Protestant) World Missionary Conference held its first meeting at Edinburgh, Scotland, on the basis of national representation. One of the problems raised by the Conference was missionary work in Central and South America. Many of the churches were conducting missions in those countries. But the problem was shelved for fear that "this topic might offend the Roman Catholic Church which is the dominant religious body in the whole territory south of the Mexican border." The more liberal-minded delegates considered this a weakness, which they attributed to the great differences in doctrine and policy that characterize the various churches in Christendom. To remedy the evil of non-cooperation and fear of Rome, they suggested the formation of a study group to explore and, as far as possible, resolve the points of disagreement, or at least reduce friction to a minimum.

Bishop Charles Brent, Episcopal missionary in the Philippines, is generally credited with taking up the idea suggested at Edinburgh and carrying it into effect. Later in the same year, the triennial convention of the Protestant Episcopal Church was meeting in Chicago. Brent attended the convention and asked the House of Bishops to appoint a committee inviting "all Churches which accepted Jesus Christ as God and Saviour to join in conferences for the consideration of all questions pertaining to the Faith and Order of the Church of Christ." Due to the approaching World War and its aftermath, the First World Conference on Faith and Order was not held until 1927, when representatives from sixty-nine churches met at Lausanne in Switzerland to lay the foundation of the future World Council of Churches. The actual birthday was August 22, 1948, when "the bells of a thousand steeples of American churches proclaimed to the world that the official representatives of 147 churches from all great communions except the Roman Catholic, were assembled at Amsterdam to offer their united prayers to God for the way He had led them to that hour." When, six years later, America was host to the World Council, the membership had increased but the original enthusiasm had simmered down. Inability to agree on a definition of the Church and, therefore, on the kind of unity they desire made some leading Protestants wonder if the Council might not more profitably confine itself to a study of social problems, "from the saddle, so to speak," and scuttle all discussions of theological divergence.

The American counterpart of the world ecumenical movement has two phases: the formation of new churches through organic merger and the cooperative federation of many denominations for the sake of greater efficiency. Both types are important, not only as a vindication of Catholicism whose unity is a standing challenge to the non-Catholic world, but as evidence of the serious efforts being made to recover something of the Christian solidarity which existed before the Reformation.

Since 1900 about thirty-five denominations of numerical consequence have entered into mergers to form new churches, sometimes remerging two or three times. The Congregationalists, for example, absorbed the Evangelical Protestants in 1924 without changing their name; seven years later they joined the Christian Churches to become the Congregational Christians; and in 1957, after a generation of controversy and litigation, they united with the liberal Evangelical and Reformed body to form the two million member United Church of Christ. Thus after more than three centuries of relative autonomy, the Congregationalists have merged themselves out of existence. Because of their fragmented character Lutherans are often amalgamating, though generally on a minor scale, except for the United and American Lutheran Churches which cater, respectively, to conservative and liberal elements in the Lutheran tradition. The high point in organic mergers took place in 1939 when three segments of Wesley's family joined forces to reorganize the Methodist Church which had split during Civil War days over the slavery question.

Parallel with the creation of new churches out of smaller segments were three other coalescences on a much wider but less intensive scale, in which the end product was not a new entity but a denominational cooperative. In 1908, twenty-eight Reformed Churches, including Baptists, Methodists and Presbyterians, formed the Federal Council of Churches, which marks a turning point in American Protestant history. Previous efforts to get the churches to collaborate had all foundered. For one thing, they were too ambitious; their organizers were generally idealists who could think only in terms of organic union. They were also plagued by a spirit of anti-Catholicism which alienated the more conservative minds, and, above all, the basis of unification had always been conceived as doctrinal. The Federal Council cut through these obstacles or avoided them by applying

the principles of American democracy to ecclesiastical cooperation. Its five-point objectives have remained substantially
unchanged in fifty years, even after the Federal Council
became the National Council of Churches in 1950. As provided by the constitution, its purpose was to express the
fellowship and "catholic" unity of the Protestant denominations, to bring these bodies into united service for Christ
and the world, to encourage their devotional fellowship and
mutual counsel concerning the spiritual life and religious
activities, to secure a larger combined influence for the
Christian churches in all matters affecting the moral and
social condition of the people and, finally, to assist in the
organization of local branches of the Federal Council where
the full weight of national Protestantism could be brought
to bear on the community level.

Although the largest, the Federal Council was only one
of several like agencies that sought to bridge the denominational differences in American Protestantism. A Home Missions Council, the National Protestant Council on Higher
Education, and the United Stewardship Council had all been
founded by denominational boards to make their work
more effective. But this was not enough. As these agencies
evolved their programs, they found overlapping and divisions of responsibility. Closer cooperative action was needed.
Further study and negotiation were finally terminated in
1941 at an historic Atlantic City conference which recommended "the creation of a single corporate agency to succeed all of the existing national councils." This met with
enthusiastic acceptance and after nine more years of planning emerged as the National Council of Churches with a
current voting constituency of thirty-five denominations,
including one National Catholic and six Eastern Orthodox
churches, having an aggregate membership of thirty-eight

million. Another forty lesser bodies are affiliated with the Council, besides organizations like the Y.M.C.A. and the American Association of Theological Schools.

On a lower key, a group of fifteen fundamentalist bodies formed the American Council of Christian Churches in 1941, ostensibly to coordinate evangelical sects that were out of sympathy with the liberal trend in the National Council. But the impact of this protest federation has been minor, both for lack of members and because the strongly negative bias has made enemies on every side. Catholics are attacked for trying to control the government, Protestants for diluting the Bible and the Jews for cooperating with Communism. "This group," according to John Mackay, late president of Princeton Theological Seminary, "while paying lip tribute to the Bible and Jesus Christ, represents an unbiblical Christianity. Wherever they go and in all they say about those whom they love to malign and traduce, they act without the slightest interest in truth and in terms of a Jesuitical ethic."[2] When reporting this comment, Religious News Service omitted the reference to "Jesuitical ethic."

The World Council of Churches

The constitution of the World Council of Churches covers nine sections, of which the most important defines the doctrinal basis of membership and the extent of its authority over member churches. Significantly, the dogmatic foundation is disposed of in one sentence, stating that "the World Council of Churches is a fellowship of churches which accept our Lord Jesus Christ as God and Saviour." Visser't Hooft, General Secretary and guiding genius of the Council, admits that "theologically speaking the basis is probably not the best that could be found." However, it has the advantage of emphasizing that "our unity is not found in ourselves but in our common relatedness to a common Lord."[3]

Apparently, therefore, the Council recognizes the divinity of Christ and requires profession of this doctrine for active membership. But one of the anomalies of the organization is the discord to be noticed on the three levels on which its voice may be heard, namely, the official declarations of the governing body, the express statements of outstanding authorities within the society, and the open profession of faith by member bodies in the World Council. Whenever the Council officially, and anonymously, touches on the subject, it seems clearly enough to teach the natural divine filiation of Jesus Christ, who is "God's Son become Man," who is "God and Man."[4]

Not so clear are statements of such conciliar lights as Paul Minear, delegate at Lund for the Conference on Faith and Order, according to whom "recent scholarship is underscoring the fact that Jesus' teachings are impossible. Does anyone today seriously consider giving money to all, loving all, forgiving all? Can we refuse marriage to divorcees, abandon wealth and property and family? Do we serve only one master, take no thought of the morrow, seek to become last of all, least of all, servant of all?"[5] Completely denying Christ's divinity is the teaching of the Congregational Church Manual which asks, "What made Jesus divine?" and answers, "His divinity was achieved. Had he yielded to temptation he would have weakened, and ultimately destroyed his divine nature."[6] Yet Congregationalists, now as the United Church of Christ, are one of the leading bodies of the World Council, whose very definition of the Church as a "fellowship" has been incorporated into the Council's constitution.

Commentators on the Council never tire of repeating that it is not a super-church but a democratic society which allows free discussion and imposes no duties in faith or morals, except such as the churches may wish to assume by themselves. "It has no constitutional power of any kind over the participating churches. It is a consultative body and will not legislate for the churches. It has duties but no rights. It is an instrument for the use of the churches, but to what extent it will be used remains a matter for each and all of the participating churches to decide."[7] In the words of its constitution, "the World Council should offer counsel and provide opportunity of united action in matters of common interest," with no question of setting up an ecclesiastical structure and much less of requiring assent to any doctrine of the ancient creeds.

When the Council met in plenary session at Evanston, it produced a solemn manifesto which was drafted by the Committee on Faith and Order, voted on by the delegates and "communicated to the Churches for appropriate action." As the fruit of several years' study by the best minds in the Council it may be taken as an accurate statement of the two cardinal issues that vex the Protestant mind and that have created the ecumenical movement. The first is to find some intelligible ground of unity among the Christian churches separated from Rome, and the second to explore the nature of their disunity, with a view to finding a means of unification.

Hoping to discover some vestige of unity among the member churches, the theologians of the World Council prejudged their case by stating that "the New Testament conceives of the unity of the church, not as sociological, but as having its essential reality in Christ himself and in his indissoluble unity with his people."[8] Instead of defining unity both in terms of its divine Founder and of its human components, who profess and practice a common faith, unity is said to belong only to Christ Himself, who, clearly, is the one Mediator between God and man. In answer to the question, therefore, whether the New Testament teaches that the Church of Christ is one, the Council would say, yes, but in a novel sense. It is one only because Christ is one, because He is the one source of our reconciliation with the Father, because through Him alone we receive the Holy Spirit and hope for the glory of heaven. To use a comparison, we may speak of the human race as unified because all men are created by one God, or of a human family as united because all the children were born of one father and mother.

But is this all? Did Christ give His Church only the integrity which comes of His being the one Lord and Saviour of mankind? Essentially and substantially, we are told, this is sufficient. True, Christ also desired His Church to have a second kind of unity, consisting in the union of its members with one another, which may be called "the oneness of the church in its earthly pilgrimage." But this is only a tendency toward unity, that "will not be totally achieved until God sums up all things in Christ," that is, after the last day. So as not to be mistaken in its meaning, the Council expressly stated that, "In this *eschatological* perspective all our human divisions are provisional."

An analogy from St. Paul illustrates the two types of unity, one given and existing, the other to be manifest and still in the making. "In each Christian there is the 'new man' who has been crucified with Christ and yet must be daily mortified. So the Church is already one in Christ, by virtue of his identification of himself with it, and must become one in Christ, so as to manifest its true unity in the mortification of its divisions."[9] In ecumenical theology, the Lord has given His Church abundant means for the gradual, though never total, manifestation of unity among the members of the Mystical Body of Christ.

Painfully aware of their mutual discord, the denominations in the World Council wanted to assure themselves that "the undivided Christ is present among us, in spite of our divisions." To this end they narrated the various gifts received from God, which suggest at least some measure of uniformity. As regards faith, "we all wait upon one Father, through the one Holy Spirit, praying that we may be ready to hear and obey when he talks of the things of Christ and shows them to us." As regards the Scriptures, all the churches read them, "and proclaim that the gospel forms them in the faith that the word speaking through them draws us to himself and into the apostolic faith." Relative to the sacraments, "we all receive his gift of baptism whereby, in faith, we are engrafted in him even while we have not yet allowed it fully to unite us with each other." Moreover, "we all hear his command 'do this' and his word 'this is my body . . . this is my blood' in the sacrament of the eucharist, even while our celebration of the Lord's Supper is not yet at one table." In like manner, "we all receive a ministry of the word and sacraments, even while our ministers are not yet recognized by all and not understood in the same sense."

Here the Council made a strange distinction between the terms "common" and "uniform" as applied to the churches. The gifts of Scripture, baptism, the Eucharist and the ministry are not indeed being used in a uniform manner. But at least "the fact of our *common* though *diverse* use of these gifts is a powerful evidence of our unity in Christ." As a present reality it affords some consolation since justice "compels us now to examine seriously how it is that our disunity as churches contradicts our unity in Christ."[10] This self appraisal, it may be added, is the most promising feature of the ecumenical movement.

Unfortunately, when the Council came to examine how the great divisions in Christian history are to be estimated, its analysis shaded into ambiguity. Objectively, according to the Evanston Assembly, the alienation of one Christian body from another should be considered sinful, but subjectively all the schisms and heresies in Christianity have been sincerely, even necessarily, instituted.

During the first millenium some people believed that others were departing from the God-given structure and faith of the church by unfounded doctrines. Thus came the schism between the East and West, completed by the year 1054 and, except for temporary and partial reunions with Rome, still extant in the "Orthodox" churches which number almost 200 million communicants. Others believed that "God had called them to such reformation of the faith and order of the church as would restore it to its primitive purity." They felt the work could not be completed within the framework of Roman Catholicism, and brought into being the churches of the Reformation, derived from Luther, Calvin and Zwingli, and since proliferated into scores of denominations. "Some believed that the faith must indeed be reformed but within the framework of the ancient and historic episcopacy." The Anglican and Old Catholic communities, therefore, became separated both from Rome and from most of the Reformed churches. Finally, "some believed that the established church of their day would not give free course to the word of salvation." So the older free churches and the Methodist connection felt themselves forced to organize independent organizations.

In this group belong some of the most influential bodies in the World Council, which are founded on the principle of "self-determination" in matters of faith and discipline.

The basic remedy for disunity proposed to the churches is blind self-surrender, "even unto death." Churches that have cherished certain doctrines and traditions for centuries are to offer them up "in uniting with other churches, without complete certainty as to all that will emerge from this step of faith." Various measures are suggested to give tangible proof of this self-surrender, which lies at the heart of all unity movements outside the Catholic Church.

First, and of paramount importance for healing the discord in Christendom, is humble repentance. "Not the repentance we may expect of others, but that we will undertake ourselves—cost what it may—even when others are not willing to follow." This means a sincere acknowledgment before God that "we have sinned so as to be caught in the net of inexplicable evil and rendered unable to heal our divisions by ourselves."

After repentance should come thankfulness to God "for the actual oneness he has given to us." Concretely the gratitude becomes effective if the present members of the Council resolve to "stay together and beyond that, as the Holy Spirit may guide us, we intend to unite."

The guidance of the Holy Spirit must come through "our Lord speaking to us through Holy Scripture." Whatever difficulty this involves, arises from the fact that "we still struggle to comprehend the meaning and authority of Holy Scripture." Hence the recommendation to make an earnest study of the word of God and, above all, to be obedient to "what we are told" by the inspired text. Then "we are on our way toward realizing the oneness of the church in Christ in the actual state of our dividedness on earth."

Special and studious attention should be paid to the function of baptism and the Eucharist as instruments of unity. "For some, but not for all, it follows that the churches can only be conformed to the dying and rising again in Christ, which both sacraments set forth, if they renounce their eucharistic separateness."

And lastly, "the measure of our concern for unity is the degree to which we pray for it. We cannot expect God to give us unity unless we prepare ourselves to receive his gift by costly and purifying prayer." Especially valuable are communal prayers, for "to pray *together* is to be drawn together." Therefore, "we urge, whenever possible, the observance of the Week of Prayer for Christian Unity, January 18–25, or some other period suited to local conditions, as a public testimony to prayer as the road to unity."[11]

In order properly to evaluate the foregoing statement of ecumenical principles, we must first recognize it as a compromise between disparate elements in the Council of Churches. At one extreme are those who believe there is strength in doctrinal and ritual differences, for whom the Council should be only a federated cooperative with no ambition to any sort of organic merger. They are "keenly sensitive to the gains in vitality" which come from church disunion. At the other extreme are the "Orthodox" groups, for whom the unity of the Church already *exists* and, in fact, is to be found within the exclusive limits of their own communion. This claim was so jarring on the sensibilities of certain Protestant churchmen, they publicly asked what business the Orthodox had in belonging to the World Council. Feeling on the point is quite mutual.

Between these extremes lies the majority of denominations in the ecumenical movement. They are undecided either on the nature of the church or on the kind of unity it is supposed to have. Some maintain the unity is an existing reality, within certain theoretical boundaries. Their problem is to define these boundaries, within which the church must be united and beyond which diversity is allowed. Others define the church as purely invisible, "a community known only to God." The problem is to give better expression to this existent—so far mostly invisible—union among the divided members. Still others consider the church essentially visible, but without restricting limits, capable of embracing "all those who profess and call themselves Christians, however diverse their belief and practice."

Faced with these discordant opinions, the Council had to make a choice and settled on the Lutheran theory of man's utter depravity after the fall. Accordingly, disunion among the churches is certainly sinful, but unavoidable, in view of our corrupted nature. Thus, "we may think of the church as we are able to think of the individual believer, who may be considered at one and the same time both justified and a sinner." In other words, the Lutheran idea of man's justification becomes also the speculative basis for the church's simultaneous unity and disunity. Even as individual believers are and ever remain sinners, although "justified" by God, in Christ who alone is *just;* so the churches are divided among themselves, while united in their founder, Jesus Christ, who alone is *one.* Disunity, therefore, is no less inevitable in the churches of Christ than sin in the individual Christian. They cannot help being divided, any more than he can help committing sin. After all, the members of the Church are human, suffering from the common effect of Adam's fall that vitiated the nature of man. If any semblance of unity can be found in the Church, it must be something extrinsic, a kind of appropriation, where the unity of Jesus Christ is imputed to the society He founded. Really and formally, the Church is not united and cannot be, this side of heaven, by reason of her fallen members in whom the virtue of charity, which makes for solidarity, has been utterly destroyed.

What practical conclusions should be drawn? To be consistent the theologians of the World Council should have resigned themselves to the *status quo* and not have presumed to change the unchangeable. Fortunately, though illogically, they went on to offer a series of remedies to "heal our disunity as churches," thus negating their doctrinal supposition while, from the Catholic viewpoint, opening the way to a possible solution of the gravest problem in Christianity.

The success of the world ecumenical movement will depend in large measure on what sentiments become dominant in the member churches. If the rigid Reformation concept prevails, according to which the Church's unity is invisible and her disunity inevitable, then the ecumenical movement is destined to fail. The churches of the World Council may continue to cooperate in solving their social and economic problem, with tangible benefits to everyone concerned; but real unitive progress will never be made where radical differences in faith and worship are conceded, on principle, to be irremediable.

Typical of this attitude was the judgment of the *Christian Century*, commenting on the Evanston Assembly. "Always at Evanston," it complained, "there were grim disunities which the World Council may at limited times and to limited degrees transcend, but which it has hardly even begun to dissolve." In fact, "Evanston will not be remembered for having carried forward the cause of Christian unity. It might possibly (though we hope not) be remembered for having shown how far off and blocked off the goal of unity is." Then by way of prophecy, "if four more assemblies handle theological or dogmatic themes as badly as this one did, say the nature of biblical authority in 1960, the nature of the church in 1966, the nature of salvation in 1972, and the creedal basis of the Council's own being in 1978—and if the world itself hasn't blown up by that time, the Council almost certainly will."[12]

A more hopeful and balanced judgment comes from those who take their stand with the actionists in the World Council. Without examining too closely the speculative reasons of why they are divided or in self-defense trying to rationalize their disunity, the optimists prefer to work and pray "as the Holy Spirit may guide us." The defeatist attitude was excoriated by the Council's Secretary General, who knows that on this point rests the whole future of non-Catholic ecumenism. There are many, he said, who feel they have reached the limit of all that can be hoped for. The World Council would thus become a narcotic rather than a stimulant. "We must react against this temptation of accepting the present established disorder of our ecclesiastical world simply because it has been made to look less shocking as it has been provided with an ecumenical varnish." By contrast, the sanguine element in the Council of Churches looks to find "the way that leads beyond mere cooperation to a true unity which will make it clear to the whole world that as there can be only one Body of Christ, so there can be only one Body which is the Church of His people."[13] Without prejudice to their own position as members of the only true Church of Christ, Catholics may sympathize with the latter sentiments. In union with the Holy

See, they can see here "the inspiration of grace from the Holy Spirit," leading all men of good will to the unity of one Lord, one faith, and one baptism.

American Mergers and Federations

In comparison with the world ecumenical movement, American efforts to solve Protestant disunity are more practical and geared to raise external efficiency more than to find dogmatic agreement. The reason for this different approach runs deeper than appearances suggest. American practicality has something to do with the emphasis, and the absence of a doctrinal tradition like the European is also a contributing factor. But really the problem of unity in the States has a character all its own, deriving on the one hand from the sheer number and variety of sectarian bodies and, more seriously, from the diluted form of Christianity which most Protestant churches in the States have allowed themselves to adopt.

Organic mergers of two or more denominations were normally the healing of old dissensions. Divided religious groups solved their original differences and came together again. Or if they were never actually together before, they had common antecedents in stemming from a common religious family. In the last fifty years, the Lutherans figured in three reunions of smaller sects that were separated in America because of immigration and geographical distance. So also the Presbyterians were rejoined on four occasions, twice with a sect of the same denomination and twice with the Reformed Churches which trace their lineage to the same Calvinistic origin. Consequently, the historic basis of the ecumenical movement of the merger type is the consciousness of a common source. This was strikingly emphasized in *The Declaration of Union* by which three Methodist bodies reunited in 1939 to form the largest Protestant denomination in America. All three uniting components, the Declaration read, "had their common origin in the organization of the Methodist Episcopal Church in America in 1784 A.D., and have ever held, adhered to and preserved a common belief, spirit and purpose, as expressed in their common Articles of Religion."[14]

On closer analysis, the Articles of Religion are found to be nothing else than a redaction of the Anglican Thirty-nine Articles drawn up by the Methodist founder, John Wesley; which Methodist churchmen today honor by inclusion among the things to be believed, but which they officially declare not to be binding in conscience. Nevertheless, a common historical origin, here the break from Anglicanism, and at least token adherence to a common ritual and creed generally urge separated denominations to recombine their forces under the same ancestral name.

Does any doctrinal change occur when the churches unite? Do they gain or lose in dogmatic stability? Generally they lose. With ecclesiastical authority rejected on principle, mergers take place on the basis of mutual—and therefore minimal—agreement. When the merger between the Congregational and Christian Churches was first proposed in 1895, it was unsuccessful because, among other things, the Christians were suspected of denying the Trinity. One apologist for union admitted that "Their rejection of all man-made formulas and creeds has sometimes led to the idea they are Unitarians, because they will not adopt the word *Trinity* which they do not find in the Bible." It took thirty-six years before the merger was finally achieved. By that time the Congregational and Christian Churches had both become liberalized to a point where creedal differences no longer stood in the way of "fellowship," and where "theology, precisely defined, had ceased to be the primary concern of the churches and their leaders."[15] With rare exception, the more doctrinally fluid a denomination, the more likely it will fuse with other bodies; and conversely, dogmatic fixity discourages unionizing tendencies.

On the level of national federations, American Protestantism has reached a measure of success that fifty years ago would have been thought impossible. Every phase of religious activity—education, radio and television, pastoral services, social welfare, home and foreign missions, public relations, research and survey—is now thoroughly organized under the aegis of the National Council operating on a multi-million dollar budget and serving every corporate need of the member churches. Twenty-four periodicals including two weeklies and seven monthlies, and a thousand radio and TV programs every week communicate to the nation at large the principles and ideals of Protestant Christianity. There is nothing like it in American history.

But here, too, the price of external success was compromise. For years the Unitarians had asked to be admitted to the federation and were consistently refused. Their creedal position was said to be too liberal. They deny the Trinity and their concept of God is only a shade removed from pantheism. In a parody on the Apostles' Creed prepared by a high-ranking Unitarian minister, the first article reads, "I believe in a single, eternal, all-inclusive, all-pervading Life Principle whose source and perfect embodiment is God, who finds varying degrees of embodiment in all forms of life." Ostensibly then, the motive for refusing admission to the Unitarians was based on principle. But when the president of the Council was directly questioned, he conceded it was a matter of expediency. "If we let in the Unitarians, we let out the Lutherans," that is, if creedless liberals like the Unitarians were accepted, conservative groups like the Lutherans would leave. Actually no doctrinal commitment is required for membership in the National Council, and no doctrinal conformity. Along with the Baptists who reject infant baptism are Lutherans who believe the opposite, and along with Episcopalians who profess a historic episcopate are Congregationalists who deny the same. In fact, two fully accredited members are Quaker denominations whose theory of the Inner Light allows them every liberty in matters of faith: accepting or denying the divinity of Christ, believing or doubting in heaven and hell, and for all Quakers, discarding the whole sacramental system. "Throughout their history," writes their modern prophet, "they have preferred to seek for the baptism of the Spirit without the use of water, and to experience a communion of the soul with the living Christ without the use of bread and wine."[16] Yet the Society of Friends is so highly respected in the Council of Churches that its ecumenical spirit has more than once been held up as a model for others to imitate.

The worst victims of this doctrinal miscegenation are churches whose membership still retains something of traditional Christian ideals and a consequent horror of any compromise with the deposit of faith. Under title of *The Ecumenical Movement and the Episcopal Church*, the Anglo-Catholic segment of Episcopalians protested against their church's active participation in the National Council. "The deep and throughgoing contradiction and opposition between the teaching of the Protestant Churches (in the Council) and the Anglican Church" are manifest, they felt, to anyone who understands the two entities. How explain Episcopal membership in an alien body, this "mischievous intimacy in ecclesiastical activities and responsibilities"?[17] It cannot be explained except on a theory of divided allegiance within the Episcopalian body, in which liberal elements are willing to sacrifice dogmatic integrity for the sake of material efficiency.

With all its compromise and defects, however, Protestant ecumenism in America shows certain obvious merit. It has lessened the strain among the various denominations. A century ago Protestant denominations spent much of their time trying to prove one another wrong. With the start of the twentieth century a definite change took place; the denominations decided to accept rather than fight one another. Instead of opposing one another, they are now co-operating in projects and areas that were always a source of conflict. Thus one of the principal services sponsored by the National Council of Churches is "Evangelism," which promotes the spiritual interest of the member bodies. Recognizing that promotion work must be non-sectarian, the Council has steered clear of denominational polemics and concentrated on such basic items as public worship and prayer.

Beginning the first Sunday in January, the Council sponsors a Universal Week of Prayer, "to emphasize that prayer is a vital force for developing a closer relationship with God." The third Sunday of February is a Universal Day of Prayer for Students, "to unify in prayer Christian students throughout the world." The first Friday in Lent is a World Day of Prayer, and all during Lent an advertising campaign urges people to a more faithful observance of the pre-Easter season as a period of prayerful sacrifice. Every April, a National Christian College Day calls attention to the work and needs of church—affiliated colleges throughout the country. Starting the first Sunday in May is National Family Week to "provide motivation for home and church cooperation, the rededication of home and family to God." On the fifth Sunday after Easter (in the Christian calendar since 450 A.D. as a Rogation day) is Rural Life Sunday "to emphasize the meaning of Christianity for rural life and of rural life for Christianity." Labor Sunday emphasizes the religious aspects of manual and clerical work. World-Wide Communion Sunday in October promotes attendance of all Christians "at the communion table of their own church." During Advent a campaign of advertising urges "communities to put Christ into the center of Christmas, and to make the celebration of the birth of Christ more spiritual, less commercial." For ministers in the armed forces a regular retreat program has been organized to give the chaplains a Protestant equivalent of the Spiritual Exercises. A recent development is Bible study clubs.

However, it is especially in public education that the reduced tension among American Protestants shows promise of spiritual benefit to the country. As denominationalism recedes, the chances are improved for introducing at least a minimum of religious training into tax-supported institutions without the fear of arousing opposition from vested sectarian interests.

The great danger, of course, is neutralization. In melting their respective differences the churches dissolve some of their doctrinal substance. As a rule, churchmen who are most ecumenically-minded are the least conscious of dogma. They often look with complacency on the "bickerings over trifles" among the conservatives who believe that the first essential to Christian unity is doctrinal uniformity. "There was a time," they admit, "when theological differences loomed large to Americans." And they are still important to a few. "But today the average Protestant churchgoer just doesn't care about technical differences separating denominations." The result is a new American creation, the complex of "religion in general," from which Protestants have least to expect and most to lose. After generations of a virtual monopoly in forming the religious aspect of American culture and going beyond religion to inform the culture as a whole, Protestantism is being displaced by a temporalized national feeling which uses the Christian vocabulary and retains a variety of noble impulses but outside the framework of principles taught by Jesus Christ.

XII

THE MEANING OF PROTESTANTISM

PROTESTANTISM is an elusive concept of which we can find
as many definitions as writers on the subject. Even diction-
aries are not a great help. Two hundred years ago Samuel
Johnson defined a Protestant as "one of those who adhere
to them, who, at the beginning of the reformation, protested against the errors of the church of Rome." Modern
lexicons are clearer but still describe, without defining, a
Protestant as a member of one of the Christian churches
that repudiated the papal authority, and were severed from
the Roman communion at the time of the Reformation.
Hence in popular language the term is applied to any
Western Christian or member of a Christian church, outside of the Catholic faith.

Further complications arise from the reluctance of Protestants to accept the connotations of their name. It was admittedly derived from the protest of Luther's followers at
the Diet of Speyer (1529), where they refused to accept
the agreement by which Lutheran princes would allow
their states to practice the new religion while demanding
the same rights for Catholics. It is further conceded that
the subsequent extension of the term may be justified as an
official protest which became "the only thing that all the
multifarious institutions and cultural manifestations known
as Protestant have in common. This is the opposition to the
Roman Catholic Church and all Catholic thought as ex-

pressed in literature, art, science, and culture in general: an opposition in the name of individual responsibility before God."[1] But the negative implications grate. So appeals are made to etymology to prove that Reformation culture is quite positive. The Latin *protestari*, as found in Quintilian and frequently in law, means to profess, bear witness or declare openly; which makes it nearly equivalent to *profiteri*. In both cases the preposition adds the idea of openness or publicity to that of witness or declaration. Even Shakespeare is quoted to support the argument. "Do me right," says Benedick to Claudio in *Much Ado About Nothing*, "or I will protest your cowardice."

However, this sensitiveness about the name has no place in serious theological writers. Men like Calvin and Schleiermacher among the classics, or Barth and Tillich at the present day make no apology for the negative elements of their faith. They glory in them as the clearest way of describing a form of Christianity which is Christian without being Catholic. Our analysis will follow the pattern set by those who, after reflecting most deeply on their own beliefs, found certain features that may be called characteristic. Their agreement will be more universal on what should be rejected of Catholic principles, and less common on adequate substitutes. But this, too, is part of the genius of Protestantism.

Mediation of the Church

While Protestants may admit the foundation by Christ of a religious society, they deny that any church has the right to consider itself the vice-gerent of God and commissioned by Him to lead men to their destiny. In the Catholic conception they see the Church confused with the kingdom of God and her authority assimilated to that of the transcendent Deity.

Over the years the leaders of Protestant thought have resisted this claim with a passion which suggests how keenly they recognize it as the keystone of the Catholic religion. In his closing address to the World Council of Churches, Reinhold Niebuhr frankly confessed that the unity of the Catholic Church is impressive and, in some respects enviable, in comparison with Protestant divisions. But the Romanists, he explained, maintained this union at the price of a monstrous heresy. They presumed to "exalt the Church as the 'extension of the Incarnation,' as essentially divine, as the mediator of God's judgment rather than as the locus in human history where the judgments of God can be heard, whether upon the righteous or the unrighteous. This heresy was to obscure the chasm between the human and the divine, which the prophets of Israel understood so well; to pretend that there were priests who were privy to God's counsels, were in control of God's redemptive powers and purposes; and were in possession of the keys of heaven."[2] It would be hard to improve on this passage for clarity on the most radical cleavage that separates Catholic from Protestant Christianity. All other differences are subordinate or merely corollary.

Every shade of Protestantism makes the same disclaimer, although naturally for different reasons. Evangelicals refuse to believe in the Church as a representative of God because for them the Scriptures are sufficient guide on the road to salvation. Pietists of the Moravian type profess to have a constant, confidential intercourse with Christ; their mystical union with the Saviour more than supplies for dependence on ecclesiastical mandate. Quietists like the Quakers prefer direct contact with the Inner Light which, they say, frees a person from adherence to any church or obedience to any creed. Liberals find it incredible that intelligent men should submit to the Church's discipline on the grounds of her authorization from God. Religion, in their vocabulary, is a private and personal matter. There must be no ecclesiastical discipline for heresy. And any institution which seeks to fetter the human spirit by creedal conformity is, in Harnack's phrase, "enslaving souls to the despotic orders of the papal king."

Closely identified with this attitude toward the Church in general are the corresponding sentiments on the Roman primacy. Competent writers understand the crucial function of the papacy in Catholic life and worship. Some are less clear than others and the language they use will differ according to personal feeling, but without exception they place the papacy first among the objects of "Protestantism's Everlasting No" because Catholicism puts submission to the pope foremost among its requirements. "Those who submit to the pope and all his claims are Roman Catholics; those who do not are not. All other differences sink into insignificance in comparison with this. Rome recognizes no *rapprochement* until its basic dogma of papal authority is accepted, no further *rapprochement* is necessary because everything else naturally and necessarily follows."[3] While oversimplified, the fundamental accuracy of this judgment cannot be denied. Indeed obscurity on this point has led more than one well-meaning Protestant to consider his religion "almost Catholic," while leaving the primacy and papal infallibility as somewhat accidental properties.

Since the *bête noire* of Protestant theology is the Church's claim to being a divine legate, either collectively or epitomized in the papacy, it will pay to examine this difference more closely. Why, we ask, should Protestants be so offended by what Catholics take for granted? Why this scandal of Christianity, as so many have called it?

We may conveniently divide the Protestant world into two camps: those who still believe in revelation, along with certain mysteries like the Trinity and the supernatural order; and those who call themselves Christians after they have scuttled everything but a pragmatic acceptance of Christian dogma—they "believe" in the mysteries as convenient hypotheses. Both types will repudiate the Church's profession of speaking with absolute assurance of the things of God. But the reasons in each case will be different.

Those who admit that God has miraculously intervened in human history, that "at sundry times and in divers manners He spoke in times past to the fathers by the prophets, and last of all has spoken to us by His Son"—will say that men should receive this communication in the humility and obedience of faith. The only question, but a large one, is where to find the revelation, how discover its meaning and be sure that God has actually revealed what I am so willing to believe? Opinions differ widely, but substantially they agree that the Holy Spirit is the final and sufficient illuminator. "Christians are individually taught by the Spirit of God so that they are slaves to no one as they study the Scriptures. Jeremiah prophesied of the blessings of the New Covenant, indicating that in the days of the Messiah there would be no need for mutual teaching. The Apostle Paul tells us that we are now in that new era, for we are all taught of God."[4] Or more vaguely, "deep within us all there is an amazing inner sanctuary of the soul, a holy place, a Divine Center, a speaking Voice, to which we may continuously return."[5] What possible need for a cumbersome hierarchy to enlighten the mind of God?

At the other extreme are those who do not believe in

revelation, except in the earthly sense of rationalizing on the objects of nature. For liberal Protestantism, all creeds must pass the bar of reason and experience; our minds are capable of thinking God's thoughts after Him; our intuitions and reason are the best clues that we have to the nature of God and of our relations to Him. A few facts may change convictions that have become hallowed by custom and time, and the truly religious man is the one who freely yields himself to the evidence of the world about him, without constraint from any agency beyond his own will. Against this backdrop, the Catholic Church symbolizes repression of human intelligence and distrust of the sacred instrument of knowledge. "We have to reckon today," complains the liberal, "with an aggressively obscurantist, anti-intellectual temper. If it had its way it would fetter free inquiry—have you observed the reaction of the Holy office to Papini's book on the Devil?—stifle any kind of criticism, keep belief fixed and static, encourage the view that change is somehow subversive and that anyone who advocates new ideas is probably a fellow-traveler who should be watched."[6] In this theory, the Church's claim to being privy to God's counsels is twice offensive: she proclaims the existence of revealed truths that have no basis in reality, and then pretends to a monopoly on their interpretation, which only credulous dupes are willing to believe.

Following in the wake of Kantian philosophy, liberalism (in the title of Kant's book) places *Religion Within the Limits of Reason Alone* and then proceeds to define the kingdom of God with no bearing on revelation or a supernatural end. In the childhood of Christianity, belief in the Church's teaching was doubtless very useful, but as the human race develops and reaches maturity it should give up the things of a child. In the words of Immanuel Kant, "the gradual transition of ecclesiastical faith to the exclusive sovereignty of pure religious faith—founded on reason alone—is the coming of the Kingdom of God."[7] The opposition to Catholic principles could not be more complete. Behind this antinomy lies a fundamental despair of the mind's ever coming to grips with reality. Skeptical of our ability to know the inner nature of things and therefore to recognize divine intervention when it comes, the autonomous reason never leaves the cell of its own speculation, but prefers to call idolatry what, perforce, it cannot understand.

Sacraments and Saints

Along with their rejection of Catholic authority, Protestant Christians repudiate the sacramental system and the Mass and have incorporated this attitude into all their confessions of faith. While most Protestant bodies still retain the two ordinances of Baptism and the Lord's Supper, even these are not sacramental in the Catholic sense of a visible sign instituted by Christ which gives grace in virtue of the rite itself (*ex opere operato*), provided that no obstacles are placed in the way. The same with the Mass. Communion services never conceive the Eucharist as a true sacrifice, in which the body and blood of Christ are offered to the heavenly Father in propitiation for sin. Apparent exceptions, as among the Episcopalians, are Protestant heresy and actually concessions to Catholicism.

How explain this negativism? We can see how nominal Christians who call themselves Protestant but have lost their faith in the supernatural will have nothing to do with reputed channels of a grace in which they no longer believe. But why should those who profess a higher than natural destiny and the need for divine help not go along with the sacraments and the sacrifice of the Mass?

The first explanation is a logical result of denying the Church's position as earthly mediatrix with God. What the Reformers rejected was more than ecclesiastical authority in the realm of doctrine or external government. They protested against the "usurpation" by Rome of the whole gamut of instruments by which sinful mankind becomes reconciled with God. It would have been naïve for Luther and Calvin to disclaim the Church's right to dictate the means of salvation and yet accept the most important of these means from the Church's hands.

However, this is not the whole story. Other malcontents had also left Rome but without dropping the sacraments. Outstanding examples are the Dissident Orientals and the Old Catholic churches in modern times. The reason for the Protestant de-sacramentalism must be sought in a novel concept of justification that requires no assistance from visible sources but relies immediately on God. The theory that faith alone justifies, that all a man needs to be saved is an implicit trust in the divine mercy, dispenses with any mediums for sharing in the benefits of the Cross. Furthermore, Protestants who still believe in sin and justification have no idea of that habitual condition which Catholic theology describes as sanctifying grace. If the sinner who is justified remains in his sin; if the merits of Christ are only imputed to him without actually uniting him to God—then clearly any system of producing holiness is either a misnomer or a figment of Christian piety. There must first be admitted a principle of supernatural life inherent in the soul and capable of growth to speak intelligently about developing its vigor by assistance at Mass and reception of the sacraments.

Comparable to the Protestant removal of the sacramental system is the attitude toward saints and especially the Blessed Virgin Mary. Polemic writers obscure the issue when they criticize alleged abuses in praying to the images of saints "not as aids to devotion but as channels, if not actually fountains, of miraculous power." The objection runs deeper than accusing Catholics of superstition because they endow material objects like pictures and statues with magical efficacy. Catholic piety is charged with placing human instrumentalities between God and man and thereby conditioning the disposal of grace on the will of a finite creature like Mary. In fact Mariolatry, or giving divine honors to the Mother of Jesus, has come to symbolize the whole prejudice of the Reformation against Catholic veneration of the saints. Anticipating the general council, Pope John XXIII identified this bias as a major obstacle to the reunion of Protestant churches with Rome.

We may distinguish three levels of Protestant thought on Mary's place in Christianity. At the two extremes are High Church Episcopalians whose devotion to the Mother of Christ is almost or entirely Catholic, and radicals who do not rise above equating the Marian cultus with pagan mythology. "Apollo has no revelatory significance for Christians," says Paul Tillich, "the Virgin Mother Mary reveals nothing to Protestants." In between lies the majority mind of Protestantism. Briefly stated, Mary is the most honorable of women, but a sinner like the rest of mankind and, consequently, impotent before the throne of God.

Within the framework of this position, however, we must again distinguish between essentials and accidentals.

Judging by the amount of writing on the subject, we might suppose the basic problem was Mary's Immaculate Conception, her Virginity or bodily Assumption into heaven. When Pius XII announced he was going to define the latter doctrine, the Anglican bishops drafted a formal protest that "the Roman Catholic Church has chosen by this act to increase dogmatic differences in Christendom." Similar criticism was raised against the Immaculate Conception in the last century, and many Protestants are uncomfortable with the Apostles' Creed which professes faith in "Jesus Christ, who was born of the Virgin Mary."

Actually, these elements are secondary to the main difference between a Catholic and Protestant Mariology. Catholic devotion to Mary is ultimately based on the divine Maternity. "When once we have mastered the idea that Mary bore, suckled, and handled the Eternal in the form of a child, what limit is conceivable to the rush and flood of thoughts which such a doctrine involves? What awe and surprise must attend upon the knowledge that a creature has been brought so close to the Divine Essence."[8] Accordingly a great deal of scandal over Marian piety derives from obscurity about the person of Christ. A century ago, Newman pointed out that if we look through Europe, we shall find, on the whole, that just those nations have lost their faith in the divinity of Christ, who have given up devotion to His Mother. And more recently a spokesman for the World Council of Churches declared it was "no accident that absence of devotion to Mary commonly goes with lukewarmness of devotion to her Son. For I suspect that some of the objections to the words 'Mother of God' spring unconsciously from a lack of deep conviction about the Deity of Christ."[9] In proportion as faith weakens in the Incarnation and Christ is conceived as only human or symbolically divine, the acceptance of Mary's dominant role in Christian worship becomes difficult and finally impossible.

Still the problem remains, because not a few Protestants, who profess the divinity of Christ without qualification, are opposed to giving Mary any value in the economy of salvation. They are willing to call her the Mother of God and the first Christian; to be loved and so to lead us to the love of Christ; to be imitated and so to lead to the imitation of Christ; to be called happy and blessed among women, and so to lead us to the praise of God. But that is all. She may not be invoked as intercessor with God, or honored as our mediatrix with Christ.

Mary's mediation is, therefore, the crucial issue on which Catholic and even the most biblical Protestant theology divide. The reason lies hidden in the Protestant concept, or better, denial of merit. Since the fall of Adam, all men are conceived and born in sin, and enemies with God. Later justification covers over the depravity of human nature like a cloak, without removing the sin. The ravages are so deep that freedom, in Luther's phrase, was completely destroyed, and we have nothing left but the name. Without liberty of choice, merit is impossible; and without merit, we cannot speak of saint or degrees of sanctity or, what depends on holiness, intercessory power with God. We are all equally powerless, during life to do anything meritorious for heaven and after death to intercede for those who are still living on earth.

In this scheme, the only purpose of having saints would be as models to encourage us with resignation to an immutable fate. There is no question of imitating their virtues, and surely not of asking for their aid. The hierarchy of God's friends whose good works made them, in varying degrees, prayerful mediators in heaven, disappears after we cut everyone down to sinful uniformity. Nothing we do has any merit in the eyes of God, and even the Mother of Christ was no exception. She can do no more for us than the least of those who are saved; she was just as much a sinner as they, and is now just as helpless in obtaining the graces that we need.

Both factors are integral to Protestant theory: that no human agency, whether mortal or in glory, can mediate between God and man; and even though (contrary to fact) mediation were possible, no person has more influence with God because of greater merit, since merit vanished with the loss of freedom. Saints become historical memories of absolute predestination, and the Blessed Virgin only the object of the greatest mercy.

Subjective Christianity

If we would define Protestantism by a short formula, we might call it subjective Christianity, whose positive contents are derived from Catholicism and whose radical error is a denial that faith belongs essentially to the intellect.

All that we know of Protestant culture points to its heavy emphasis on the subjective side of the Christian religion. Different churches had different orientations, but the general trend was the same. The "out-going" Catholic ritual centered in the Mass and directed to God was replaced by the "in-taking" sermon for the people; external forms of worship were removed in favor of internal meditation; interest in promoting the apostolate became an exclusive concern for one's own destiny; doing good for others under the counsels turned into preoccupation with sin and the assurance that a believer was one of the saved. Where Catholicism made obedience to ecclesiastical authority one of the marks of a Christian, the Reformers assured their disciples that no society, however ancient and professedly divine, has a right to stand between the soul and her Creator. Where Catholic theology insisted on good works, and the practice of virtue and mortification, Protestants were told to rely entirely on faith; and where the Church required the sacraments as a condition for grace, the Reformation dispensed with these ordinances, even with Baptism, as a means of salvation.

But if Protestantism were sustained by subjectivism or negative elements only, it would have passed out of history long ago. It has positive and objective features, too, which are not properly its own but borrowed or derived from the Catholic religion. Mysteries of faith like the Incarnation and the Redemption, principles of Christian morality and methods of church government, ritual customs, forms of worship and even a Catholic vocabulary have entered the stream of Protestantism to give whatever vitality the inheritors of the Reformation still possess after four centuries of separation from their common source.

The dependence on the Catholic Church is too widespread and universal to be fully analyzed. It is more than historical, and envelops the sectarian bodies like an atmosphere. When someone described Protestantism as "a kind of parasite living upon the Church, one that would die should the Church die, one also that draws all its nutriment from the Church," he was crude. But the principle he expressed is true.

First in the order of influence was the origin of the Reformation. Its leaders had been practicing Catholics: Luther, Zwingli, and Knox were priests; Cranmer a bishop; Calvin a student for the ministry. After breaking with Rome they kept so much of their former religion that the two major schisms in Protestant history, the Anabaptists on the continent and the Non-Conformists in England, were re-action movements to excessive Romanism. To this day the confessions of faith of all the major denominations are Catholic derivatives. Cranmer's *Homilies* and Calvin's *Institutes* are filled with Reformation fancies, but not to the exclusion of such thoroughly Catholic doctrines as the Trinity, the necessity of grace and the eternity of hell. It may seem incongruous that the same manual should tell seminarians that "the marks of Antichrist plainly agree with the kingdom of the Pope," and expatiate on the two natures in Christ, the Virgin Birth and the resurrection of the body in the very words of the general councils summoned by the popes. But it shows how deeply imbedded Catholic doctrine can remain in a Protestant body alongside the most violent anti-catholicism.

More pervasive is the impact which Catholic teaching and customs are making on Protestant thought by way of example and emulation. For more than four centuries, the Church has co-existed with Protestant sects in every country, often in the same city or town, and even the same street. Catholics associate with Protestants in all the professions and every walk of life. Individually the influence has been mutual, with each side affecting the other; but institutionally all the evidence points to the Catholic Church remaining substantially unchanged by her contact with Protestantism, while the latter is daily and profoundly affected by its co-existence with the Church.

The most impressive sign of this at the present time is the ecumenical movement, with its drive towards Christian unity, realized in the Church of Rome and envied by those outside of her fold. But not only the Church's unity; the whole panorama of ritual and doctrine fascinates the Protestant world and helps to condition its mind. A passage from Karl Barth may illustrate this subtle influence. He is speaking of the slight effect produced by evangelical pastors when preaching the Gospel message.[10]

At those times when the task of being ministers of the divine word has oppressed us, have we not all felt a yearning for the attractive worship of Catholicism, and for the enviable role of the priest at the altar? When he elevates the Sacrament, the double grace of His sacrificial death and the Incarnation of the Son of God is not only preached in words but consummated under his hands. He becomes a maker of his Creator before the people. I once heard it announced literally at a first Mass, "The priest is another Jesus Christ." If only we could be the same. How completely the poorest of sermonettes is transfigured by the saving radiance of the Eucharistic miracle. How well-ordered and possible is the way of God to man and of man to God which leads from this center, a way which the Catholic priest may walk daily himself and indicate to others.

Reflecting that Barth is the most prominent figure in Protestant theology and these sentiments are not an isolated sample, we have some idea of what the Vatican Council meant when it described the Church as a standard lifted up for the nations and calling to herself those who are not of the faith.

The negative phase of Protestantism and its radical error are the claim that we do not believe with the mind. It might seem that Protestants who still profess Christian doctrine are united with Catholics on the character of faith. Both subscribe to the articles of the Creed, from believing in "God the Father Almighty" to "life everlasting." In reality the difference is extreme. Catholics hold that faith is an assent of the intellect to accept on divine authority whatever truths God has revealed. Protestants, unless they surrender their own principles, claim that faith is primarily an act of the will—as trust, or love, or abandonment—without prior dependence on the mind. Their opinions on the nature of faith are fluid, and theories range over the whole field of psychology. For Tillich faith is an experience in which "we are grasped by the unapproachably holy which is the ground of our being"; for Marcus Bach "we believe because we want to believe"; for Pike and Pittenger "faith is the response of a person to a Person. When a man says he believes in his wife, he does not mean that he believes that she exists or that he has a wife. He means rather that he trusts her and that he has given himself to her for life."[11] The same must be said for God. When professing to believe in Him, we do not affirm His existence but only declare our trust.

The consequences of this notion are far-reaching. If faith is not necessarily submission of mind to objective truth, what difference does it make whether I believe that God has three Persons or One, whether He became incarnate in Christ or not, whether His presence in the Eucharist is real or merely symbolic? It makes no difference. I am just as good a Christian and equally on the road to salvation whether I profess, with Luther, that "after Adam's sin man's free will was wholly destroyed," or say, with the Council of Trent which condemned Luther, that if anyone holds this doctrine "let him be anathema."

In the final analysis the very possibility of affirming that certain propositions are true and necessary for salvation rests on the prior conviction that faith is something intellectual which can be formulated in statements and definitions, to which the mind can freely assent if it wants to. Deny this principle; call faith by whatever name you wish, but say it is not creedal or intellectual, and you reduce the

Christian religion to what some investigators are agreed is the essence of Protestant thought: a feeling of dependence on a superior being, whose very existence may be called into doubt. "The proposal," writes a sympathetic observer, "that religion may be sufficiently founded on feeling comes with too great promise of relief to be lightly dismissed. Grant it, and all dogmatic authority loses its pressure at once. We are set free to be religious beings without the infinite argument and haggling over unreachable and untestable propositions. Creeds we wave aside, or else, we carry them lightly, knowing that they are at one stroke disarmed, put out of conflict with truth as otherwise established."[12] The libertarian comfort which this brings to the natural man may explain, in part, the success which the Reformation had in winning so many people to its cause, and still has in retaining the fidelity of millions who would be offended if told their religion is only a shadow of the Catholic substance they have lost. Tasting the perfectly human pleasure of believing what they please, they have no idea of that deeper satisfaction which St. Paul promised to those who bring their mind into subjection to the obedience of Christ, who profess that faith is not feeling or pious sentiment but the acceptance, on the word of God, of things that are not seen.

If we may trust the experience of mature converts, priority of feeling is the heart of the Protestant way of life. For Catholics it is almost a matter of indifference whether the soul realizes, in such a way as to visualize, the facts of revelation and the principles of the spiritual world; the point is that the will should adhere, and command the intellect to assent. But for Protestants, whose theology is fundamentally arbitrary, and among whom authority is really non-existent, it becomes natural to place the center of gravity rather in the emotions, and to mistake, as one of them put it, the imagination for the soul. The reason for them must be continually suppressed even in its own legitimate sphere; the will must be largely self-centered. And they have left only the experience of feeling as the realm in which their religion operates.

Permanent Tension

Catholics are generally baffled by one feature of Protestantism that is more easily described than defined: the evident tension that runs through the whole of Protestant culture, horizontally between successive stages in the churches' history, and vertically in every phase of their doctrine and ritual practice. It is more than a conflict between conservative and liberal elements that we find in any institution, whether secular or religious. It is certainly deeper than the familiar difference between caution and the spirit of progress, which is healthy and normal wherever men of different temperaments join together for a common end. The tension is nothing less than opposition between a "Catholic" and "Protestant" attitude in the denominations, and within the churches in their leaders and affiliated members.

We defined Protestantism as a form of Christianity whose positive contents are derived from Catholicism, and whose basic error denies that faith is an assent of the mind to revelation. This is more than a statement of fact. It describes the final earmark of the Protestant religion: an interior conflict between fidelity to Christian tradition and autonomous self-sufficiency, whose consequences and attempted solution are a matter of common experience.

Radical Instability. The first result of this inner conflict is a desire for change. We might expect to find alterations in a religious system whose founders had themselves made the revolutionary change of leaving the Catholic faith and spent the rest of their lives in opposition to their former allegiance. We have seen something of the vagaries in Protestant churches since the Reformation. Compare the unqualified supernaturalism in Luther's *Catechism* or the *Journal* of John Wesley with the compromising doctrine of their respective churches and we get some idea of the essential fluidity of Protestant theology.

This tendency is more widespread than most people think. Religious leaders are especially susceptible. Some time ago forty ranking theologians in American (and world) Protestantism were asked to reply to the question, "How my mind has changed in the last decade." Men of the stature of Wieman and Reinhold Niebuhr, Bennett and Stanley Jones, Barth, Horton and MacKay wrote their answers in detail and with disarming sincerity, revealing to the lay readers the struggles and conflict they had undergone in searching for the truth. Under title of "Ten Years That Shook My World," Niebuhr confessed that about midway in his ministry he underwent a complete conversion of thought which involved rejection of almost all the liberal ideas with which he began his career. He wrote his first book in 1927, which when now consulted proves to contain "almost all the theological windmills against which today I tilt my sword." Every successive volume expressed a more explicit revolt against what is usually known as liberal culture.

Others changed in the same direction, from liberalism to what Wieman called "some of the realities of the Christian outlook which have now become clearer." Among the converts to "neo-orthodoxy," the most prominent was Karl Barth. He began his career as a liberal who saw the future hope of Christianity in the building of a socialist society. The First World War came as a shock to his optimism. He saw the present day as a time of crisis, when judgment has been visited on the western world which ignores the distance between God and man. Its only chance of salvation, both here and hereafter, lies in awaiting the coming of Jesus Christ, risen from the dead, who will reconcile us with the Father and bring us to a happy eternity.

However, not all the changes are away from liberalism. Some are quite the opposite. And although a certain leaning to orthodoxy is apparent in many churchmen, the over-all picture shows a dogmatic decadence and gradual dilution of the Christian faith. Present estimates place the number of unchurched Americans at about seventy million, or forty per cent of the total population. These people are not even claimed as church members by any denomination. They may still retain some faith in God and even call themselves believers. But by and large, judging by their spokesmen, they have lost their belief in supernatural reality. As a matter of record, most of them came from the ranks of Protestantism, and the rest from other bodies (like the Catholic) mostly through the influence, direct or otherwise, of free-lancing descendants of the Reformations. Consequently, it is only half correct to speak of Protestantism in terms of the existing denominational structure, as found in the various churches. It must be charged with major responsibility for alienating millions of persons from traditional Christianity, beginning with deistic philosophy in England, passing through naturalism in Germany and now become the heritage, some would say, of two out of every five Americans.

If there is any question about this indictment, we have only to see what goes on inside the liberalizing churches. The rise of naturalism is creating a rift between the ordinary churchgoer and the ministry that reflecting Protestants freely admit. In Protestant Christendom today, writes an American Quaker, the beliefs and religious expectations of those learned in theology are often not only different from and more complex than those of the average man in the pew, but they contradict them. Agreement still exists, but it is no longer over beliefs. It is over passwords, passwords which the hearer may take in any sense he pleases, depending on his theological sophistication.

This type of nominalism may run deeper than differences over points of faith, or even such fundamental issues as the Incarnation and the life of grace. It may concern the very existence of God and His attributes, and our responsibilities, or lack of them, to a personal Deity. Atheism, we are told, was formerly left to those outside the church. Today the disagreement within the churches is over whether the traditional God exists and whether there is an after-life.

More often than Catholics (or many Protestants) suspect, the church services which result are a strange pantomime. "Kneeling before the same altar in the same service, saying the same creeds and singing the same hymns, one man worships the God who acts literally, another worships the God who acts metaphorically, a third worships the God who acts symbolically, and yet another worships the God who doesn't act at all."[13] The agents behind this tragedy are theologians sitting in high places in schools of divinity; men who toy with the most sacred concepts of revelation and conscience like children playing a game.

The essential unrest at the root of Protestantism also works in favor of conversions to the Catholic faith. "I have always been latently and potentially a Catholic," wrote

Sheila Kaye-Smith. "There has been no swing around from a contradictory set of ideas. I joined the Church of Rome only because I found that it was impossible to be a Catholic in the church of my baptism." Some, like Newman, asked themselves if remaining Protestants they could save their souls. Others were repulsed by the specter of infidelity from which Protestantism offered them no protection. "It was not liking for Catholicism" with Arnold Lunn, "but disliking for secularism which first set my feet on the Romeward road. For many of us have been driven back on the truth in our attempt to put as much ground as possible between ourselves and the modern prophets." The Church, we are told, is a house with a hundred gates, and no two men enter at exactly the same angle. Yet the converts are surprisingly unanimous in desiring to be freed from their Protestant uncertainties and, once converted, are almost rhapsodic about the security and peace of soul they enjoy. "There is no happiness in the world comparable to that of the experience known as conversion," according to Robert Hugh Benson. His sentiments have been shared by thousands.

This latent instinct needs to be better known, to recognize that within the body of Protestant faith and worship are elements that are not Protestant at all but Catholic; that Protestants cherish these elements, wish to preserve and protect them, and want nothing more than to increase their possession of what, objectively, is a part of their Catholic ancestry.

Correlative with a desire for change is the current stress on solidarity among the churches that we saw in the ecumenical movement. Although the motivation is very complex, somewhere near the center lies the perfectly human (and we believe divinely encouraged) wish to be united with fellow Christians, at least externally, in religious organizations on every level from the World Council of Churches down to the parish society. Among their own critics, some have called it only a camouflage to hide the interior disunity that cannot be healed but only covered over and disguised. This is unfair and less than true. What moves the Protestants to unite is partly emulation of Catholicism and partly the unwitting instinct to regain what they had lost by their separation from Rome.

Social Activism. Most typically in America, the conflict over theological principles is being resolved by devotion to social activism that goes back to the days of John Wesley and William Booth. "What a cruel satire," wrote Booth, "that a population sodden with drink, eaten up by every social and physical malady, should attract so little concern on the part of churchmen. Why all this apparatus of temples and meeting houses to save men from perdition in a world which is to come, while never a helping hand stretched out to save them from the inferno of their present life?"

We can distinguish two phases in this practical substitution of social for religious activity. Until recent times the preaching of the Social Gospel was the Protestant response to the impact of the industrial revolution with its large scale production, concentration of economic power and resultant evils affecting family life, especially in the big cities. America's outstanding prophet of the Social Gospel was Walter Rauschenbusch, professor of Church History in Rochester divinity school, who served for eleven years in the early 1900's as pastor of a Baptist church on New York City's west side. Sharply critical of Catholicism as antidemocratic, he found special fault with its practice of celibacy. God alone knows, he suggested, where the race might be today if the natural leaders had not so long been made childless by their own goodness. "The wonderful fecundity of the Protestant parsonage in men of the highest ability and ideality is proof of what has been lost." Except for this bias, the message was appealingly simple. All the talent of the ministry and machinery of church government should be used to improve the social conditions of the people, if need be at the cost of heroic sacrifice. Just as "the first apostolate of Christianity was born from a deep fellow-feeling for social misery and from the consciousness of a great historical opportunity" which produced saints and heroes, so "the championship of social justice is almost the only way left open to a Christian nowadays to gain the crown of martyrdom. Theological heretics are rarely persecuted now"—at least not among the Protestant clergy.[14] Rauschenbusch is still venerated as one of the pioneers of the labor union.

After World War I the optimism of the earlier period began to fade, first in Europe and then in America. Hope in the Kingdom of God on earth as a result of human activity lessened; the idealistic basis of the crusade was challenged on political and economic grounds. Witness the demise of the prohibition experiment, born of Methodist unrealism. By the time of World War II the movement as a creative force was diverted into other channels.

But if social gospeling is practically moribund, activism still remains the most prominent feature of modern Protestantism. Preoccupation with external activities is not limited to the United States, and involves something more than providing recreational facilities through the Young Men's Christian Associations.

The emphasis on social betterment is neither passing nor merely expedient, as may be seen from the constitution of the World Council of Churches. Although the work of the Council is divided into six sections, each dealing with a major area of the churches' labors, only two of the sections are professedly religious, those dealing with Faith and Order, and with Evangelism. The rest are exclusively or primarily concerned with social questions, international affairs and ethnic or racial problems. In practice, however, even this nominal third of the Council's religious interest is reduced to a fraction.

Though extreme and coined more than twenty years ago, there is a popular definition of a Christian still in vogue that underlies the spirit of much of Protestant thought. "Who is a Christian," they ask. "It is one whose life is built on love, who holds his brother as his other self; who toils for justice, equity and peace, and hides no aim or purpose in his heart that will not chord with universal good. Though he be pagan, heretic, or Jew that man is Christian and beloved of Christ." Even as a piece of rhetoric, it calls for severe distinctions; as a philosophy of life it denies the Christian name.

Self-Improvement. Parallel with social activism as an escape from solving the conflict in Protestant theology is another, less noble phenomenon. A penchant for self-improvement, in body, mind and emotions, has become the religious absorption of millions who call themselves Christians. Norman Vincent Peale's book on *The Power of Positive Thinking* was written, he said, to prove that "you do not need to be defeated in anything, that you can have peace of mind, improved health, and a never-ceasing flow of energy"—all by the simple device of calling upon the Higher Power that is ever ready to help you. "It is there for anybody under any circumstances or in any condition. This tremendous inflow of power is of such force that in its inrush it drives everything before it, casting out fear, hate,

[271]

sickness, weakness, moral defeat, scattering them as though they had never touched you, refreshing and restrengthening your life with health, happiness, and goodness."[15] An attractive offer, if there was one, getting so much for so little. Yet Peale is only the best known of a long line of cultists, many of whom have organized their methods into a system and built whole churches around the idea.

Almost a century ago, in 1866, Mary Baker Eddy discovered the Christ Science or divine laws of Life, Truth and Love, and named her discovery Christian Science. God, she professed, had been graciously preparing her for many years to receive this final revelation of the absolute divine Principle or scientific mental healing. She called her discovery Christian because Christ first "demonstrated the power of Christian Science to heal mortal minds and bodies." It was a discovery because "this power was lost sight of, and must again be spiritually discerned, thought and demonstrated according to Christ's command, with 'signs following.' "[16] It is a Science in opposition to mere belief, which in Mrs. Eddy's vocabulary means understanding, as against belief or mere ignorance. The object of belief is the visible world, the object of science is Spirit or God, who alone has real existence, animating the world of apparent reality as the Soul of the Universe. As a practical science, however, its purpose is not prayer or the worship of God but the shedding of sickness, pain and death by driving out the devil of belief in their existence. Another name for this exorcism is Christian Science healing.

Mrs. Eddy came from a family of Trinitarian Congregationalists, was formally confirmed in that church and never ceased to call herself both Christian and Protestant. Her followers regard themselves as inheritors of the Reformation, whose title to singularity is their insight into the healing narratives of the Gospel, that the power which Christ possessed for healing diseases by an act of the will may be had by anyone who sincerely believes in Him.

About the same time as Mrs. Eddy began her system of faith healing, the New Thought movement had its beginning in New England under the leadership of influential thinkers, notably Ralph Waldo Emerson, who rebelled against the current Calvinism of their day. Fifteen to twenty million Americans are now under the influence of New Thought, which "together with Christian Science," said William James, "constitutes a spiritual movement as significant for our day as the Reformation for its time."

As with Eddyism, the theory is uncomplicated. Reacting against Calvinist depravity, New Thought has the highest respect for the human mind, so high, in fact, that it credits our mental faculties with powers that approach the divine. "We affirm the new thought of God," runs the creed, "as Universal Love, Life, Truth and Joy, in whom we live, move, and have our being; that His mind is our mind now, that realizing our oneness with Him means love, truth, peace, health and plenty. We affirm the teaching of Christ that the Kingdom of Heaven is within us, that we are one with the Father."[17] Like Peale and Mrs. Eddy, the same confidence of a divine supply that has only to be tapped to receive all the blessings of health of body and peace of mind.

Some historians are slow to classify movements like Christian Science and New Thought as Protestant. They mistakenly identify the term only with "respectable" bodies that still have some semblance of traditional (which means Catholic) Christianity when actually the discredited groups may approach more closely to genuine Protestantism, on its negative side, of a purely subjective religion that makes no compromise with Catholic objectivity.

Direct Revelation. Protestantism as a religious system is torn between accepting Christian tradition in the spirit of the Catholic faith and rejecting this tradition as a tyranny of the mind. The easiest way of settling the conflict, we have seen, is by an appeal to divine authority, outside the Church and beyond the Scriptures, directly communicating with the human soul. Luther and Calvin made this appeal when they excluded certain books from the Bible, discarded the Mass and the sacraments, and disclaimed obedience to the Roman Pontiff. In a celebrated debate between Luther and Cochlaeus, the latter asked him point-blank by what right he opposed the decrees of the ancient Councils. "Have you," he asked Luther, "received a revelation?" Luther hesitated a moment and then said, "Yes, it has been revealed to me." When Cochlaeus reminded him that before this he had protested against such a claim, Luther replied. "I did not deny it." His opponent rejoined. "But who will believe you had a revelation? What miracles have you worked in proof of it? By what sign will you confirm it? Would it not be possible for anyone to defend his errors in this way?"[18] We have no record of Luther's answer, except that whenever hard-pressed to prove his denial of some point of Catholic dogma, he said, simply, it was commanded him from above.

This aspect of Protestant inwardness is of cardinal importance. It first explains the incredible self-reliance in the founder of the Reformation which Harnack said "fills us with anxiety"; absolute assurance that withstood all opposition, based on the conviction of having received a heavenly mandate. But more relevant to our purpose, Luther's example has been followed by his heirs to a degree that Catholics may not realize. Many churches and movements which seem to be outside Reformation genealogy are authentically Protestant when they advance divine communications in support of their sectarian bias.

When George Fox organized the Quakers in the mid-seventeenth century, it was an act of rejecting Anglicanism in favor of what he called the Inner Light. All men, according to Fox, are naturally endowed with a divine Light which they have only to recognize and follow to be saved. Profession of faith in Christ is needless for the Quakers, unless a man believes in this Light; and given such faith, it matters little what else he believes. The first function of this Light is to emancipate a person from adherence to any creed or submission to ecclesiastical authority. Hence the strange compliment that "Quakerism, whose genuine Christianity few will doubt, has best caught the genius of a particularity that is also universal, by exploring and finding common ground with mystical tendencies in Japan and of Hinduism in India."[19]

At different levels of the social scale are such groups as the Pentecostals, who believe that every convert receives an outpouring of divine grace in visible form; the Adventists, whose prophetess, Mrs. Helen White, had a series of revelations that fill twenty volumes in a modern edition; the Mormons, whose founder, Joseph Smith, was told by heavenly messenger to advocate plural marriage as a divine command; the Spiritualists, whose faith is a tissue of comuniqués from the other world and yet sufficiently Christian (and Protestant) to believe that Christ was a medium, that the Annunciation was a message from the dead, and the Resurrection a proof that all men live on after death as disembodied souls. If we are tempted to dismiss fringe sects like Pentecostal-Adventists and Spiritualists as insignificant, a sobering reminder is the converts they are making in Latin America, where most of the defections from the Catholic faith are to this brand of Protestant extremism.

Also in Europe and the United States, Protestant-sponsored Moral Rearmament had gained so many sympathizers among the Catholic laity that formal directives were necessary to expose its dangerous character. The bishops of England, Belgium and Wales, and most recently, Bishop Noa of Marquette, condemned MRA as a heresy whose motto, "When man listens, God speaks," is only a catchy restatement of Quaker illuminism that wants no human interpreter of the Holy Spirit.

Charity and Truth

In the four centuries since the Reformation, Catholics have often reflected on the mystery of God's providence in allowing so many persons to be separated, first from Roman unity, and finally (for many of them) even from the Christian faith. If nothing happens by chance with God, there must have been reasons to correspond in gravity with the event and explain, as far as we humanly can, why the tragedy was permitted to occur.

One reason was anticipated long before, by St. Augustine, when he observed that the Catholic Church has been vindicated by heresy, and those who think rightly have been proved by those who think wrongly. "Many things lay hid in the Scriptures, until the heretics had been cut off and began to trouble the Church of God with questions; those things were then opened up which lay hid and the will of God was understood. Was the Trinity fully treated before the Arians opposed it? Was penance properly de-

scribed before the Novations raised their attack? So too
baptism was not perfectly explained before the re-baptizers,
who were cast out of the fold, contradicted the teaching."[20]
Even a passing acquaintance with the Council of Trent
shows that no heretical movement in the Church's history
prompted more study of the deposit of faith and more
clarification of Christian doctrine than the Protestant
Reformation. For twenty years, from 1545 to 1565, the
combined intelligence of Roman Catholicism concentrated
its efforts on so defining the nature of grace and justification, the Sacrifice of the Mass and the priesthood, the sacramental system and ecclesiastical authority, that insights
were gained into these mysteries which the faithful had not
seen since the beginning of Christianity.

The full proceedings of Trent amount to thirty volumes
of modern size, and cover every phase of doctrine and religious discipline that was questioned or denied by the Reformers. When the Council finally adjourned and published
a confession of faith, it was with a note of finality that only
an infallible Church would have dared. "I promise, vow
and swear that, with God's help, I shall most constantly
hold and profess this true Catholic faith, outside of which
no one can be saved and which I now freely profess and
truly hold. With the help of God, I shall profess it whole
and unblemished to my dying breath." The clarity of doctrine which made this Credo possible was occasioned by
contemporary opposition.

This remains true to the present day. In their contact
with Protestants, Catholics are forced to re-examine their
position, prove their faith against the indifference or criticism they meet and, with divine assistance, acquire a
sharpness and penetration for which there is no counterpart.

However, along with these obvious benefits is a corresponding risk, which may further explain the providence of the Reformation Constant intimacy with those of another religious persuasion creates hazards of which the Church is painfully aware. If ever a Catholic feels that he cannot lose his faith or have it suffer harm, he has only to consider the mass defection of the sixteenth century or the tragic losses in our own day to be undeceived. Protestants exaggerate the number of "conversions" from Catholicism, which at most are only a fraction of those who enter the Church from the Protestant ranks. Still the National Council felt justified in publishing a sizeable brochure, *When You Come Over,* "to put into the hand of people who were coming into the Protestant churches from the Roman Catholic Church." The motives offered to make the change, or strengthen one already made, are enlightening on the advantages of being a Protestant. "You will hear more preaching in your new church than you did in your old . . . You will be received as full grown men and your counsel will be sought. You are coming to a layman's church. You will help to make many of the vital decisions that lie ahead of us . . . You can pray anywhere, any time, and in any words that come to mind." Add to this the prospect of a "democratic way" of life, of "religious freedom and an open Bible," and deliverance from the usurped authority which seeks to "dictate the form of religious institutions." All are attractive offers and all perfectly logical once you admit that "Our Saviour left us no absolute pattern for His Church. How wise He was! Uniformity is a deadly thing."[21] Only a strong faith can resist this allurement without dilution. Not being confirmed in grace a Catholic will take measures accordingly.

One final, and the best, reason why the Reformation

and its consequences were permitted by God: to give those who possess the true faith an ocean of opportunities for practicing the highest charity. Conscious of the blessings they enjoy in the fullness of revelation and grateful for the claims they have on God's mercy, Catholics are inspired to share these blessings with those who lost (or had lost for them) that which is better than riches and more precious even than life. It is a platitude of history that much of the zeal of the past four hundred years has been heightened by the fact that evangelization now includes not only the pagans and those who never received the Gospel but millions of others who call themselves Christians but do not belong to the Mystical Body of Christ.

All that we know by faith and reason tells us that God permits evils only because He foresees the good that results by His permissive will. If the love of neighbor is a divine command and the greatest love is to share one's greatest possession, then for Catholics to meet the spiritual needs of the Protestant world is indeed most pleasing to God.

NOTES

Chapter One

[1] Luther, *Werke* (Weimar edition), vol. II, p. 325.

[2] Luther's *New Testament* (1525), Preface to the Epistles of James and Jude.

[3] John Calvin, *Institutes of the Christian Religion*, Bk. I, chap. 7, num. 1–4.

[4] St. Augustine, "Contra Epistulam Manichaei," *Patrol. Lat*, 42, 176.

[5] Calvin, *op. cit.*, num. 5

[6] Edgar J Goodspeed, *The Story of the Apocrypha*, Chicago, Univ. of Chicago Press, 1952, p. 11. Copyright 1952 by the University of Chicago.

[7] Francis Pieper, *Christian Dogmatics*, St. Louis, Concordia, 1950, vol. I, p 216.

[8] Billy Graham, *Peace with God*, Garden City, Doubleday, 1953, p. 24.

[9] Albert C Knudson, "Radical Principles of Protestantism," *Protestantism A Symposium*, Nashville, Parthenon, 1945, p. 132.

[10] Paul Tillich, *The Protestant Era*, Chicago, Univ of Chicago Press, 1951, p 11 Copyright 1951 by the University of Chicago.

[11] John C Wenger, *Introduction to Theology*, Scottdale, Herald Press, 1954, p 173.

[12] Pieper, *op. cit.*, pp. 359–360.

[13] W. A. Criswell, "Whose Book Is It?" *Ashland Baptist*, March 18, 1955.

[14] Article VI.

[15] James A. Pike and W. Norman Pittenger, *The Faith of the Church* (Department of Christian Education), Greenwich, Seabury Press, 1952, pp. 19–20.

[16] James H. Nichols, *Primer for Protestants*, New York, Association Press, 1951, pp. 130–131.

[17] Oscar Cullmann, *Peter: Disciple, Apostle, Martyr*, Philadelphia, Westminster Press, 1953, pp. 211–212, and *Catholiques et Protestants*, Neuchâtel, Delachaux et Niestle, 1958, p. 10.

Chapter Two

[1] Luther, *Works*, St. Louis, vol X, p. 1590.

[2] *Ibid*, vol. V, p. 1037

[3] Calvin, *Institutes of the Christian Religion*, Bk. IV, chap. 19.

[4] C. D. Henderson, *Presbyterianism*, Aberdeen, The University Press, 1955, p. 34.

[5] William W Sweet, *Methodism in American History*, New York, Nashville, Abingdon-Cokesbury, 1953, p. 107.

[6] *Ibid*, p. 105.

[7] I Timothy 4.14.

[8] Oscar T. Olson, "Worship and the Sacraments," *Protestantism: A Symposium*, Nashville, Parthenon, 1945, p. 168.

[9] *Ibid*, p 167.

[10] Francis J. McConnell, "Ethics," *ibid*, pp. 196–197.

[11] Patrick J. Dignan, *History of the Legal Incorporation of Catholic Church Property*, New York, 1935, p. 75

[12] *The Constitution of the Presbyterian Church, U. S. A.*, Philadelphia, 1955, p. 243.

[13] C. D. Henderson, *op cit.*, p. 170.

[14] *The Living Church*, April 7, 1957.

[15] *Anglican Orders*, London, Society for Promoting Christian Knowledge, 1948, p. 14.

[16] John Henry Newman, *Apologia Pro Vita Sua*, Chicago, Loyola University Press, 1930, p. 171.

Chapter Three

[1] Alberto Rembao, "The Reformation Comes to Hispanic America," *Religion in Life*, Winter 1957–58

[2] *International Missionary Council*, New York, pp. 1–2.

[3] *What Is a Faith Mission?*, International Foreign Mission Association, New York, pp 5–8.

[4] Clarence P. Shedd, *History of the World's Alliance of Young Men's Christian Associations*, London, S.P.C.K., 1955, pp. 245–246.

[5] *Journal of the Christian Medical Association of India, Pakistan, Burma and Ceylon*, Sept. 1952, p. 271.

[6] Alberto Rembao, *op. cit*, p. 9.

[7] Prudencio Damboriena, *Cuadernos Hispanoamericanos*, Madrid, Aug 1956.

[8] "Evangelism Around the World," *Faith and Order Commission Papers*, num 18, New York, 1954, p 37.

[9] Published under the auspices of the Interdenominational Foreign Mission Association of North America.

[10] Pius XII, Letter to the Latin American Hierarchy, July 25, 1955, *Catholic Mind*, Nov 1955, p. 689.

[11] Archbishop Michael, "The Tensions of the World and Our Unity in Christ," Evanston, 1954, pp. 3–5.

Chapter Four

[1] Stanley I. Stuber, *Primer of Roman Catholicism for Protestants*, New York, Association Press, 1953, p. 140.

[2] John Calvin, *Institutes of the Christian Religion*, Book IV, chap. 19, num. 34.

[3] St. Augustine, "De Bono Conjugali," *Patr Lat.*, 40, 394.

[4] "De Fide et Operibus," 40, 203.

[5] Winfred E Garrison, *A Protestant Manifesto*, New York, Abingdon-Cokesbury, 1952, p. 145.

[6] Articles 16 and 25, respectively, of the Methodist and Episcopalian *Articles of Religion* The same idea is expressed in different words by all the standard confessions of faith.

7 *Christian Marriage*, Chicago, National Council of Churches, 1952, pp. 9–10. Copyright 1952 by the National Council of Churches.

8 Calvin, *op. cit.*, num. 37.

9 Luther, *Table Talk*, London, 1883, num. 748.

10 James P. Lictenberger, *Divorce, A Social Interpretation*, New York, McGraw-Hill, 1931, p. 96. Copyright 1931 by McGraw-Hill Book Company, Inc.

11 Anson P. Stokes, *Church and State in the United States*, New York, Harper, 1950, vol. III, p. 49.

12 Carl Zollmann, *American Church Law*, St. Paul, Minn., 1933, p. 427.

13 *The Lutheran Agenda*, St. Louis, Concordia, p. 53.

14 Morris Ploscowe, *The Truth About Divorce*, New York, Hawthorn, 1955, p. 6. Copyright 1955 by Hawthorn Books, Inc.

15 Sec. 451 020 Mo. Rev. St. 1949.

16 *Christian Marriage*, National Council of Churches, Chicago, 1952, p. 5.

17 *Dr. Martin Luthers Briefwechsel*, Frankfurt, vol. VIII, p 398.

18 S. Baranowski, *Luthers Lehre von der Ehe*, Münster, 1913, p. 124.

19 *Doctrine and Discipline of the Methodist Church*, Nashville, 1952, p. 120.

20 *The Constitution of the Presbyterian Church, U.S.A.*, Philadelphia, 1955, pp 68–69.

21 George F. Thomas, *Christian Ethics and Moral Philosophy*, New York, Scribner's, 1955, pp. 237–239.

22 *Constitution of Eire*, Section III, num. 2–3.

23 Russell L. Dicks, *Pastoral Work and Personal Counseling*, New York, Macmillan, 1951, p. 123.

24 Canon 1013, par. 2; 1086, par. 2.

25 *Acta Apostolicae Sedis*, vol VII, p 292.

26 *Rotac Decisiones*, vol XV, p 223.

27 John T. Mueller, *The Lutheran Reformation*, St. Louis, Concordia, n.d., pp. 16–17.

28 *Ibid.*

29 Georgia Harkness, *The Sources of Western Morality*, New York, Scribner's, 1954, p. 243.

30 Garrison, *op. cit.*, p. 160.

31 Luther, *Werke* (Erlangen edition), vol XVI, p. 241. *Augsburg Confession*, Art. 18.

32 Luther, *Werke* (Wittenberg edition), vol. VI, p. 160.

33 Karl Barth, *La Prière*, Neuchâtel, 1949, p. 38.

34 Paul Blanshard, *American Freedom and Catholic Power*, Boston, Beacon, 1950, p. 132.

35 *The Lambeth Conference*, London, 1958, Resolution 92

Chapter Five

1 James Gustafsen, "Christian Ethics and Social Policy," *Faith and Ethics*, New York, Harper, 1957, p. 137.

2 Luther, *Werke* (Weimar edition), vol. VIII, p. 654.

3 *Passim* in *Predigt vom ehelichen Leben* (Erlangen edition), vol. XX, and *An den christlichen Adel* (Weimar edition), vol. VI.

[4] Leon Whipple, *The Story of Civil Liberty in the United States*, New York, 1927, p. 285.

[5] *Lambeth Conference*, London, 1920, Resolution 68.

[6] *Lambeth Conference*, London, 1930, Resolution 15.

[7] *Lambeth Conference*, London, 1958, Resolution 115, also the Encyclical Letter, 1: 23.

[8] *Moral Aspect of Birth Control*, New York, Federal Council of Churches, p. 5. (Now the National Council of Churches. Used with permission.)

[9] *The Christian Ideal of Marriage*, Boston, Pilgrim Press, pp. 10–11.

[10] *Moral Aspect of Birth Control*, p. 12.

[11] *Ibid.*, p. 2.

[12] *The Living Church*, October 8, 1948, p. 8.

[13] Luther, *Werke* (Erlangen edition), vol XX, p. 34.

[14] John H. C. Fritz, *Pastoral Theology*, St. Louis, Concordia, 1945, p. 162.

[15] Commission on Social Relations, in *A Guide to the Religions of America*, New York, 1955, p. 79.

[16] William T. Holt, Jr., *The Living Church*, p. 12.

[17] *Ibid*, p. 11.

[18] G. Bromley Oxnam, "Planning Our Children," *Social Problems in America*, New York, Henry Holt, 1955, p 118

[19] *The Evanston Report*, New York, Harper, 1955, p 125.

[20] *The Christian Century*, Aug 6, 1958, p. 895.

[21] Mahatma Gandhi, *Harijan*, June 5, 1937; May 5, 1946; March 28, 1951.

[22] Laird W. Snell, *The Living Church*, Oct. 10, 1948, p. 15.

[23] Fritz, *op. cit*, p 164.

[24] Emil Brunner, *The Divine Imperative*, London, Lutterworth, 1942, p. 368.

[25] *New York Times*, Dec 9, 1935.

[26] William B. Lipphard, in *A Guide to the Religions of America*, p. 6

[27] *New York Times*, Sept. 18, 1958.

[28] Farley W Snell, *The Christian Century*, Nov 5, 1958

[29] *The Table Talk of Martin Luther*, New York, World, 1952, pp. 170, 172.

[30] *If I Marry A Roman Catholic*, New York, National Council of Churches, pp. 15, 22.

Chapter Six

[1] John Dewey, *Characters and Events*, vol. II, London, 1929, p 508.

[2] Martin Luther, *Werke* (Weimar edition), vol. XI, pp. 405–415

[3] John Calvin, *Institutes of the Christian Religion*, Book IV, chap. 20, num 6

[4] *Ibid.*, num. 2.

[5] Kirsopp Lake, *The Religion of Yesterday and Tomorrow*, Boston, Houghton Mifflin, 1925, pp. 34–35.

[6] Christopher Dawson, "The Religious Origins of European Disunity," *Dublin Review*, Oct. 1940, p. 151.

[7] R. E. Thompson, *History of the Presbyterian Churches*, New York, Scribner's, 1907, p. 363.

[8] S. E. Morison and H. S. Commager, *The Growth of the American Republic,* New York, 1936, p. 110.

[9] Samuel H. Woodbridge, *The Overthrow of the Louisiana Lottery,* 1921 (Supplement), pp. 1–2.

[10] H. U. Faulkner, *The Quest for Social Justice,* New York, 1931, p. 224.

[11] *Doctrines and Discipline of the Methodist Church,* 1936, p. 664 and 1952, p. 639.

[12] C. Zollman, *American Church Law,* St. Paul, 1933, p. 162.

[13] *Selective Training and Service Act of 1940,* Section 5 q.

[14] George Channing, "What is Christian Science?" *A Guide to the Religions of America,* New York, Simon and Schuster, 1955, p. 23.

[15] *Table of Statutory Provisions Favorable to Christian Science,* Boston, p. 10.

[16] As reported by *Time,* July 18, 1949.

[17] Letter to William Bradford, Jan. 24, 1774, *In God We Trust,* New York, Harper, 1958, p. 299.

[18] "Memorial and Remonstrance" (1785), *Ibid.,* p. 311.

[19] *Religious Liberty in the United States Today,* American Civil Liberties Union, 1939, p. 8.

[20] *Annals of Congress,* vol. I, p. 730.

[21] *Constitution of the Presbyterian Church, U.S.A.,* Philadelphia, 1955, p. 239.

[22] *The Book of Common Prayer,* New York, Oxford Univ. Press, 1944, p. 610.

[23] Peter Guilday, *Life and Times of John Carroll,* New York, 1922, p. 115.

[24] *Writings of Washington* (Sparks edition), vol. XII, p. 179.

[25] Kenneth W Cary (State Chairman of "Protestants United Against Taxing Schools"), *Christianity Today,* Oct. 27, 1958, pp. 7–8.

[26] W V Wells, *The Life and Public Services of Samuel Adams,* Boston, Little Brown. 1865, vol. I, pp. 502–503

[27] "Christian Faith and the Protestant Churches," *Social Action,* May, 1952, p. 1.

[28] Ray Allen Billington, *The Protestant Crusade,* New York, Macmillan, 1938, p. 437.

[29] *Ibid.,* p. 438.

[30] Statement of the Third Provincial Council of Baltimore, *National Pastorals of the American Hierarchy,* Westminster, Md, Newman, 1954, pp. 90–91.

[31] *American Ecclesiastical Review,* March, 1924, p 296.

[32] *Ibid,* p 247

[33] C Stanley Lowell, "If the U.S. Becomes 51% Catholic," *Christianity Today,* Oct. 27, 1958, p. 8.

[34] *Christian Century,* Dec. 10, 1947.

[35] Full text in *The Shadow of the Pope* (Michael Williams), New York, McGraw-Hill, 1932, p. 326. Copyright 1932 by McGraw-Hill Book Company, Inc

[36] *Churchman,* May 15, 1947.

[37] *Op. cit.,* March 1, 1947.

[38] *New York Times,* Jan. 12, 1948.

Chapter Seven

[1] Northwest Ordinance, passed by Congress on July 13, 1787.

[2] *Acta et Decreta Concilii Plenarii Baltimorensis Tertii,* 1886, p. 104

[3] *Journal of Christian Education,* I (1839), p. 41.

[4] *Journal of Christian Education,* III (1841), p. 2.

[5] *Journal of General Conference,* 1872, p. 44.

[6] *The Relation of the Churches to the Public Schools,* Church Federation of Greater Chicago, Chicago, 1955, p. 2.

[7] *The Christian and His Public Schools,* Statement of the American Lutheran Church, 1954, p. 2

[8] *Statement of Church and Public School Relations,* Board of Education of the Methodist Church, 1955, pp. 4–5.

[9] "Statement of the Commission on Christian Social Action," *Christian Community,* Nov. 1954, p. 1.

[10] Thomas J. Van Loon, Board of Education, The Methodist Church, *Religion for Public School,* quoting favorably from the American Council on Education.

[11] A. C. Stellhorn, *Lutheran Schools,* St. Louis, Lutheran Education Association, 1953, pp. 4–5.

[12] "Public Education and Religion," *International Journal of Religious Education,* National Council of Churches, 1956, p 24.

[13] Arthur S Adams, "The Partnership of Independent and Public Schools," *The Role of the Independent School in American Democracy,* Milwaukee, 1956, p. 54. Dr. Adams is president of the American Council on Education and an active member of the Protestant Episcopal Church.

[14] *National Baptist Educational Convention,* 1888, p. 31.

[15] Anson P Stokes, *Church and State in the United States,* New York, Harper, 1950, vol. II, p 660.

[16] "Pluralism—National Menace," *The Christian Century,* June 13, 1951.

[17] Nevin C. Harner, "A Protestant Educator's View," *American Education and Religion,* New York, Harper, 1952, pp 85–86.

[18] Francis Pieper, *Christian Dogmatics,* St. Louis, Concordia, 1953, vol. III, p. 365.

[19] "Christian Faith and the Protestant Churches," *Social Action* (Congregational Christian), May, 1952, p. 1.

Chapter Eight

[1] George F. Thomas, *Christian Ethics and Moral Philosophy,* New York, Scribner's, 1955, pp. 309–310.

[2] Pius XI, *Quadragesimo Anno,* Washington, N C.W C, 1935, p. 27.

[3] *The First Assembly of the World Council of Churches,* New York, Harper, 1948, p. 80.

[4] *The Evanston Report,* New York, Harper, 1955, p. 118

[5] *Ibid,* p 121

[6] Press Release (Evanston Assembly), No. 66, pp. 1–4.

[7] *Human Events,* Jan. 21, 1959, p. 4.

[8] *Reinhold Niebuhr, His Religious, Social and Political Thought* (Kegley and Bretall edit.), New York, Macmillan, 1956, p. 140.

[9] *Christianity Takes A Stand* (Wm. Scarlett edit.), New York, Penguin, 1946, p. 41.

[10] *Radical Religion*, Autumn, 1948, p. 5.

[11] Paul Tillich, *The Protestant Era*, Chicago, Univ. of Chicago Press, 1951, pp 166, 259–260.

[12] L. Nelson Bell, "Christianity and Communism," *Christianity Today*, Jan. 19, 1959, p. 19.

[13] *New York Times*, Jan 19, 1959.

[14] Arnold J. Toynbee, A *Study of History*, London, Oxford Univ. Press, 1948, vol. I, pp. 211–212.

[15] *Ibid.*

[16] C. Mirbt, *Quellen zur Geschichte des Papstums*, Tubingen, 1901, p. 270.

[17] Paul Hutchinson, "Protestantism in the Crisis of These Times," *Christian Century*, April 3, 1957.

[18] *What the Negro Wants*, Edited by Rayford W. Logan, Univ. of Carolina, 1944, p. 1.

[19] *Christian Century*, Feb. 5, 1958, pp. 164–166.

[20] Division of Christian Life and Work, National Council of Churches, New York, 1957.

[21] Waldo Beach, "A Theological Analysis of Race Relation," *Faith and Ethics* (P. Ramsey edit), New York, Harper, 1957, p. 208

[22] *The Evanston Report*, p. 152

[23] Waldo Beach, *op cit.*, p. 222.

Chapter Nine

[1] St Hilary of Poitiers, "Liber Contra Constantium," *Patr. Lat.*, 10, 598–599.

[2] Francis Pieper, *Christian Dogmatics*, St. Louis, Concordia, 1951, vol. II, p. 60.

[3] Reinhold Niebuhr, *Human Destiny*, London, Nisbet, 1946, p 73.

[4] Henry D. Gray, *A Theology for Christian Youth*, New York, Nashville, Abingdon–Cokesbury, 1941, pp. 55–56.

[5] Francis Pieper, *op. cit.*, vol. III, p. 269.

[6] John T Mueller, *A Summary of the Teachings of the Evangelical Lutheran Church*, St Louis, Volkening, 1946, pp. 13–16

[7] *The Westminster Confession of Faith*, chap. 3, sec. 3–5

[8] John Wesley, *Sermon I*, 3; *Sermon XC*, 3.

[9] Robert E. Cushman, "Salvation for All," *Methodism*, Nashville–New York, Methodist Pub. Hse., 1947, p. 112.

[10] Paul Tillich, *The Shaking of the Foundations*, London, S.C.M., 1954, pp 159–163.

[11] James Luther Adams, "Tillich's Concept" in *Protestant Era*, Chicago, Univ. of Chicago Press, 1948, p. 316.

[12] These judgments were expressed, in sequence, by William B. Lipphard, James A Pike–W. Norman Pittenger, and Henry D. Gray.

[13] S. J. Gamertsfelder, *Systematic Theology*, Harrisburg, Pa., Evangelical Pub. Hse., 1952, p. 589.

[14] Billy Graham, *Peace with God*, Garden City, Doubleday, 1953, p 215.

Chapter Ten

[1] *Proceedings of the Southern Baptist Convention*, 1866, pp. 65–66.
[2] C. W. Hall and D. Holisher, *Protestant Panorama*, New York, 1951, p. 91.
[3] "Madison Journal," June 12, 1788, *In God We Trust* (The Religious Beliefs and Ideas of the American Founding Fathers), New York, Harper, 1958, p. 314.
[4] "Republican Notes on Religion" (1786), *Ibid.*, p. 124.
[5] Angus Dun, *Prospecting for a United Church*, New York, 1948, p 13.
[6] Truman B. Douglass, "Our Cooperative Witness to Our Oneness in Christ," *Christian Century*, Jan. 8, 1958, p. 44.
[7] C. W. Ranson, *World Wide Evangelism in this Generation*, Aug 24, 1954, p. 6
[8] Truman B Douglass, "The Job Protestants Shirk," *Harper's*, Nov. 1958, p. 46
[9] Charles C Morrison, *The Unfinished Reformation*, New York, 1953, p. 86.
[10] James H. Nichols, *Primer for Protestants*, New York, Association Press, 1951, p. 87.
[11] *Una Sancta*, vol. XIII, 1956, p. 5.
[12] Morrison, *op. cit*, pp. 42–43.

Chapter Eleven

[1] *World Council of Churches*, Geneva, 1954, p. 1.
[2] *Christian Beacon*, Jan. 5, 1950.
[3] *The Story of the World Council of Churches*, New York, 1954, p 21.
[4] *Third World Conference in Faith and Order*, London, 1953, p. 18
[5] Paul Minear, in *Contemporary Thinking About Jesus*, New York, 1944, p. 310.
[6] *What the Church Has to Offer*, Commission on Evangelism of the Congregational Christian Churches, Boston, Pilgrim Press, p. 13
[7] *Story of the World Council*, p. 21.
[8] *Our Oneness in Christ and Our Disunity as Churches*, Adopted on Aug. 29, 1954, p. 1.
[9] *Ibid*, pp. 3–4.
[10] *Ibid.*, pp. 5–6.
[11] *Ibid*, pp 8–10.
[12] *Christian Century*, Sept 22, 1954, pp. 1124–1125.
[13] *Third World Conference on Faith and Order*, p. 130.
[14] *Doctrines and Discipline of the Methodist Church*, Nashville, 1952, pp. 7–8.
[15] *Manual of the Congregational Christian Churches*, Boston, 1951, p. 29.
[16] Rufus M. Jones, *The Faith and Practice of the Quakers*, London, Methuen, 1927, p. 80.
[17] Elwood C Boggess, *The Ecumenical Movement and the Episcopal Church*, New York, pp. 14–16.

Chapter Twelve

[1] Gerhard Ritter, "Protestantism," *Schaff-Herzog Encyclopedia of Religious Knowledge*, Grand Rapids, Baker, 1955, p. 914.

[2] Reinhold Niebuhr, *Our Dependence Is Upon God*, Evanston, Aug. 29, 1954, p. 4.

[3] Winfred E. Garrison, *A Protestant Manifesto*, New York, Nashville, Abingdon-Cokesbury, 1952, pp 176–177.

[4] John Wenger, *Introduction to Theology*, Scottdale, Herald Press, 1954, p. 173.

[5] *Faith and Practice*, Philadelphia, 1955, p. 170.

[6] Robert J McCracken, *Man's Right to Knowledge and the Free Use Thereof*, New York, 1954, p. 7.

[7] Immanuel Kant, *Religion Within the Limits of Reason Alone*, Chicago, Open Court, 1934, p 105.

[8] John Henry Newman, *Difficulties of Anglicans*, London, Longmans, 1907, p. 28.

[9] T. M Parker, "Mariology," *Ways of Worship* (Theological Commission of Faith and Order), London, S C M. Press, 1951, p 283.

[10] Karl Barth, *The Word of God and the Word of Man*, New York, Harper, 1957, p. 113.

[11] James A. Pike and W. Norman Pittenger, *The Faith of the Church*, Greenwich, Conn., Seabury, 1951, p. 31.

[12] William Hocking, *The Meaning of God in Human Experience*, New Haven, Yale Univ. Press, 1928, p 39

[13] William W. Bartley, "I Call Myself a Protestant," *Harper's*, May, 1959, p 50.

[14] Walter Rauschenbusch, *Christianity and the Social Crisis*, New York, Macmillan, 1917 (twenty-first printing), pp. 414–418.

[15] Norman Vincent Peale, *The Power of Positive Thinking*, New York, 1953 (tenth printing), p. 267.

[16] Mary Baker Eddy, *Science and Health with Key to the Scriptures*, Boston, 1934, p. 116.

[17] Charles S. Braden, *These Also Believe*, New York, Macmillan, 1957, p. 137

[18] Ernest L. Enders, *Luthers Briefwechsel*, Stuttgart-Leipzig, 1886, vol. III, pp. 174 ff

[19] William E. Hocking, *The Coming World Civilization*, New York, Harper, 1956, p. 135.

[20] St. Augustine, "Enarrationes in Psalmos," 54:22, *Corpus Christianorum*, vol. 39, pp. 672–673.

[21] *When You Come Over*, National Council of Churches, New York, pp. 4, 14, 21–25.

INDEX

89–90, Methodist Church on, 88; National Council of Churches on, 87–88; pleasure basis recognized by social scientists, 98–99; Presbyterians on, 91; Protestants against mixed marriages because of Catholic stand on, 104–105; Protestant charges against the Catholic Church regarding, Scripture argument in favor of, 91–92; World Council of Churches on, 95–96

Birth prevention among the ancients, 85

Blessed Virgin, attitude of Protestants toward worship of, 255–258

Bolivia, inter-racial population in, 170–171

Brazil, inter-racial population in, 170–171

Brent, Charles, pioneer in ecumenical movement, 224–225

Brunner, Emil, on the "law" of sexual urgency, 100–101

Bultmann, Rudolph, on the Incarnation as mythology, 13

California tax exemption law upheld, 125–126

Calvin, John: against Church's authority over the Bible, 5–6, against the sacrament of orders, 23–24, contribution to American Church and state relations, 113; denies marriage is a sacrament, 59–60; different from Luther on Church and state, 111; establishes theocracy at Geneva, 111; determining the canon of Scripture, 5–6; on why Church "usurped" authority over marriage, 64

Calvinism, South Africa race problem and, 175–176

Calvinist predeterminism, effect on South African race relations, 175–176

Canterbury, Red Dean of, on Communism, 169

Capitalism· Protestant contribution to the rise of, 160–162; World Council of Churches on, 163

Carey, William, pioneer missionary to India, 43

Carroll, John, reasons why Catholics shown tolerance, 124–125

Catholic: education defended by Protestants, 152–153; immigration, numbers and result thereof, 128–130; losses to Protestantism, 278; population increase since colonial times, 132, population ratios in leading American cities, 217, schools, authoritarianism of, 153–154; schools, divisive character of, 154–155; schools, teach heresy, 156–157; schools, undemocratic, 155, schools, why Protestants oppose, 153–157; statement on birth control in New York controversy, 103–104

Catholic Church: accused of sexual preoccupation, 99–100; denied as having determined the Bible, 15; opposed for authority to interpret Scripture, 17–18

Celibacy· reasons given for Catholics, 76–77; Walter Raushchenbusch on clerical, 269–270

Chesterton, G. K., on the consequences of denying Christian dogma, 105

Chile, missionary propaganda for, 55–56

China, Methodist revision of Apostles' Creed in, 53–54

Christ: divinity obscured where Blessed Virgin not honored, 256–257, doctrinal differences on divinity of, 184–186, teaching on second coming of, 200–202

Christian Science. as Protestantism, 117, basic tenets of, 272–273; healing protected by law, 117–118

A NOTE ON THE TYPE

IN WHICH THIS BOOK WAS SET

This book is set in Caledonia, a Linotype face created in 1939 by W. A. Dwiggins, which is by far one of the best book types created in the last 50 years. It has a simple, hard-working, feet-on-the-ground quality and can be classed as a modern type face with excellent color and good readability. The designer claims Caledonia was created by putting a little of each of Scotch Roman, Bulmer, Baskerville and Bodoni together and producing a lively crisp-like book type. This book was composed by Progressive Typographers, Inc., York, Pa., printed by the Wickersham Printing Company of Lancaster, Pa., and bound by Moore and Company of Baltimore. The typography and design of this book are by Howard N. King.

CPSIA information can be obtained at www.ICGtesting.com
Printed in the USA
BVOW10s0413300114

343367BV00004B/296/P